COMMUNITY WATER DEVELOPMENT

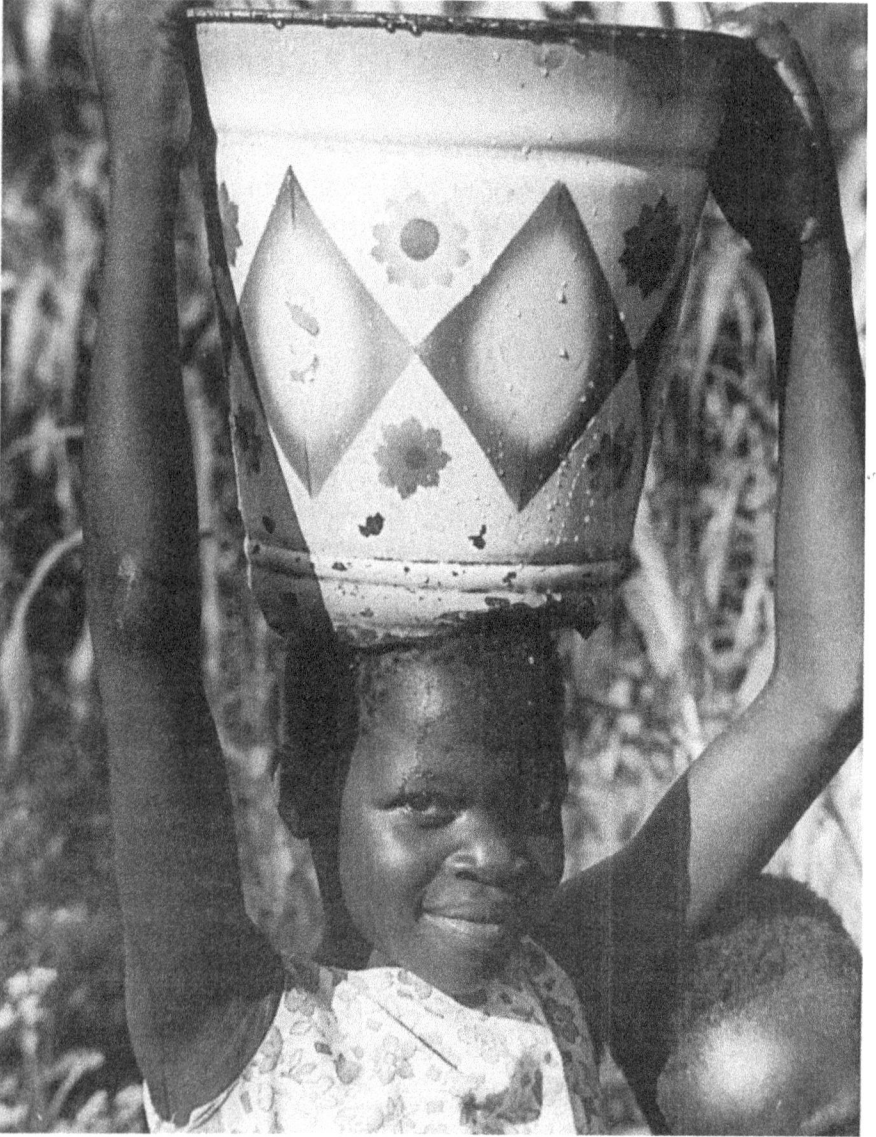

Community Water Development

Selected and edited by
CHARLES KERR

INTERMEDIATE TECHNOLOGY PUBLICATIONS 1989

Intermediate Technology Publications Ltd.
103–105 Southampton Row, London WC1B 4HH, UK

ISBN 0 94668823 0

Typesetting by Inforum Typesetting, Portsmouth
Printed in Great Britain by BPCC Wheatons Ltd, Exeter

Contents

ACKNOWLEDGEMENTS

The publishers would like to thank WaterAid, UNICEF, Jeremy Hartley, Peter Morgan of Blair Research Laboratory, the World Bank and ITDG for the use of photos as credited.

A NOTE ON CURRENCIES

Although the articles in this book cover a number of different years in the 1970s and 1980s, the following conversion rates, dating from September 1988 will give the reader a general idea of the values involved.

	£ sterling	*US $*
Botswana	3.31 pula	1.95
India	24.10 rupees	14.29
Kenya	30.85 shillings	18.29
Malaysia	4.49 riggits	2.66
Morocco	14.14 dirhams	8.38
Nigeria	7.92 naira	4.69
Papua New Guinea	1.46 kina	0.87
United Kingdom	1.00	0.59
USA	1.68	1.00
Zimbabwe	3.12 Z dollars	1.85

ACRONYMS

AT	Appropriate Technology
CA	Consumers' Association, UK
DANIDA	Danish Appropriate Technology Association
GTZ	German Appropriate Technology Organization
IDRC	International Development Research Centre
IDWSSD	International Drinking Water Supply and Sanitation Decade
IRC	International Reference Centre for Community Water Supply & Sanitation (The Netherlands)
ITDG	Intermediate Technology Development Group
ODA	Overseas Development Administration (UK)
OXFAM	Oxford Famine Relief Agency
REDR	Register of Engineers for Disaster Relief
SCF	Save the Children Fund
TOOL	Technical Development with Developing Countries (The Netherlands)
USAID	United States Agency for International Development
UNDP	United Nations Development Programme
UNEP	United Nations Environment Programme
UNICEF	United Nations Children's Fund
UNIDO	United Nations Industrial Development Organization
VSO	Voluntary Service Overseas (UK)
WASH	Water for Sanitation and Health Project (USA)
WEDC	Water and Waste Engineering for Developing Countries
WHO	World Health Organization

Preface

Media reports of drought and famine seem to have appeared all too frequently in recent years. Yet, in most cases, the situation has only become 'newsworthy' when death tolls have reached tens of thousands of people.

Many of these disasters occur in areas where the absence of clean water is something that the people have had to live with for a long time; and many millions of other people in the Third World—who will never hit the headlines—live in similar conditions, far out of reach of clean supplies of water and without basic sanitation.

From the time of its foundation in 1965, ITDG has been all too aware of the problems associated with the lack of safe water and adequate sanitation facilities. One of ITDG's earliest projects involved low-cost water storage reservoirs in the Sudan and articles on water and sanitation have always been prominent in ITDG's quarterly journal, *Appropriate Technology*, established in 1973.

With the launch of the IDWSSD in 1981, ITDG decided to make a contribution by starting a new journal featuring articles on appropriate technologies for safe water and improved sanitation. The first issue of *Waterlines* appeared in 1982, thanks to the financial support of Canada's International Research and Development Centre (IRDC), and has continued with the support of agencies which sponsor bulk subscriptions to field-workers who would otherwise be unable to order the periodical.

This book contains articles selected from *Waterlines* and *Appropriate Technology*. The main objective of the journals is to pass on practical, down-to-earth information to community planners and field-workers in developing countries who are tackling the problems day by day; a vital link in the chain along which information is disseminated for the Water Decade.

As Technical Editor of *Waterlines*, I analysed the contents of the first four volumes, drawing the conclusion that the articles provided good coverage of most aspects of rural water supply and sanitation in developing countries. Supplemented by material from *Appropriate Technology* the articles set out original concepts and field experience for the development of appropriate technologies. It was suggested that their publication in book form would preserve the information as a valuable reference for planners and workers in the field.

At an early stage it became obvious that separation in two volumes would be necessary; it was decided that the articles could best be divided under two titles, namely *Community Water Development* and *Community Health and Sanitation*. Inevitably, although each volume could stand alone, there are several articles in each relevant to the other: sanitation must progress simultaneously with water supply improvements as emphasized in many articles.

Because of the high standard of the articles and space restraints, a major problem has been to decide which articles to leave out. A secondary problem has been the question of whether to update the original articles. It was decided to minimize editing to retain the articles in their original context. Each has been dated and a further reading list has been included to replace the original references. An ancillary problem is that of changes in currency values; these have fluctuated widely and the conversion chart on page ix should give some guidance.

This volume has been divided into eleven chapters, each preceded by a short introductory note for continuity and explanation. Chapter 1 develops the appropriate technology approach and the importance of community participation to adapt to local needs. The next two chapters deal with underground sources, both shallow wells and tube-wells. These are followed by two chapters on surface sources, proceeding from rain-water harvesting on micro-catchment principles to the conservation of stream and river flow diverted by weirs or collected behind dams.

The choice between pumping methods with reference to some alternatives is discussed in Chapter 6, followed by the testing and development of handpumps and their maintenance in the next two chapters. Transport and storage is considered in Chapter 9 with particular reference to alleviating the burden of water-carrying by women. Education and training are discussed in Chapter 10, and planning and management in Chapter 11. The latter includes modern problems and possible solutions for the traditional *falaj* system in Oman which has important lessons for community water development projects.

All credit for this book must go to the many authors who have contributed so much to *Waterlines*. My special thanks for their support and encouragement to the *Waterlines* Editorial team, and to Chris D'Souza for undertaking all the real editing of this book.

Charles Kerr
1988

CHAPTER 1
Technology for the People

'Appropriate technology' is a term used to describe both a method and a movement. It is the appropriate application of scientific knowledge to development and also the movement, started in the 1960s, and which is now active all over the world.

Peter Stern outlines the development of the movement and the application of appropriate technology to water development in the Third World. John Pickford goes on to highlight the importance of community participation and the adaptation of intermediate technology to local needs 'as if people mattered'. Jim Howard follows up with his call for engineers to learn from their heritage about the basic skills and technologies needed to develop simple water supplies. The long-term approach of Dan Schellenberg, working with self-help groups in rural Kenya, is described by Simon Batchelor. Finally, based on their experiences in two large-scale projects, the Dutch appropriate technology organization TOOL, warn that it is essential to investigate peoples' needs and to seek their participation in finding the right solution.

These articles provide an introduction to the philosophy of appropriate technology for community water supply and some guide-lines on its implementation through participation and self-help.[1,2]

Appropriate technology for water
PETER STERN

The view that much of Western technology is inappropriate to developing countries has been expressed by a few thoughtful people for nearly 60 years, but most of this time the world in general was not willing to listen to what they had to say.

In 1965, Fritz Schumacher founded ITDG in London for the purpose of developing programmes on technologies for rural life in developing countries. Water was one of ITDG's main concerns, and in its early years the ITDG Water Panel was actively engaged in promoting low-cost simple technology in water conservation and storage.

In considering the water needs of the Third World it is important not to over-simplify the issues. Needs can be divided into those vital to sustain life and additional needs required to enable people to live fully and effectively. Even where basic needs only have to be met under an emergency, this is a temporary solution and sooner or later water requirements have to be seen in the context of a development rather than an emergency situation.

The more common use of technology for meeting the water needs in the Third World is concerned with improving some existing facility. It may be a case of increasing the yield of a source; bringing water nearer to dwelling places; removing the health hazards of polluted water; making better use of a source for watering animals or irrigating crops or fishponds. Whatever the needs, technical solutions can usually be found. In the 1950s and 1960s, when money went further than it does today and when funds for aid and development were more plentiful, many of those involved in development believed that it would only be a matter of time before technology would be able to satisfy the water needs of all the people in the Third World. For hydraulic engineers the catchword was 'control'. It seemed that once river systems could be controlled and their resources harnessed, the problems of surface water sources would largely be solved. And so hydraulic research became absorbed with the design of control structures, controlled discharges and erosion control, and books and papers were published on the control of water.

It would be wrong to suggest that the Third World has gained nothing from this type of activity, but the gains have been small compared with the effort and resources expended. The pursuit of technology for its own sake is a neutral activity. Schumacher was very concerned about the domination of the world by technology, and asked, 'Can we develop a technology which really helps us to solve our problems—a technology with a human face?' Technology applied in ignorance of its consequences in human terms is counterproductive. This can be illustrated by some examples.

Technology problems

It was believed 20 years ago that borehole supplies should be extended and developed throughout the Third World and thus many massive drilling programmes were started, sometimes with very little preliminary hydrogeological investigation.

Most of these programmes were undertaken jointly by an international or bilateral aid agency with a recipient government water department or authority. With little concept of the value of the investment made on their behalf, the people would begin to enjoy its benefits. All would go well for a few years. New machinery required little attention beyond routine maintenance and even when unmaintained and unlubricated, the machinery survived for a while. But sooner or later the equipment would begin to deteriorate and a few weeks or months after that there would be a major breakdown and the water point would cease to supply water.

A second example may be found in the construction of dams and storage reservoirs. Dam construction was part of the controlling water crusade 20 or 30 years ago, and small earth dams became a popular feature of the development programmes of many Third World countries. There is nothing wrong with storing water for a useful purpose, but the dam-planners were inclined to be carried away by their enthusiasm.

During the 1960s, the Water Development Department of Uganda constructed over 100 earth dam storage reservoirs in the drier northern parts of the country. Few of these have been put to any use other than serving as watering places for cattle during the dry seasons. By 1983 many of the dams and spillways were in a poor state of repair and several had been destroyed.

The third example may be seen in the many water supply schemes for small urban and semi-urban communities which incorporate water treatment systems. It is a common experience in many developing countries to find a water treatment system intact in that raw water extracted from a river source follows a correct route through sedimentation tanks to sand filters and then into contact tanks for sterilization. But because of the unavailability of chemicals and spare parts, staff shortages and inadequate supervision, raw, untreated water passes on into the service reservoir and thence to the consumer. Here again, many of these installations were provided under aid programmes, and donors and their technical advisers cannot avoid sharing some responsibility for the outcome of their interventions.

Rainwater

One of the most widespread and directly accessible sources of water is rainfall itself. Although rainfall harvesting has been practised in some parts of the world for several thousand years, it was given little attention until the 1960s when the techniques were revived and adapted to modern use. Today, all over the developing world, micro-catchment systems are collecting rainfall from the roofs of buildings, paved land surfaces and natural ground to provide water for domestic use and agriculture.

In many upland areas water supplies are derived from springs. Although the water emerging from a spring is usually pure and unpolluted, the indiscriminate use of a spring source for collecting water, bathing, washing clothing and watering animals pollutes the source and the surrounding area. The protection of springs is often an important feature of low-cost water improvement programmes.

The development of shallow groundwater also offers opportunities for appropriate technology in the construction of hand-dug wells, underground galleries and shallow tube-wells, which can sometimes be driven by manual labour.

Many kinds of simple human-operated water-lifting devices have been used in different parts of the world for hundreds of years. With devices such as swinging baskets, scoops and buckets there is little scope for technical innovation. In other cases such as the counterpoised lift (or shadoof, as it is known in the Middle East), rope and bucket systems, various chain-lifting devices and different types of water-wheel, appropriate technology has been applied to improve efficiencies in some cases, but on the whole these devices have remained much as they have always been. Most of the scientific interest in improving water-lifting technology for the Third World has centred on the reciprocating handpump.

Water lifting requires energy and the most readily available source of energy to human beings is human power. But it should be remembered that the human individual is not a large power unit when compared with the mechanical power sources available in the modern world today. For pumping water in the Third World, and bearing in mind that it is often women and children who do the work, human power is usually taken as 100 watts per person. The human body is capable of developing much more power in short bursts, but tests carried out in Africa have shown that 100 watts per person is about right.

Animal power is used traditionally for raising water in many developing countries throughout North Africa, the Middle East and Asia. Animals are used in two ways:

○ For direct lifting by hauling a rope or ropes to raise a bucket.
○ For operating a water-wheel or chain of buckets through gears by walking on a circular track harnessed to a pivoted arm.

The first method is usually employed in semi-arid pastoral areas for raising water for stock and domestic use. The second method is more appropriate to the prolonged continuous watering required for irrigation. As continuously working animals require about 40 per cent more food than grazing animals, this extra food has to be taken into account. If all animal fodder is provided on irrigated land, one working animal would need about 0.8 hectares of land for its food production.

AT developments

Wind power is today a popular source of alternative energy, and the direct use of the sun's energy for mechanical power has attracted the attention of scientists and engineers for over 100 years. The development of the photo-voltaic cell which converts sunlight directly into electrical energy has been a breakthrough in solar energy conversion. Although solar pumping systems consist of highly sophisticated technology, the equipment produced for practical use is robust. The systems require little operational attendance beyond keeping the equipment clean and the pumps free from sediment. On the other hand if there is an electrical failure it would be quite beyond the means of local resources in most developing countries to trace and cure a fault, and servicing and repairs could be very costly indeed.

Another form of natural energy which has been used for some 2,000 years is the energy of falling water. During the past decade there has been a recovery of interest in small-scale hydro-power systems.

The storage of water is a topic which has attracted much attention from promoters of AT and this has led to a number of interesting developments. The simplest form of small, localized storage is the rainfall catchment tank. This is not new and excavated tanks and cisterns have been in use in North Africa, the Middle East, Asia and elsewhere for hundreds of years.

In the 1960s C. W. Lauritzen of the US Department of Agriculture was one of the most active workers in the USA on the research and development of plastics for waterproofing small reservoirs for rainfall catchment. At about the same time Michael Ionides of ITDG was evolving a technique using layers of thin polyethylene and clay for waterproofing excavated tanks in Western Sudan.

For storage below ground the walls of the tank have only to be water-proofed because the ground itself supports the weight of the water. But above ground the walls have to be both waterproof and strong enough to hold the weight of the water they contain. There is a wide range of ready-made commercial tanks available, but usually these are too costly for small rural communities. Alternative AT solutions have included ferro-cement construction and cement plaster with basket-work reinforcement.

A very important application for AT concerns the treatment of water for domestic uses. Slow sand filtration, a system which was in common use all over the world before the development of the rapid sand filters of the modern waterworks, is a treatment which is appropriate for developing countries.

Mr Abdel Mageed, a distinguished water engineer from the Sudan, made a powerful plea in his contribution to the discussions at the Second African Water Technology Conference in Nairobi in April 1984, for a better understanding of Third World aspirations. He reminded the participants, the majority of whom came from countries outside Africa, that inevitably the development objectives of every Third World country were to achieve the same living standards for the majority of their people as were enjoyed by the majority of the people in the more developed countries. In his view, AT, as generally understood, is an interim solution.

This, of course, is a very valid argument. In a world which clamours for economic justice and help for the poorest of the poor, there is no logic in maintaining two standards, one for the haves and one for the have nots. But as the Brandt Commission has been at pains to point out, this gap, which is widening all the time, can only be closed by drastic voluntary changes in the world's economic systems. Looking at the controlling forces which govern our economic systems, there would seem to be little hope of voluntary change unless more notice can be taken of the non-material values of life so that economics, in the words of Schumacher, might find a human face.

It is to be hoped that the powers which are exerted so forcibly to maintain economic advantages will be relaxed when more attention is paid to the basic wisdom which was expressed 2,000 years ago in the words: 'If anyone has material possessions and sees his brother in need but has no pity on him, how can the love of God be in him?'

(Waterlines Vol. 3 No. 4, April 1985)

People and the Decade— technology and community
JOHN PICKFORD

The International Drinking Water Supply and Sanitation Decade is obviously about water and sanitation, but it is equally about people. The objective of the Decade is to provide water and sanitation for people, not for crops or hydro-power or transport. Drinking-water supplies are needed for nearly two billion men, women, boys and girls. Even more people need sanitation.

Anyone who has travelled amongst the people of Africa, Asia and Latin America has seen people queueing at public taps or drawing foul water from virtually dried-up pools; women and children carrying terrible loads of water; human excreta in the street and flies by the million in and around people's homes. All these show the effect on people of the present deficiencies in water supply and sanitation—deficiencies which should be eradicated in the Decade.

An overall assessment of the global situation may be important and we are often inundated with statistics detailing the numbers of hundreds of millions of people suffering from various diseases or the relationship between their country's gross national product and the percentage of this, that, or the other. However, these cold facts and figures are less convincing than the distress of individual people caused by inadequate water supply and sanitation. A television film of a family in an undrained squatter hut creates an upsurge of popular concern; no one can fail to be appalled by the grotesque bulbous legs of a sufferer from elephantiasis; and we are appalled if a mother dies in childbirth because of deformity caused by carrying heavy loads of water. While people's suffering can be understood, it is difficult to imagine such conditions being multiplied to give the thousands of millions needing clean water and proper sanitation.

These millions of people will be, or should be, at the receiving end of programmes and projects devised to achieve the Decade's objectives. No less important in the Decade are the people who should make that achievement possible—the planners, plumbers, pump-operators, politicians and professionals. They are the 'human resources' without which money, pipes, cement and other material resources are useless. Human resources have to be mobilized for the Decade: a great variety of effort is required from a great variety of people and it is absolutely essential that this input is co-ordinated.

Community participation

I had an interesting example of collaboration when visiting the *katchi abadi* area of Baldia in Karachi. My visit was in response to a call for engineering advice and I vividly remember a meeting in the office of the Turk Colony Welfare Society. At the meeting were Quratul Ain, the Community Organizer (a sociologist), Karim Daya (a mason), a representative of the welfare society and me (a professional engineer). We talked for a long time and sketched several soakpit designs. In the end we came up with a solution which I think was only possible because *all* of us were there. Without any one of the four, an important component in planning would have been absent.

The soakpits of Baldia are especially interesting because of the high degree of involvement by a squatter community where co-operation would not normally be expected. In fact, one of the reasons for the earlier departure of the Dutch Advisory Mission was a sociologist's report of lack of community solidarity. I had visited the area earlier, before the Dutch left, and it seemed true that Baldia had no group willing to take on sanitation for the 150,000 or so inhabitants. At that time there was no organization capable of developing facilities on the scale required.

However, there were people—all kinds of people. Few had previous experience of 'acceptable' sanitation, but all knew that the existing dry latrines were appalling and that they paid scavengers their hard-earned money to empty them. Starting in a small way, a programme evolved and people who previously associated for entirely different purposes became involved in sanitation. Once some action could be seen, other people became interested.

Another good example of co-operation between engineers and people is a rural water programme in Malawi. Here thousands of people have worked together in excavation and pipe-laying and all the associated facets of vast water supply schemes. Some of the individual projects are large in size and take a long time to complete, so stimulating the people's co-operation is extremely important and difficult—but nonetheless it has been successfully achieved. As many as a hundred thousand people have worked on a single project, the construction taking two years to complete. Lindsey Robertson, the man behind the programme, wrote that its success depended on these principles:

○ The system evolved from the bottom upwards as a response to a real need.
○ The community was involved in the project at all levels and through the whole cycle of planning, implementation and maintenance.
○ As a result of this involvement and because of its basic importance to the success of the programme, a sense of pride and ownership in the project was generated within the local community.
○ In addition to being competent the engineer should have a high degree of motivation with qualities of leadership and sound judgement, which enables him to evolve appropriate management techniques suitable to the rural project situation.

Robertson added that this did not happen overnight; it took ten years of patient understanding and persistent hard work.

Other projects which help achieve the Decade's objectives are quite small. A few people in a village dig a well. In another village a little outside money is used to purchase material for a dozen sanitary latrines; the householders repay their loans for material provided and the money is recycled until all the people have good latrines. In another country a hydraulic ram and pipes are given to a group of families who then provide all the labour to install a water supply from a stream hitherto reached only by a long and arduous trek. And so on. Millions of small projects are needed to make up the programmes that in turn make up the Decade.

Appropriate technology

Water and sanitation for all these people calls for appropriate technologies. Professional engineers are particularly interested in the technology aspect of sanitation and should be eager to ensure that the technology applied in the Decade is of a really high standard. It should be the best possible in the circumstances, whatever they are.

Careful engineering design and construction are even more important for poor people than for the more affluent. It may be disastrous for poor people when a facility breaks down and cannot be repaired because of a fault inherent in the design or construction. If the initial scheme was paid for from their own resources they will probably be unable to make the effort a second time; if an outside agency helped the attitude is likely to be 'you've had your share—no more now!'

Too often in the past second-rate engineering has gone into the water and waste facilities of Africa, Asia and Latin America. Too many schemes have failed simply because the engineering was not good enough.

From a purely engineering point of view, there is always a danger of thinking only in terms of design and construction. The goal may be the commissioning of a scheme; for instance water flowing through a pipe for the first time, a latrine being used for the first time, or when a local dignitary switches on a pump.

This has always been a criticism of consulting engineers especially when they come from overseas, although the fault may lie with the clients' brief rather than the consultants themselves. However, the danger of the 'completion date complex' applies just as much to local engineers if construction is separated from subsequent maintenance. The engineer must give more thought to the people who should be benefiting from his work two, 10 or 20 years after completion.

I have heard engineers working as consultants for water/sanitation projects in developing countries boast that they do not agree with 'appropriate technology'. I have also heard civil servants in Third World countries declare that they are against appropriate technology. One even said he was 'totally opposed' to it!

It is hard to take this statement seriously. *All* technology should be appropriate. *All* engineering should be appropriate for its location. *All* engineering work should be designed and made so that it provides the best engineering solution for the purpose for which it is intended while making the best use of the resources available.

It is often said or implied that appropriate technology is in some way inferior to the sophisticated technology of the industrial world. This is confusing the meaning of the words appropriate technology with terms like 'intermediate' or 'alternative'.

It was Fritz Schumacher who first coined the words intermediate technology. Indeed, the subtitle of his book *Small is Beautiful* includes the words *as if people mattered*. He did not initially use the term 'appropriate technology' because he felt that they merely posed additional questions: appropriate to whom, for what, where and when? It was up to the people involved to choose the answers to these questions. However, having noted the rising unemployment, increase in national debts, and growing reliance on expatriate inputs to technological activities in Third World countries, he saw that the Third World had few choices.

The traditional technologies were simple and labour intensive but low in productivity, whereas modern technologies were productive, but capital intensive and labour-saving. They were also large scale, centralized and heavily dependent on foreign resources, skills and even markets. Intermediate technologies could be labour intensive and capital-saving, simple and small; and would use local resources more fully.

The development of technologies intermediate in complexity, and their adaptation to local needs as if people mattered, widens the choice of technologies which may be appropriate, but also requires high-quality scientific and technical expertise. However, there is a growing acceptance by Third World leaders and international agencies of the value and importance of making funds and resources available for such work.

Sewerage and sewage treatment for affluent residential areas are similar everywhere and use well-known engineering techniques. On the other hand, the engineering requirements for truly appropriate self-help sanitation for poor squatter areas are only a part of the job because allowances have to be made for the people and the community. For *appropriate* work an early consideration is the health of the people and its converse, the local diseases caused by inadequate sanitation: the prevalence of various worms and diarrhoeal illness. In a way, community health improvements are techno-logical and therefore not too far removed from the thinking processes of a proficient engineer. Similarly, economic and financial topics are based on mathematical and logical ideas which are akin to the basics of engineering.

However, in addition to engineering, health and economics, there is a completely new dimension which influences appropriate technology. The degree of self-help and the type of sanitation are greatly affected by the people and the community; in turn sanitation influences the people and the community.

The success of such sanitation (and also of rural water supply) projects depends on the will of the people to succeed. Somehow or other the people must be motivated; they must have the will to achieve perceived objectives. Provision of a good water supply is a positive goal which people can easily recognize. Sometimes sanitation is seen in the same light—as a goal in itself. For example, the possession of a latrine of a particular kind often enhances the owner's prestige, and villages or other communities may compete for the privilege of a new communal latrine.

However, such positive objectives are less likely than viewing sanitation as a means of overcoming bad conditions. Disease may not be seen as the result of bad sanitation, but the inconvenience or cost of removing excreta may be so serious that a householder is motivated into action (if he knows what to do). It is more likely that bad conditions are accepted as part of fate, or the hand of Allah, or simply not seen to be bad.

Help from professionals

It has been said that political will is the first requirement for achieving the Decade's objectives. The politicians of many countries have had sufficient will to ensure that national programmes for the Decade were prepared.

In some countries the politicians and civil servants (who convert political will into political action) retain links with the underprivileged majority who lack water and sanitation. Elsewhere, successful politicians and top adminis-trators are as isolated from poor people as the worst imperialists before independence.

They live in large houses with constant running water and toilets con-nected to sewers or septic tanks. In some countries the seat of government has been deliberately isolated. Following the example of the British Raj's creation of New Delhi seventy years ago, independent Pakistan moved its capital to the new city of Islamabad, Brazil built Brasilia and now Tanzania and Nigeria are pouring hundreds of millions of pounds into their new capital cities. All these capitals have 'modern' water supply and sewerage.

The personal lives of many politicians and top civil servants are completely divorced from those of the poor people in their countries, who have no satisfactory water and sanitation. So their will to implement Decade objectives depends on their sympathy for the underprivileged. This may be selfishly motivated by the need for votes or popular support, but it may be activated by a genuine desire to improve the lives of their compatriots.

A similar motivation must exist among the technologists involved in the Decade. The appropriate technologist must relate to the people, whose attitudes are influenced by their history and traditions, their religion and culture, their health, their material condition, their family size and many other external factors. With people, the logical pattern of $x + y = z$ is not apparent as it is with the design of sewers or reinforced concrete structures. People are, or seem to be, illogical. Their hopes and fears, their regrets and ambitions are often obscure, even to themselves.

Yet these very traits of personality influence people's readiness to be involved in water supply and sanitation improvements. To be successful, the engineer working for Decade objectives must be aware of this human dimension.

The approach to people must be sympathetic, and the existence of their individual hopes and fears must be acknowledged. This in turn requires a readiness to listen to the people and to accept the unwelcome idea that in many ways the users of sanitation systems themselves are better at making appropriate choices than the 'experts'. Their ideas and their attachment to old ways must be incorporated into projects. Above all, whatever is good in their present water and sanitation practice should be accepted and developed, rather than being replaced by the latest designs from some international organization.

Thus, appropriate technology for water supply and sanitation is not something any idiot can do, as some sophisticated technologists imply. It is, in fact, much more demanding than conventional work.

At the professional level, water supply and sanitation have conventionally been treated as civil engineering functions. In recent years, with growing sophistication, especially in treatment processes, there has been a greater scientific input. On the whole, education and training as a civil engineer seems the best background for the leaders of Decade implementation, although other engineering specialists, and geologists and scientists as well, can all become appropriate engineers with suitable training and experience. Superimposed on the engineering background the professional in charge of implementation must acquire proficiency in management, incorporating an understanding of finance and economics.

Courses provided by the WEDC Group at Loughborough University of Technology and in developing countries are designed to contribute to the Decade's success. They cover aspects of health; civil, mechanical and electrical engineering; geology, chemistry and microbiology; management studies and the 'people' dimension. All these are needed to make the technology appropriate.

Coping with this wide spectrum demands people of high calibre who are motivated to learn because their learning will benefit the underprivileged majority.

If the Decade is to succeed, all those who provide the human resources for putting it into practice must continually think about the people who are to benefit. Human resources can often be provided by the community which is benefiting from a particular water project, thereby increasing its identification with the Decade programme.

The impetus of the Decade will continue and the best engineers in developing countries and the best engineers from the North who are working in developing countries must accept the challenge of finding appropriate technologies for a vast range of circumstances.

(Waterlines Vol. 1 No. 2, October 1982)

So much to learn

JIM HOWARD

The International Drinking Water Supply and Sanitation Decade of the 1980s has much to learn from the past. The basic techniques of digging or hand-drilling wells are as relevant now as they were hundreds—or thousands—of years ago. Records show that the ancient Egyptians and Chinese were familiar with well-drilling methods to the extent that they at least put down tubular holes into the ground to obtain water.

In about 2100 BC Henu, who worked under the Pharaoh Mentuhotep III, reported: 'I went forth with an army of 3,000 men. I made 12 wells in the bush and two wells in Idehit.' In Cairo, 'Joseph's well' is one of the world's oldest-known wells: dug in solid rock to a depth of 90m, the upper part measured 6m by 8m. Water was raised in buckets on continuous chains, the buckets in the lower part of the well being powered by mules. A spiral stairway was provided around the well for the mules to pass.

In the more recent past, as a child, I lived in a part of North London where a river (heavily fenced to keep out small rogues like myself) wound its way through the housing and factories. It was called the New River and meant little to me until I started my engineering studies.

I then learnt that Sir Hugh Myddleton completed in 1613 a scheme to tap springs at Chadwell and Amwell in Hertfordshire (20 miles or so outside London) and bring a flow of wholesome water to London. This was to supplement the stinking Thames and other surface waters being drunk by Londoners of the day. The New River still functions 300 years after its construction. It must have supplied untold millions of people over this period with a health-giving water supply.

New applications for old techniques

These examples show the same concern expressed by Oxfam's field engineers in Sudan, Uganda, Rwanda and elsewhere, who report their daily progress, problems and achievements in the spring catchment and open dug-well operations which Oxfam are organizing and financing.

They are faced with such basic questions as where to obtain cement or well-ring moulds, whether to use local or imported tools, or whether tripods and winches can be afforded. What de-watering methods can be used while digging? What level of training should be given to local people? Who pays the labour—bonus rates or incentives or not? What, if any, safety measures—clothing, helmets—should be taken?

The most basic technologies for digging wells, hand-boring tube-wells, protecting springs and filtering water through sand are still relevant today. Oxfam are digging more and more open wells, urgently seeking ways of hand-augering for ground-water surveys, trying to develop knowledge of sand filters to upgrade surface-water quality for poor communities. These are some of the oldest techniques in the world yet we are still struggling to understand them.

A few years ago, I travelled to Tanzania, where I visited Dutch and Tanzanian engineers drilling hundreds of tube-wells by hand. This was a most exciting and imaginative project, which involved developing 'new' tools and 'new' skills, with substantial results. Yet what had happened to the knowledge of hand-drilling between the early Egyptians and Chinese and the current Dutch operation? Where is the learning and the passed-on skill?

A few more questions spring to mind. How many water engineers nowadays really know about dug-well techniques, and how many have actually helped to dig wells physically with their hands? How many engineers have used hand-boring equipment to survey for water or actually bored successful tube-wells, such as the Dutch engineers are doing? How many engineers have spent time searching the countryside looking for suitable springs to develop for simple water supplies? That is what a few field engineers are doing today in the Sudan, Rwanda, Somalia, Ethiopia, Uganda, Kampuchea and India. That is what Myddleton and his colleagues did in the early seventeenth century.

Fellow civil engineers may explain why it is not necessary for them to do these activities. They are the planners, the administrators, the organizers.

Well-digging is carried out by peasants, small farmers or paid labourers.

Somehow the engineer has ceased to be concerned with the soil-digging, rock-breaking, well-lining and well-development problems. There is a serious gap between what we think we know and what we really do know.

For example, every water engineer concerned with the developing world thinks he knows a great deal about these old techniques; but what modern engineering training includes well-digging, hand-boring or spring-catchment techniques as a basic part of the course? In books about the last century one reads of groups of working men called well-sinkers—where can they be found now? Are the widely-discussed and recognized lists of tools and equipment available for low-cost water-development schemes? If these lists do not exist, is this not a major oversight, leaving each project to fend for itself with a hotchpotch of inadequate equipment and training? Who is going to put this deficiency to rights?

Of all the hundreds of publications I have seen concerning the IDWSSD few are as important as the modest but excellent book published by ITDG, *Hand dug wells*[3] (S. B. Watt and W. E. Wood) and the outstanding booklet *Shallow Wells*[4] by the Dutch consulting firm DHV. The Dutch have much to share on their simple ground-water experiences in Africa. The Dutch operation may seem expensive. Yet in Britain it costs about UK £1 million to train a single fighter pilot. The aircraft he will fly might be worth more than Oxfam's total income for a year, of which only part is spent on water projects! This reveals a strange and distorted sense of priorities in our society, where millions of our fellow humans may die for the lack of safe water supply; a society which would rather dismiss the Water Decade as a failure than examine the pathetic support given to the Decade by many governments.

We water engineers, people concerned with life-giving water and public health facilities for our fellow men, have a remarkable engineering heritage. People of great talents and determination have laboured to bring water to their communities in past centuries. Surely we can learn from their efforts?

(*Waterlines* Vol. 2 No. 4, April 1984)

Introducing appropriate technologies step by step
SIMON J. BATCHELOR

Many writers on technology extol the virtue of really getting to know the people we are trying to help, of learning about their needs and priorities; but how many projects have time to allow for this? Most funding agencies want immediate results from their financial outlay. Progress reports are due after six months or a year. The textbooks say a period of familiarization is required, but pressure from performance-orientated donors often cuts this short, or at the very least combines it with a prototype project.

I was therefore pleasantly surprised to see Dan Schellenberg's work in Kenya in 1984. Working mainly with cashless small landowners, his ability to disseminate appropriate technology stems from getting to know these people over a long period of time.

The early years

Having been a traditional missionary for many years preaching the Gospel as his father had done, Dan Schellenberg began to wonder if there were not more he could do. He wanted 'to get Christianity to be an agent of freedom, not just a post holding up the system'. His aims were to improve the people's life-style and encourage the men to come home from the city where they usually go to seek cash-earning work. After two or three years of just living with the people, he decided to concentrate on what he calls the 'middle class' —those families with approximately five acres of land and one or two cows.

The Kamba people, who live near Kitui/Yatta, have a fairly typical rural African life-style. The area has numerous smallholdings which vary in size from less than one acre to 20 acres. These *shambas* generally house the family's wife and children, while the husband is in the city. Traditionally, maize, sorghum and beans are grown on the *shamba*, with little or no reliance on market vegetables. These crops fail every other season.

During these first two or three years, Dan was supported by churches in America. Despite Dan's liaison with the donors, his 'lack of results' almost got him fired. He was able to build an accurate picture of the people's problems. He came to understand that the changes in society in recent years had weakened the decision-making mechanisms of the community. He began to restore the traditional village meeting to involve the community in the generation of ideas. He sees the first few years as a period of encouraging in his friends an increased awareness of the concept of 'home' and of the large-scale economic forces which often weaken the community's self-reliance.

Only after these years of building trust and friendship was Dan able to obtain some constructive discussion on possible solutions to the community's problems. The most immediate and obvious need was water during the dry spell. The area had rivers but these became contaminated during the dry season and were often many kilometres from the *shamba*. However, determined not just to donate money, Dan decided that the first step was to generate cash that could be used to create a water supply.

He chose to work initially with seven groups which still had some men in them. Five were families and two were groups of families, spread over the Yatta area. These groups had two oxen each, or donkeys or cows which they used to plough their land with a traditional harness.

The first technological offer from Dan was an improved ox or donkey harness. Developed by the Dutch at Nairobi University, dozens were already being used in Kenya. The harness takes the power from the shoulders of the animal and not as with the traditional harness from the spine. It allows the ox merely to lean forward in order to break the static friction needed to plough.

The harness cost 250 Kenya shillings (Ksh) (UK£12.50), whereas the average monthly income in the city is about 600 Ksh. After a suitable trial period, the group sharing the improved harness proved that one ox could do the work of two using the traditional type.

There was a variety of benefits from this discovery; one was a discussion on agriculture. As Dan explained the harness, he created an atmosphere that was open for suggesting and discussing improved agricultural techniques. The discussion led to the development of a covenant relationship within the group. The members of the community agreed on a plan of action: If the community kept its part of the bargain Dan would keep his.

The major benefit of the harness was to release one ox for sale, which fetched about Ksh 2,000. This money was used to build a 20,000 gallon rain-catchment tank.

The tank was simply a reasonably well-placed hole in the ground lined with concrete. The 20,000 gallons of water supplied domestic needs and, with a little management, there was excess water to sell to neighbours during the dry season for a total of between Ksh 1,500 and 2,000. Each *dèbe* (20-litre container) of water cost 10 to 40 cents, or was exchanged for work in the busy seasons. Social pressure within the community prevented those with a water tank exploiting those without.

Water from the catchment was very muddy, despite the use of simple sand filters, so there was a risk of disease. This was overcome by an upward flow filter made from sand and charcoal, at a cost of approximately Ksh 100. As its construction required only a single bag of cement, it could be made at the same time as the lining of the catchment tank.

Construction of the tank provided a practical introduction to the principles of land management and, in particular, erosion control. Trees had to be planted to prevent the water washing away the hill as it ran into the catchment. This sort of planting contrasts sharply with the traditional practice of planting annual crops, where the soil is exposed to erosion. A leguminous forage tree (a *Lucaena* species) which also bears protein-rich beans was introduced by Dan and accepted by those with rain catchment tanks. A second type of tree planted immediately next to the tank contained sap that could be used to flocculate the sediment. A twig from the tree placed in a bucket of water would rid it of most of its sediment before it passed through the charcoal filter.

At this point the farmer and his household had achieved a marked improvement in their life-style with a potential extra income of Ksh 4,000 a year.

In most cases it took a year or so for the novelty of this new income to wear off and for people to re-invest it. During this settling period, people bought radios, watches and other luxury goods, as items of interest and prestige. This was by no means a bad thing as radios add to a family's general education with a large input of information.

During this time some market gardening was done, using the water from the catchment tank. With some planning and the sale of these vegetables to neighbours in the dry season, people found that the income from the water could be doubled.

Branching out

Several paths of growth branched from this point. People who learnt the new skills which Dan introduced became craftsmen, and were able to work with concrete. The plastering technology used in lining the water catchment tank was used in the construction of simple concrete bins for storing grain. This grain was dried for use when harvests failed; it naturally required a longer cooking time. Having introduced firewood management at the same time as tree-planting for erosion control. Dan found that an improved stove fitted into the homesteaders' thinking.

The introduction of grain stores and stoves was different from the other innovations in one important way. Although the original seven families Dan was working with built them, no one else asked how to build the stove or grain store, unlike the rain catchment tank where neighbours who could afford to do so had built them on their own land.

The reason for not taking up the store was simple, said the homesteaders. All things had spirits, some good and some bad, either blessed or cursed by God. The catchment tank obviously had God's blessing as He filled it with water. But the store? It showed neither good nor bad omens, so the people were prepared to wait several years before trusting it. The solution was for Dan to lay hands on it and pray for God's blessing. This simple act opened the way for more than 20 grain stores to be built.

The top-loading stove was unacceptable because of a local custom, which requires a wife to pass food over her genitals a few times a year before serving it to her husband. The problem was solved by building a seat (to warm the woman), giving the stove a side opening, and praying. This led to between 20 and 30 stoves being built within a few months.

All this was done without money from outside; Dan's only contribution was information. Yet an aid agency with a budget of Ksh 10 million working on stoves near Dan's project had only 100 in the field.

Biogas

The homesteads still depended on paraffin for lighting. A natural choice of technology to increase self-sufficiency was biogas. The first digester was made by Dan and consisted of three oil drums and an agitator, with three other oil drums to make a pressurizer. With a home-made lamp designed by Catholics in Kenya's Western Province, the system cost under Ksh 2,000.

The cow or ox not sold at the beginning of the project supplied dung for the digester. Human excreta was also used. An interesting social change caused by the digester occurred among the men. Before the introduction of the digester, men would not admit to going to the toilet. So even if a pit latrine had been built, a man would not use it but continued to go into the bush. This was an obvious risk to health. The biogas, however, was different. Giving four extra hours of good light in the evening, it increased the family's enjoyment of life; it now became noble to contribute to the digester. Dan testifies to being in discussion with a group of men and someone standing up and saying, 'I'm just going to contribute to this evening's light.'

Three years after the introduction of the ox harness, water from the catchment was being used in many situations: the market garden, to water the cow, for cooking and washing and in the biogas plant. A simple windpump, produced by the Salvation Army in its Workshop for the Handicapped at under Ksh 2,000, shifted all the water required.

Windpump

The windpump was developed from a combination of ideas from several people. It had a portable tower 15 feet high and its own stand, to allow it to

Sketch to show water from the sunken tank being filtered using power from the windpump

be moved around the homestead. The blades were steep-pitched for easy starting and stalling and to prevent over-speeding. The diaphragm of the pump was designed to be replaced with rubber from old tyres.

The suitability of the design is demonstrated by two anecdotes. Firstly, the strength of the Ksh 60 bearings can be shown by the fact that they ran for six months with no grease and without a mark on them. Secondly, Dan began to puzzle at the extraordinarily long life of the diaphragm on one particular machine, as he had not changed it for more than nine months. It then came to light that the man of the family, attracted back from the city by developments at home, had changed it twice with no help from Dan, and without even telling him.

At this point the family, complete again, had a regular supply of food and water, lighting, a well-managed farm and, perhaps most important, a future not dependent on the state of the government or a supply of oil.

By December 1983 the original seven groups were using the windpump and more were interested. There were variations between the seven groups in the rate of uptake and the innovations. For instance, stores have been built without a catchment tank. The ox harness is known to have encouraged a poor family which was hesitating over buying a cow for milk to purchase one, when they realized it could be used to plough as well.

(*Waterlines* Vol. 3 No. 3, January 1985)

Why TOOL changed to small-scale projects
GERT VAN DER BIJL and MARC HOFSTRA

TOOL, the Dutch appropriate technology organization, had been involved in two relatively large-scale projects: one in Ghazipur in northern India, and the other in Sukabumi, on the south-western tip of Java, Indonesia. Both projects had promising technical results but neither noticeably improved the position of the target group, the poorest of the poor.

This showed TOOL that, although a reliable technology is extremely important, economic and social conditions are the decisive factors in whether a project is successful. Appropriate technology requires appropriate projects, and small projects are more likely to affect the lower strata of the population. They require less complicated project management and allow greater flexibility for local people to participate. Adjustments can then be made to match changing circumstances. Small projects tend to fit in better with existing local activities; they can more easily be taken over by a local organization, even if it lacks management capacity. Small projects also have a better 'cost to benefit' ratio than large ones.

Windmills in Ghazipur

The windmill project in Ghazipur developed after TOOL made contact with the Organization of the Rural Poor (ORP) in the northern Indian state of Uttar Pradesh. ORP was established to help the rural poor obtain credit to finance projects to improve their standard of living. During discussions with ORP, it was decided to introduce windmills to pump groundwater for irrigation.

In the Ghazipur area, 85 per cent of the population depends mainly on agriculture for its living, and only the rich farmers could afford to buy a diesel or electric pump. Farmers who owned pumps could also put pressure on those who did not, by selling them water. Those who had no pumps only produced enough food for their own families. Their main source of cash income was off-farm employment, but they sold any small surpluses of food they might have. The TOOL-ORP project aimed at making irrigation with windmills feasible for these farmers.

After a period of preparation, the project started in 1978. In 1979, a workshop to produce the windmills was established near Ghazipur. It was originally planned that local blacksmiths should make the windmills themselves, and also learn how to repair and maintain them. This proved impossible in practice, because the blacksmiths lacked the knowledge and tools to make high quality windmills. So Dutch windmill specialists trained Indian technicians in Ghazipur, and produced well-made windmills of the 12 PU 500 type, which has 12 steel blades and a rotor diameter of 5 m.

The design was developed by the Working Group in Development Techniques (WDT) at Enschede, The Netherlands. The windmills were installed free of charge at selected farms. Up to the end of the project in 1981, 15 windmills had been installed for testing. Only three were actually bought by farmers, and none of these were farmers with very small amounts of land who were supposed to be the target group. Even after six years, small farmers in Ghazipur showed a distinct lack of interest in the windmills.

It proved very hard to introduce windmills to Ghazipur, for a number of reasons. A significant problem was that the windmills' output was out of phase with the traditional seasonal pattern of crops in the area, and the farmers' capacity to adjust their farming calendar was overestimated. For instance, wheat was normally irrigated in November, but the wind was too feeble in that month to raise water. This meant that sowing had to be delayed until the third week of November when the wind had picked up, which would be likely to reduce the yield.

Windmills performed most effectively during the hot, dry summer in Ghazipur, so farmers needed to grow crops such as sugar-cane intercropped with onions during the summer season to make them economically attractive. Water-melons bear fruit (and need water) in summer, but labour is scarce then and it is very difficult to sell crops in the summer.

A second problem was the inequalities in the amount of land held by each farmer, and the fact that the land of many farmers was split into several plots, as a way of spreading risks. Almost 70 per cent of the population of Ghazipur either had no land at all or less than two and one half acres, the optimal acreage for the windmill. Unlike other types of pump, the output of water from a windmill is impossible to regulate, which makes it difficult to sell the water. If it had been traditional for farmers in Ghazipur to co-operate, the problem could have been overcome. However, this was not the case, and attempts to encourage the purchase of windmills by groups of farmers failed.

Lack of credit was a third problem. During the period of the project, the price of windmills varied between 7,000 and 10,000 Rupees (Rs) (Rs 8 = US $1), and a loan for this amount would have to be repaid at about Rs 2,400 a year. Compared to the annual income of small farmers, Rs 1,300 to Rs 3,500, this is a huge sum. It should also be remembered that small farmers are far better off than the marginal and landless farmers.

Small farmers could therefore only afford a windmill if they could get loans or subsidies. The Government of India subsidizes 25 per cent of the cost to small farmers and 33 per cent to marginal farmers. Additionally, the Government of Uttar Pradesh provides a 50 per cent subsidy for farmers who own less than two and one half acres. However, illiterate farmers found it very difficult to secure these subsidies, and even if they had, they would have needed supplementary loans.

Between the start of the project in 1978 and the point when the Dutch pulled out in 1980, considerable transfer of technology had taken place. Afterwards, most of the technicians from the project worked at the Institute of Engineering and Rural Technology in Allahabad, which has been desig-nated one of the country's National Wind Energy Research and Develop-ment Centres and is responsible for manufacturing hundreds of windmills for the National Windmill Demonstration Project. But there was no effect on the living conditions of the poor. The Ghazipur project showed that just developing a technology was not enough to ensure its success.

Technologies in Indonesia

Similar problems arose in another project in Sukabumi, Indonesia, set up by the University of Technology, Eindhoven, and the TOOL Foundation in 1976, ending in 1983. It aimed to develop a range of technologies for the poorest sector of the population, and was carried out by the Development Technology Centre (DTC) of the Bandung Institute of Technology with technical support from TOOL and financial support from the Dutch Government.

The technologies included simple handpumps, windmills, low-cost water filters, ferrocement water tanks, tapioca and paddy dryers, biogas digesters, rice-hull storers and ferrocement fishing boats. The technologies were tested widely in the area. The needs of the people were investigated and surveys were carried out on the impact of the technologies on the users. Reports and manuals were the result of this effort.

The emphasis was then shifted from the development of appropriate technologies for rural needs to commercial technologies aimed at local entrepreneurs and craftsmen. In practice, it was found that most of the rural technologies developed by DTC had benefited the middle classes. The project had also concentrated too much on developing technologies *for* the poor rather than *with* them. As in Ghazipur, it was too much of a risk for the small-scale farmers to take. Interestingly, the local population was hesitant to promote the tapioca dryer as it was feared that the Chinese business community would pick it up because they were more innovative than the poorer people. However, the project certainly played a role in helping appropriate technology become accepted as an important concept in development by Indonesian universities, development organizations and extension officers.

There are several lessons to be learnt from these examples. It is important to investigate the needs of the target group before the start of any project: attention should not be given only to the technological solutions. The technologies should not be a fixed 'package' as described in the two examples above. The local population's participation should be sought in looking for solutions to the problems which have been identified. The local counterpart organization has an important role here, so it must be chosen very carefully.

The local counterpart in the Ghazipur project, the Organization of the Rural Poor, seemed to have a bad image among the rural population; in any case, it did not really have the resources to mount such a large project. The Development Technology Centre in Bandung, being affiliated to a university, consisted mainly of technicians without strong links to the rural poor. Putting appropriate technology into practice required both investments and risks from the small farmers at Ghazipur and Sukabumi, but poor farmers had to play safe and aim for security and immediate profits. Improved technologies should demand few investments of the users and should not demand too great a change in their routine.

Development organizations need to be wary of introducing completely unknown technologies, whether they are small- or large-scale. Existing local technologies are seldom investigated by organizations which come in from outside, but these should be improved and built upon, as they are more likely to meet the needs of the rural poor.[5,6]

CHAPTER 2
Shallow Wells

Well-sinking is one of the basic technologies advocated in Chapter 1. The article by John Allsebrook is just as valid today as when it was written over ten years ago. When planning well-sites, it is essential to study and understand ground conditions. The approach expressed in the title 'Where shall we dig the well?' also shows an early appreciation of self-help community development. The next article, by Simon Watt and Bill Wood, previewed their book which continues to be a standard work on the subject.[3] Their article outlines the advantages and limitations of simple wells lined with reinforced concrete. It is followed by an article by Robert Trietsch who had been involved in Dutch drinking water programmes in Tanzania from 1972. There, auguring wells by hand-operated equipment proved a good alternative to hand-digging. Robert Trietsch is the author of another recognized classic which described the Shinyanga and Morogoro projects in detail but which is, unfortunately, out-of-print. *Low-cost Water Supply, Part 1*[7] is a good alternative. 'Wells for Mali' is a record of the experiences of Euro Action ACORD working with existing co-operatives in the drought-stricken northern areas of Mali. Here, corrugated-iron sheeting was the chosen material for lining hand-dug wells and investigations were speeded up by using motorized rigs. Finally comes a case study from the Sahel, based on material provided by Bob Mann and Derrick Knight. As this article concludes, 'Where the land, and therefore its people, are this poor, the division between surviving and not surviving is thin. Small-scale efforts such as described in this article can make a difference'.

The vital importance of rehabilitating existing wells and constructing new wells cannot be overemphasized.

Where shall we dig the well?
JOHN ALLSEBROOK

The whole subject of water supply revolves around rain. Where, when and how much falls and what happens to it after it has fallen. Conditions vary widely from place to place as, obviously, there will be greater fluctuations where one has three months' rain followed by a nine-month drought than where rain falls frequently throughout the year. However, the basic behaviour is the same and six (rather obvious) principles apply:

○ Water will not flow uphill.
○ Water will not flow through clay or dense rock.
○ Water passes only slowly through sand and is liable to move the sand with it.
○ Water flows freely through rock fissures and between stones.
○ Rainfall results from, and depends upon, evaporation from exposed water surfaces and transpiration from plants.
○ Only rain which has fallen upon and soaked into porous ground can provide the underground water store from which wells can draw.

To plan a well-digging project successfully, three natural conditions must be considered: climate, geography and geology. The diagrams on page 26 do not pretend to give all the answers; with such a wide subject, there must be some generalization. They do, however, help to explain a wide variety of situations and provide basic guide-lines for seeking effective solutions.

Geology examines how the Earth was formed and how succeeding layers were deposited, eroded, and the resultant debris redeposited elsewhere. The areas which particularly concern us are which strata are porous and which impervious, their sequence and where they are exposed and able to receive rainfall percolation.

In the very early stages of the Earth's formation, the land rose and fell in relation to sea-level and, after the various layers of mud and sand and rock had been deposited, a wrinkling and tipping of the land and its deposits took place. This was followed by a gradual erosion of the layers by the wind, by ice and by water. The up-tilted strata have outcrops (where the rock is exposed to the surface) which can receive rainfall percolation, and where debris is deposited. Where the debris material is porous, the resultant pockets of material can receive and collect rainfall percolation and provide aquifers into which a successful well can be dug. When rain falls, something like half goes back into the atmosphere, either as evaporation or through transpiration from plants. The rest either soaks into the ground if this is porous, or runs off (as from an umbrella) if it is impervious. There are cases where the ground might be described as semi-porous, or reluctantly porous. In these places, the amount of water percolating into the ground can often be increased by building little dams across the slope in order to slow down the run-off water and give it more time to soak in. An additional benefit of such dams is a reduction in soil erosion.

Deciding where to dig the well

The figures which follow show various geological situations and the water supply conditions and levels associated with them.

Women are very often the regular carriers of water (WaterAid/Framework)

Children also have to collect and carry water. Nepal (UNICEF/Nick Wheeler)

Upgraded well, with a raised plinth (WaterAid/Jeremy Hartley)

An upgraded well with a concrete surround, and a windlass structure (Blair Research Laboratory)

Rain falling on the porous landscape shown in Figure 2.1 will produce a saturated water level. Often there is a river flowing in the valley with a water level the same as that of a pond dug nearby and at the top of the horizon of saturation, called the water-table. If a borehole is drilled (or a well dug) up the hillside, the water-table will be found to be higher than it is in the valley. This is evidence that the underground flow is normally moving from the surrounding catchment area towards the valley and not from the river. However, there is a possible exception: on low ground, if extreme drought dries out the area and the river is bringing water from a distant source that is continuing to flow, this water will soak into the valley alluvium (alluvium is water-borne matter deposited on low-lying lands).

Figure 2.2 illustrates a more complicated situation. The lie of the land is similar to that of the previous figure, but there is clay on top of the hill which acts like an umbrella. Rain falling on to the clay cannot soak in so it runs off and soaks into the porous ground at the edges of the clay cap; in fact, 'swallow-holes' may be formed. (In this case swallow-holes were eroded through the clay to the porous ground.) Again, a good supply of water may be obtained from a borehole near the valley but a borehole drilled through the clay capping will probably give only a poor yield because the joints and fissures between the rocks have never had the chance to be washed clear of silt by rainwater passing through them. Here again, the gradient of the water-table from the high ground towards the river can be seen.

Figure 2.3 shows a hill with a porous capping and underlying clay rising above the valley. If the capping is a loamy sand, then it will hold water rather like a sponge, forming a water-table and letting water ooze away to form springs where the porous ground meets the clay and cannot soak down any further. If it is a small area, the store of water will not last very long into a drought, but if it is a larger area then it will go on yielding a supply throughout the dry season, within the limitations of the area and character of the strata. When there is an abundant rainfall, springs will flow at the higher spring-line, but these are likely to fail in dry weather. The springs on the other side of the hill will persist much longer and will tend to maintain lush pastures on the slopes below them, or even a perpetual stream.

In Figure 2.4, another porous stratum on top of a clay stratum is shown. In this case, however, there is another, higher, layer of clay. Area A is porous and water falling on to it soaks in, whereas area B is impervious. A look at an ordinary map of such an area will indicate which area is impervious and which is porous because there will be drainage ditches marked on B but few, if any, on area A. The borehole on the left, marked C, will go straight into porous strata and should get a good water supply. The borehole at D will go through clay before it enters the aquifer; it will tap water which has fallen on catchment A and has percolated underground to D. When the hole enters the aquifer, water will rise to a rest level at the water-table, as shown. This is known as subartesian pressure. At borehole E, the clay ground has fallen to

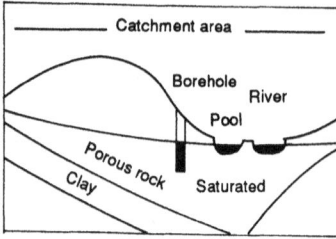

Figure 2.1

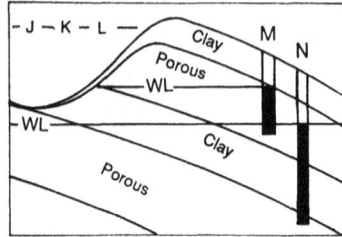

Figure 2.6

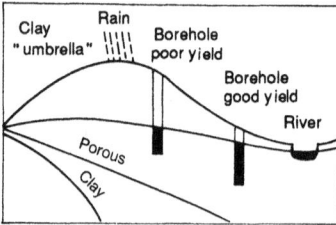

Figure 2.2

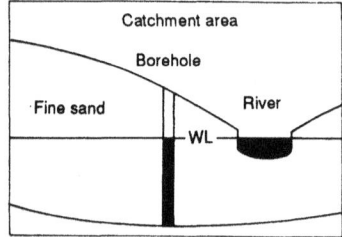

Figure 2.7

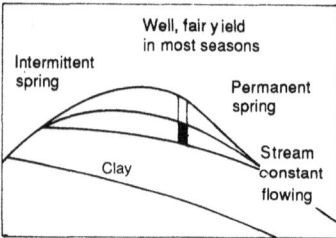

Figure 2.3

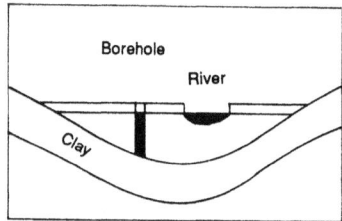

Figure 2.8

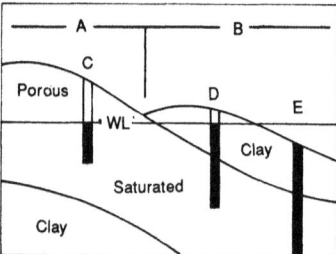

Figure 2.4

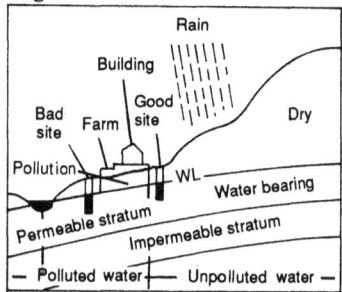

Figure 2.9

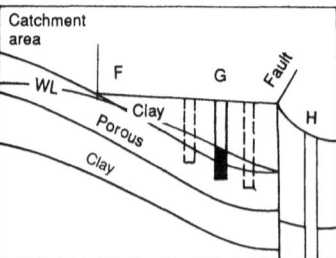

Figure 2.5

Factors affecting the availability of ground water

below the water-table and water will flow from the borehole by true artesian pressure. (An artesian well is one bored deep enough so that water rises to surface of the ground by internal pressure.)

Figure 2.5 illustrates a similar but more complicated situation. One or more boreholes at G are some distance from the edge of the outcrop and catchment at F. Heavy pumping at G has lowered the water-table, because the porous strata is rather dense and the fissures and crevices therein restrict the freedom of flow. In the same way, a pipe which is too small will starve the flow at the end. In situations like this it is necessary to limit the permitted rate of pumping so that the water-level does not go down out of reach. There are also other important situations where pumping must be restricted: where the catchment area is not big enough to collect enough replenishment from rainfall to meet the pumping demands and where excessive lowering of the water-table may encourage the inflow of salt water from another direction. Figure 2.5 also shows a geological fault and it is obvious why a borehole at H is likely to give a disappointing result because the strata have slipped so that the continuity of the porous layer is interrupted and the flow actually valved off.

Figure 2.6 is rather like the earlier diagrams, but there is a hill with a clay capping over a porous one, followed by another band of clay and another porous zone. These strata are all dipping down so that the right hand area is covered with clay. It might be supposed that there would be a porous catchment area on the left-hand slope, but it is masked by clay washed down from the capping at L. Consequently, the borehole at M will not get a continuing supply of water because it receives no replenishment. When first drilled, however, a borehole sited here might find a small supply of water accumulated over a long time. A deeper borehole, as at N going down through the second layer of clay into the lower aquifer, may tap an excellent yield and here the water-level will respond to that under catchment area J.

The situation shown in Figure 2.7 illustrates the problems of fine sand. Sand can be so dense that only 100 or 200 gallons of water per hour can be obtained from a well or borehole. This does not mean that there is no water there; only that it moves so reluctantly through the sand that it will flow slowly into the well, carrying sand with it and resulting in collapse. One method of dealing with the problem in a site such as this is to dig a large-diameter well or pond into which water will ooze through the large area of its floor slowly enough to be at 'non-sand-disturbing velocity'.

To return to the subject of difficult sand conditions, an alternative method is to sink a number of tube-wells, at intervals, for instance of 5 to 10 m, as on-site dewatering projects, then to couple them together. In one case, a combined yield of some 1, 00 to 2,000 gallons of water per hour was obtained from such a group. Although each hole only gave about 100 gallons per hour, by pumping from the tube-well system, a farmer will have enough water to do a good irrigation job on several acres.

Figure 2.8 shows a shallow valley aquifer overlying clay. This was evidently formed from debris carried by the river from somewhere upstream and deposited there. Its character, stony, sandy or clay, will depend on the conditions of the upstream strata. Within the limitations of these characteristics and the area concerned, alluvial beds like this, even small ones, can yield useful supplies. However, being shallow, they are vulnerable to pollution.

Regarding pollution, Figure 2.9 hardly needs explanation. Clearly pollution, such as a farmyard built on porous stratum, will soak down. Rain falling there will help it on its way so a well or river downstream would get polluted, thus a 'pure' site would be found upstream.

It is interesting to do an experiment to show how much water there is in saturated ground. A pond is a visible store of water from which one might pump, but evaporation takes place from its surface. Records have shown that this averages around 15 inches annually in England. In very hot desert areas, it can be up to about seven times as much. An aquifer is like a pond filled with stones and as the water has no exposed surface, there is no direct evaporation. This is one advantage of underground storage, but how much water can a pond filled with stones hold?

A see-through plastic box filled with small stones makes an effective model to illustrate this point. When water is poured in until the water-table comes up to ground-level (and seen through the transparent wall) it will be noted that the container accepts a rather surprisingly large amount of water into the crevices between the stones. Actually, it varies at around 10 per cent of the aquifer's depth, according to the size of the grains, granules or stones. Obviously the depth of the aquifer is significant, and, according to this percentage, if it were 10 feet deep, roughly one foot of water would be in store and available for use. If irrigation is involved, this is the way to go about making the calculations. A borehole can be sunk into the model aquifer by pushing into it a perforated tube-well. Water enters through the holes and rises to the water-table. One can now pump using a simple syringe as a crude pump. If the water is discharged near the borehole it will soak in and circulate but if it is taken away to another area or if it evaporates or transpires from irrigated plants then the underground store will be depleted.

This brings us back full circle to the question of how much rain falls and where to find porous outcrops, into which rain can soak and replenish the aquifers. When planning well sites it is necessary to study and try to understand the conditions that nature has established.

(Appropriate Technology Vol. 4 No. 1, May 1977)

Hand-dug water wells lined with reinforced concrete
SIMON WATT and BILL WOOD

Digging wells by hand is the most widely used method of well construction in many rural areas of the world. Some of these hand-dug wells are lined with brick and masonry, penetrate to great depths, and have been in continuous use for centuries. The more common hand-dug well, however, is usually of a more temporary nature, being simply an open unlined hole dug into the ground in the dry season to reach the stored ground water that has infiltrated downwards from rain-water and surface water.

Better knowledge and the use of modern materials, tools and equipment has transformed this traditional hand-dug well from a crude open hole in the ground, liable to collapse, dangerous to its users both during and after construction and with an infamous reputation as the source of bacterial and parasitic diseases, into a safe structure based on sound engineering principles, and a hygienic and reliable source of water. It is still one of the cheapest methods for providing a small water supply for a rural area, and while construction is slow and laborious compared with other well construction techniques, it has many advantages.

Construction is simple and straightforward. It consists of excavating a hole in the ground by hand, removing the material to the surface, and lining the sides of the hole to prevent collapse; when water is struck a pre-built tube inside the first lining is sunk as deep as possible into the water-bearing strata.

Hand-dug wells and self-help programmes

Self-help well construction programmes are designed to provide the minimum of assistance to allow the users to build a cheap well that conforms to the necessary technical standards. There are many different methods of well construction, which drill, bore, or drive a small-diameter well from the surface, but experience has shown that hand-dug wells have the advantage of great simplicity; they can be built with the minimum of skills, and administration is not as critical or costly compared with the construction of small-diameter wells which need constant and skilled attention at all stages.

The first task of a self-help programme is to organize the purchase, delivery and storage of materials, equipment and tools. Expensive items of equipment used during construction can then be moved from one well to another as they are needed, allowing the cost of the equipment to be shared between many separate wells.

Many different materials can be used to line hand-dug wells: bricks, masonry, fabricated steel or plastic sections have all been used, but perhaps the most adaptable and versatile material is a thin shell of reinforced concrete. Reinforced concrete can be mixed and poured by unskilled workers and the reinforcing steel can be fixed with the minimum of supervision. It requires only a small thickness for structural soundness (7.5 cm in good ground and up to 15 cm in bad ground); it can be cast *in-situ* behind shutters in the well to make a permanent lining that bonds to the excavated walls and is strong enough to support the walls of the well and any superstructure that is needed; it can be cast on the surface to make rings that are lowered into the well as required; it is durable and can be made watertight to keep out surface water pollution, or porous to allow water to flow into the well and it can flex without breaking providing that enough reinforcing steel has been included.

Compared with the different methods used to construct small-diameter wells, reinforced concrete lined hand-dug wells have many advantages (though some of these can also apply to other linings):

○ The equipment used in construction is simple and lightweight: thus it can be carried by hand to almost any site, however inaccessible by road.
○ The method of construction uses craft skills which are often known to the well users, and which can be easily taught to untrained people; this reduces the amount of supervision that must be given. Each stage of the work can be physically seen and handled, and there is no danger of the lost or jammed tools which often presents serious difficulties in the construction of small-diameter wells.
○ The bulk of the materials needed to make the wells will be available locally, except for the cement and steel reinforcing rods.
○ Shutters, hand tools, pulley blocks and so on can be purchased or made up and carried from site to site to spread the cost over many wells.
○ The large diameter of a hand-dug well allows water to percolate into the well overnight from slow-flowing aquifers, to be stored for use during the following day. It also allows a simple rope and bucket to be used to lift out the water; commercial mechanical pumps have a notorious record of failure in rural areas due to the lack of maintenance.
○ One of the most important advantages of choosing this method of well construction is that it often adapts and improves on traditional methods, both expanding the skills of the local well-diggers and providing a familiar water source to the users.

Hand-dug wells have obvious limitations. Excavation is generally slow and laborious. While successful wells have been sunk by hand to depths of over 150 metres, half that depth is normally considered to be the limit of practical sinking. Sinking through hard rocks is a very slow procedure by hand, although problems can be overcome by using an air compressor and pneumatic tools or explosives.

The major drawback with hand-dug wells is the difficulty of penetrating more than about 5 m below water-level, with the result that the well will often be empty during the dry season when the water-level falls. For this reason, wells are left unfinished when the water-level is high, and sinking is completed when it has fallen.

Hand-dug wells are usually left open at the top to allow a rope and bucket to be used for water lifting; the well is then open to contamination from polluted wastes on the rope or bucket, or from rubbish that is thrown or falls into the well.

If the well is going to be deep below 60 m, provision may be needed for ventilation for the well-diggers.

Construction of reinforced concrete-lined hand-dug wells

The well consists essentially of three parts:

○ A well-head structure with a head wall to prevent rubbish and surface wastes from running into the well, and a drained apron for the users to stand on as they lift their water. The well-head structure also provides a base for the pumping mechanism.
○ A thin watertight shell of reinforced concrete, lining the well shaft from the surface to the water-bearing strata.
○ A porous intake section plug telescoped inside the main lining and sunk into the water-bearing strata (Figure 2.10).

The **well shaft** is constructed first. Using the dig-down build-up method, a circular hole is excavated carefully from the surface down to the water, with a diameter of some 1.45 m; this diameter allows two men to work down the well at any one time. The reinforcing steel is placed around the sides of the well, shuttering is lowered down from the surface and erected at the bottom, and concrete is poured between the shutters and the excavated walls.

The reinforced concrete lining is usually poured in lifts of 5 m, with each lift containing a concrete curb built into the sides of the well to prevent the lining from sinking downwards under its own weight: the well-shaft lining is therefore self-supporting. If the sides of the hole begin to collapse before water is reached, then the well is lined immediately up to the surface. In very bad ground, the depth of the lifts may be less than one metre.

The porous **intake section** allows water to flow into the well whilst holding back the soil particles in the water-bearing strata, preventing them from collapse. The intake section is designed so that it can be sunk deeper into the base of the well when the water-level falls during the dry season.

The intake section can be constructed in several different ways. It is generally built from pre-cast concrete rings or blocks at the base of the previously lined well shaft, standing free of the walls on a concrete cutting ring. The water-bearing strata is excavated inside the telescoped tube, which sinks down under its own weight. If motor-powered pumps are used to lower the water-level, the section can be sunk to give 3 or 4 m of final water depth

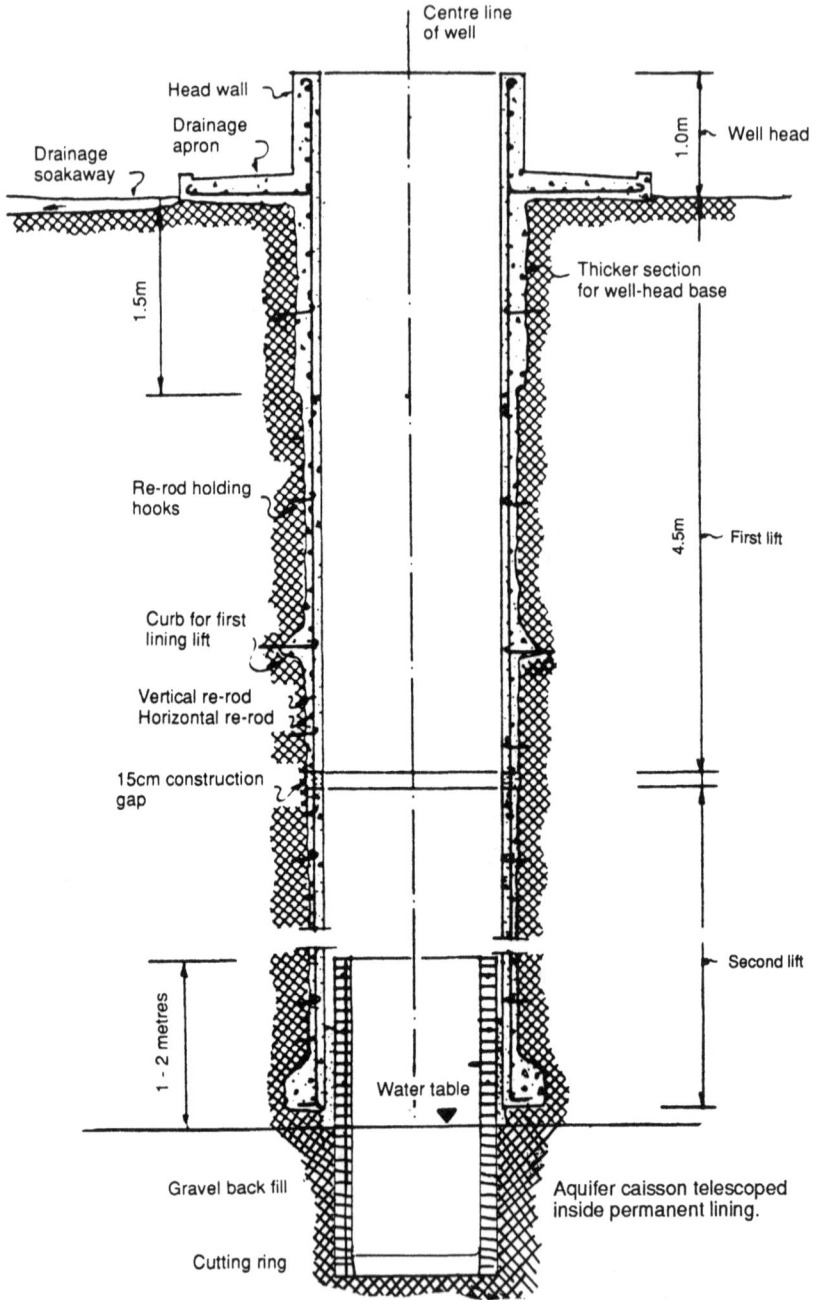

Figure 2.10   *Cross section through finished well*

in the well, giving a good reservoir of water; without pumping, the section can be sunk only 1 or 2 m below top water-level.

The intake section is left telescoped 2 m inside the well shaft for later deepening, and to allow for any settlement. Movement of this section will not, therefore, cause the well-shaft lining to fracture. Finally, a porous base plug made from layers of sand and gravel, or a concrete disc, is installed inside the intake section to prevent the movement of the water-bearing strata into the well.

The **head wall** is one of the most important parts of the well from the point of view of hygiene, and it is the last part of the well to be built. It prevents surface wastes from running into the well mouth and helps contain rubbish and animals from falling into the well. It is built about 1 m high, and is thin enough to discourage the well-users from standing on the top whilst they draw their water; this prevents the eggs of Guinea worms, discharged from the ulcers of infected persons, from washing into the well and infecting others.

The concrete apron, 2 m wide, provides a firm foundation for the well-users. It is drained and the spilled waste water is led away at least 5 m from the well to a drainage ditch.

Many of the serious diseases that cause illness and even death to mankind are related in some way or other to water and its use. If the well is properly and carefully maintained, and the users understand the need for strict hygiene in their use of the well and its vicinity, then the well will make a major improvement to the general level of their health and welfare. If the well is poorly constructed and used, however, or if contaminated wastes are allowed to enter the water either from the well head or by soaking in from nearby latrines, then it will become a source of infection and will spread diseases amongst the users. Educating the well-users on the importance of looking after and using the well properly is one of the most important tasks in any well-construction programme.[8,9]

(*Appropriate Technology* Vol. 3 No. 2, August 1976)

Shallow wells for low-cost water supply in Tanzania
ROBERT TRIETSCH

In 1971 the Dutch Government started its development aid activities in the drinking water sector of Tanzania with the preparation of a water master-plan for the Shinyanga Region, an area in the north-western part of the country, about 200 km south of Lake Victoria. One of the recommendations of the Shinyanga Water Supply Survey, to embark on the large-scale construction of shallow wells in the region, was put into practice: in 1974 the

Shinyanga Shallow Wells Project began, sponsored by the Dutch Government.

The aims of the project were:

○ To form a construction unit to build a total of 700 shallow wells.
○ Research on and development of low-cost and simple solutions for well construction and the local manufacture of tools, equipment and pumps.
○ Training of counterpart personnel to ensure the continuation of the programme after direct Dutch participation in the project ended in July 1978.

Finding water

Various techniques for establishing successful well sites were tried, including geo-electrical surveys. Eventually a standard approach was selected, with test holes drilled using hand augers. This method avoided the necessity of using sophisticated equipment which would require highly-qualified staff, and spare parts which would not be readily available.

The method has been used successfully ever since, and works as follows. Potential well sites near villages are indicated by a hydrogeologist, on the basis of available aerial photographs and geological or hydrological data. A team of two surveyors is then sent to the site to perform a test drilling.

Using hand-auger equipment a 10 cm-diameter test hole is made. When the first water is struck, a casing pipe is inserted into the hole to stop it collapsing. Drilling is continued inside the casing with 7 cm-diameter drilling equipment and a bailer, until a second aquifer is struck. A pumping test is carried out with a hand-operated pump, the 'jolly jumper', on this second aquifer and the water quality is tested.

Experience has shown that it is possible to make survey test holes more than 20 m in depth using this hand-operated method. It can be carried out by relatively untrained personnel and, because of the light weight of the equipment, a Land-Rover is normally sufficient for transporting the entire survey team and its equipment.

If the pumping test shows that it is possible to pump continuously at a rate of 1,000 litres per hour or more, the aquifer is suitable for constructing a small-diameter well. With smaller outputs, of say 500 litres/hour, survey drilling is normally repeated at other sites, to find a better well location if possible. If this fails, larger-diameter wells may have to be constructed. Because of their larger volume, water will collect in these wells overnight and augment the direct inflow, to achieve an adequate output.

The quality of the shallow ground-water in Tanzania is generally good, but may occasionally have a high fluoride concentration or be slightly saline. Therefore fluoride concentration and the electrical conductivity of the water as an indication of its salinity are the only characteristics which need to be checked.

At the start of the Shinyanga Shallow Wells Project no one had experience of the large-scale construction of shallow wells in Tanzania. For that reason it was decided to dig wells by hand as this would most closely resemble traditional methods.

From the very start it had been intended to have the well construction activities eventually continued by the Tanzanian counterpart organization, without any outside support. Thus any construction method relying on equipment that was not readily available in the country and/or would require foreign currency for its operation and maintenance was considered unsuitable.

Hand-dug wells (Figure 2.11)

For each well, a circle with a diameter of about 1.5 m was staked out around the successful survey test hole, and a hole with this diameter dug as deep as possible. As soon as the ground-water table was reached or whenever instability of the walls rendered digging inside the well dangerous, concrete well rings (inner diameter 1.25 m, wall thickness 10 cm, height 1 m) were lowered into the hole and digging continued to the required depth. The rings

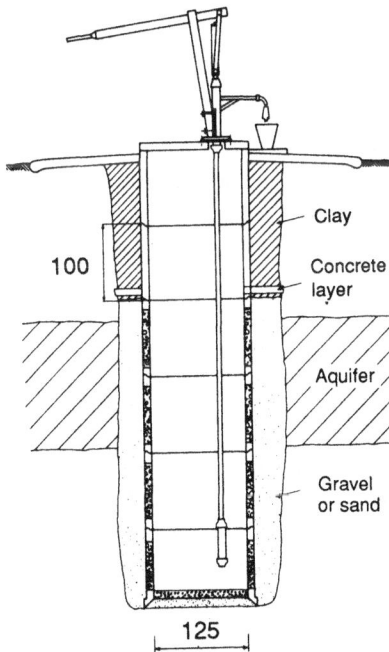

Figure 2.11 *Cross-section of a hand-dug well*

sank under their own weight (a metric ton) when the soil underneath was removed, and new rings were added to form a concrete lining for the well.

The only reinforcement needed was a 6 mm diameter reinforcing rod round both the top and the bottom of each ring. Porous rings were used, made of concrete containing no fine material, whereas the remaining rings were made of normal concrete.

Some shortcomings became apparent with the 1,000-plus wells made in the Shinyanga region by this method. For instance, in good aquifers, the speed of the water entering the well hampers construction. If only one well is to be constructed, a solution is to dig the well as deep as the level of inflowing water will allow, and finish digging in the dry season, when the water-table is at its lowest. This method is not suitable for large-scale construction projects, where the well has to be dewatered during the construction and cannot be left.

Suction pumps could be used for dewatering if the ground-water-table is less than 7 m below ground-level. Diesel- or petrol-driven pumps are not suitable for use inside wells because their poisonous exhaust gases would affect the well-diggers, so electric pumps were used in the well, with generating sets at ground-level.

Fine sand may be washed into the well due to the reduced water pressure inside, if it has to be dewatered during construction. In some areas of Shinyanga, thin clay layers tended to collapse because the sand which had supported them was washed away. This blocked the aquifer.

Maintaining motor pumps and generating tests in rural areas of developing countries is not an easy task and may be next to impossible without access to foreign currency. This is a problem that counterpart organizations in developing countries often come up against. There is also a danger of electrocution if electricity cables are accidentally cut with spades or pick-axes.

Another problem was that hard layers, such as laterite, may slow down construction considerably. In any case, it takes a lot longer to make a hand-dug well than to hand-drill one, so it is consequently a much more expensive operation.

Hand drilling

Augering wells with hand-operated equipment of 200 to 300 mm diameter (Figure 2.12) has proved to be a good alternative to hand-digging and is suited to developing countries. There is no need to dewater the well during construction, and the equipment is not only cheaper but can also be maintained and repaired locally. Costs per well can be reduced by at least 30 per cent.

The drilling equipment comprises an auger drill with various bits in two diameters (230 mm and 180 mm) plus casing pipes. The hand-drilling set is

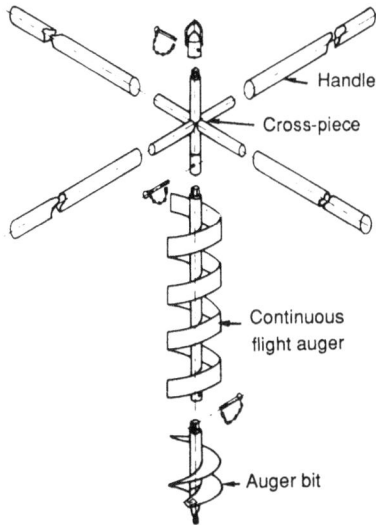

Figure 2.12   *A heavy hand auger of the type used in Shinyanga*

suspended from a tripod. It is screwed into the ground by between four and eight men, and if necessary the downward force is increased by having some of them sit on top.

The method of drilling is essentially the same as that described for the survey. The smaller-size equipment is used inside the casing, and the bailer is used for removing the soil once an aquifer has been reached. At the required depth, a partly slotted PVC filter/casing pipe combination is inserted in the borehole, and this is finished in essentially the same way as a traditional tube-well, by sustained pumping to remove the fine material from the formation around the casing until clear water is pumped.

This hand-drilling method has been used since 1977. When, in 1978, the focus of Dutch development aid in the water supply sector was shifted from Shinyanga Region to Morogoro Region (about 200 km south-west of the capital, Dar es Salaam), the Morogoro Construction Project started using the same hand-drilling method and no hand-dug wells have been made.

Since then, a number of well construction projects have been established in Tanzania, sponsored by various donor organizations. Of these, the projects in the Tanga and Singida Regions also use hand-drilled wells, whereas the others rely on the more traditional hand-dug wells.

A variation on the Shinyanga method is being used in a Dutch-assisted project for the Lake Basin Development Authority at Kisumu, Kenya. There, soil conditions are less favourable for drilling wells, but digging can often be carried out without having to use a lining, and the wells can be dewatered with handpumps. In these wells a PVC filter/casing pipe is put at the centre, and the remainder of the well is filled with crushed stone

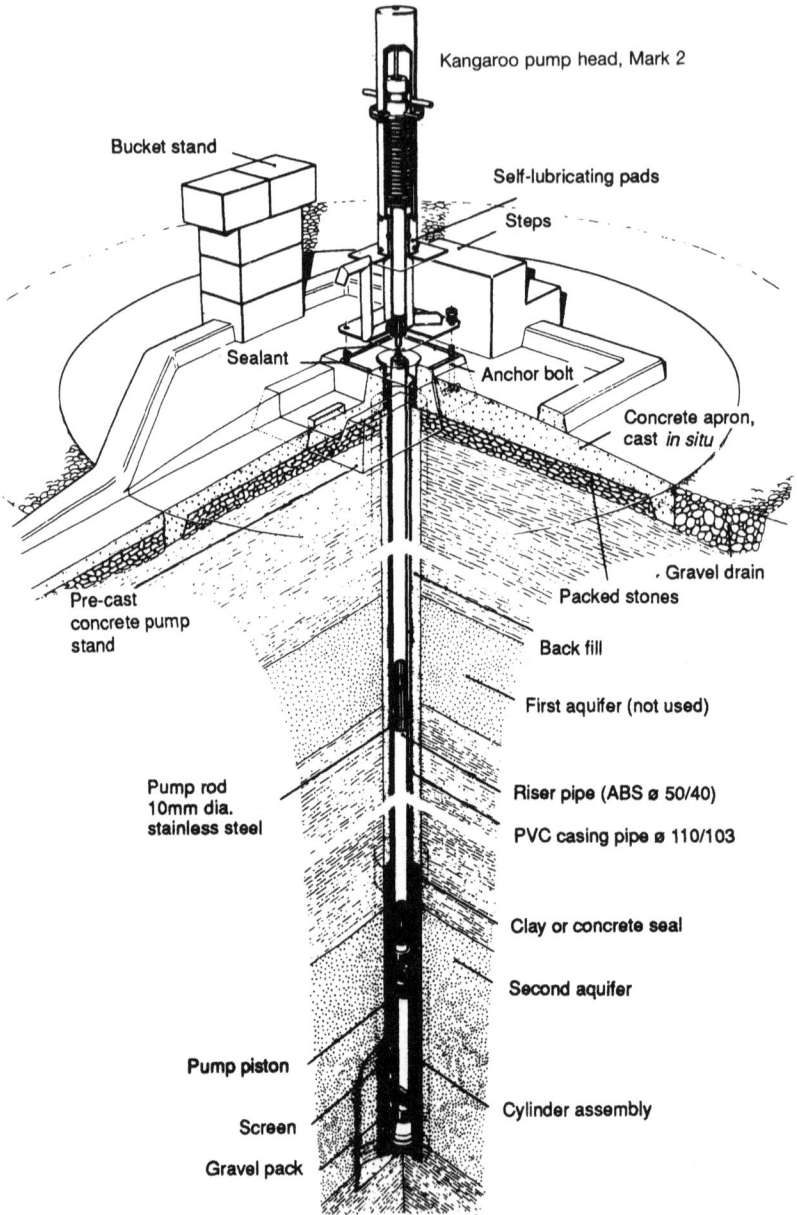

Kangaroo pump head, Mark 2

Bucket stand

Self-lubricating pads

Steps

Sealant

Anchor bolt

Concrete apron, cast *in situ*

Gravel drain

Pre-cast concrete pump stand

Packed stones

Back fill

First aquifer (not used)

Pump rod 10mm dia. stainless steel

Riser pipe (ABS ø 50/40)

PVC casing pipe ø 110/103

Clay or concrete seal

Second aquifer

Pump piston

Cylinder assembly

Screen

Gravel pack

Figure 2.13   *A completed hand-drilled well in cross-section*

chippings. This gives a considerable reduction in costs, as the expensive concrete rings are not needed. The effective storage capacity of the wells is about 50 per cent of the gross well volume, which is considerably larger than that of a drilled well, although undoubtedly lower than a ring of the same dimensions. This type of well may thus be very suitable for areas with poorer aquifers, where at least some storage is required.

All wells in the programme, whether dug or drilled, have a pre-cast concrete pump stand on top, which is cast in a concrete apron that is provided with a spill-water gulley. Sometimes, special washing slabs are constructed some 20 m downstream of the well, in order to minimize contamination of the well site itself.

All wells are equipped with handpumps. A version of the Craelius handpump was originally used in Shinyanga, but the high cost of maintaining pumps in a region of such scattered populations motivated the project team to look for a pump with fewer hinges and pivot points. This led to the construction of the so-called 'Kangaroo' pump which works by a spring-loaded plate operated by foot.

Other types of pumps (the SWN 80 and 81 series) were also developed, in co-operation with a social welfare workshop in The Netherlands. These pump types have been developed with only one thing in mind: to reduce maintenance requirements as far as possible.

Meanwhile, the Prime Minister's Office in Tanzania started a nationwide drive to stimulate the villagers to maintain wells and handpumps and to carry out small repairs when necessary. Until such time as this campaign has proved to be successful in practice, however, pumps of the (almost) 'maintenance-free' type will remain indispensable. Through the Morogoro Wells Construction Project these pumps are being made available to regional water engineers and donor-financed projects in other regions.

Waterlines Vol. 3 No. 1, July 1984)

Wells for Mali

An interview with MARC RAEYMAEKERS

Euro Action ACORD (EAA) has been working with existing co-operatives on improving and redigging wells in the drought-stricken northern part of Mali. This area, which borders the Sahara desert and forms part of the arid region known as the Sahel, has a population of little more than 650,000 in an area the size of Western Europe. Some of the people are concentrated along the banks of the river Niger in permanent settlements, but the Taureg and Maur nomads roam part of the mountainous region to the north-east. The 260,000 sq. km around Kidal is known as the 'Adrar des Iforas'; the mountainous land of the Iforas people.

Sheer distance—it is 1,300 km to the capital, Bamako, and the nomadic life-style of the population, which is of course designed to minimize the effect of humans and their animals on an area where resources are very thinly spread, means that very little has been done to provide even the most basic of services such as wells since the French colonizers left the Adrar des Iforas. The area was a militarized border zone without a civil administration and cut off from the rest of the world for many years. It is still politically sensitive.

Rehabilitation plan

The Kidal area was hard hit by the droughts of 1969 and 1972–3. In 1974 it was estimated that 80 per cent of the nomads' herds, on which they rely totally, had perished. Exact figures are not available, as the owners are unwilling to reveal the extent of their wealth.

The first phase of the general rehabilitation was to provide revolving funds to replenish the livestock for the nomads, and this was completed by 1979. It then became obvious that wells would have to be repaired or redug in order to maintain the herds.

In the Adrar des Iforas, pasture and water tend not to occur in the same area. According to Taureg sources, 50 km is the maximum distance that animals can trek between the two before they begin to die in large numbers. Water is so scarce that it is often sold from motorized tankers at around UK £0.30 a litre by Taureg entrepreneurs with control over water-holes.

Administratively, the Kidal area rehabilitation plan is under the Direction Regional de la Co-operation (DRC) at Gao, 450 km away. The subsidiary of the National Co-operative Service probably has about 40 personnel in the entire area who work with local co-operatives. Another DRC office opened at Timbuktu in 1978.

In June 1978, delegates from co-opratives in the Kidal area insisted on the necessity of a well-digging programme. January 1979 saw the launching of the Mali Five-Year Plan, which included the improvement of water points.

The DRC's initial proposal to EAA, which had been working on the general rehabilitation scheme since 1974, was that a team of 12 expatriates be brought in to dig wells in the Adrar des Iforas. This was rejected by EAA as the local population would not be involved at all, so the programme would stand little chance of success. In 1980, the DRC came up with a second plan, which involved the nomads being reorganized into the co-operative structures which already existed in theory to put 40 wells in good order over a period of four years.

The wells in the area are between 25 and 45 m deep and 1.2 to 1.4 m in diameter, dug in sand overlying rock. The plan was accepted, although agreement between the Taureg groups as to wells to work on was not easy. Tauregs were the warlords of the Adrar des Iforas, and much local politics is involved.

Well-digging

The Tauregs do all the preparatory work for well-digging: preparing the site, digging as far as the water-table and providing the construction materials. Then the EAA/DRC well-digging team takes over. It is headed by an expatriate technical officer, an employee of the DRC, with another expatriate as logistical assistant and six Malian well-diggers.

Existing wells are often lined with wood, which has many serious drawbacks. Wood is extremely scarce in this semi-desert area and either tends to be attacked by termites or rots so that the well needs relining after a couple of years. With the population spread over such a wide area, there is not sufficient labour for such maintenance and the ecological damage is considerable. Stone has similar disadvantages, while cement is even more precious. The production of concrete requires gravel of the correct grade and large amounts of water. While each well is under construction, the nearest water source may be miles away.

After some research, ARMCO corrugated iron sections seemed to be the best lining material. These curved sheets bolt together in threes to line the well, and the technical officer keeps supplies well under his control to prevent damage in transit.

The well-digging team has three heavy second-hand flatbed trucks. The first carries a compressor and a concrete mixer. A small amount of concrete, however expensive, must be used to form a raised sill around the well to reduce contamination from outside. The DRC insists on this even though the people using the well would find it easier to draw water from a ground-level surround. The second and third trucks transport other tools and the lining sections.

Without sampling equipment, the first year of the programme was difficult and demoralizing. The team might dig 40 m in an area where the water-table was uneven and still not hit water. An important acquisition was two motorized diesel-driven rigs, which can drill down to a depth of 120 m in 10 hours.

After an initial six months of setting up in 1981, the first phase of the programme started in the second half of 1981, finishing in the second half of 1982. The location of water points was facilitated since the French Foreign Legion had surveyed the area's water resources during the colonial era.

Six or seven new wells were dug where the old ones were unrepairable and others were restored to good condition. The team hopes to proceed at a rate of 10 wells a year in the second part of the programme.

There are also plans to construct three or four subsurface dams a year in the vicinity of the wells to replenish the water-table. These will abut on to the existing walls of the wadis (dry river-beds) for support and be 1 to 1.5 m high. However, mechanized equipment would be required to construct dams, as large amounts of labour are not available. Other possible developments and offshoots of this programme will be considered when it is evaluated in the near future. Simple kits to test the salinity and acidity of well-water have been sent out to Mali by EAA.

One very heartening pointer to the future hope of involving people, recruited as unskilled well-diggers, is that after a mere three months' training they were able to dig some sound 8 to 10 m deep wells for gardening use without supervision, while expatriate members of staff were on holiday. This bodes well for setting up new teams run by well-diggers trained on the job.

(Waterlines Vol. 1 No. 4, April 1983)

Sahel case study: the Gambia

From material by BOB MANN and DERRICK KNIGHT

Water is the most pressing need if the Sahel is going to make headway towards its goal of food self-sufficiency by the year 2000. In the Western Division of the Gambia, the Gambia Christian Council (GCC) has been co-operating with the Ministry of Agriculture and Natural Resources since 1975 to dig wells and establish dry-season gardens to grow vegetables and fruit trees.[10]

During 1978–9, the GCC made its own well-digging equipment and has three well-digging teams in action. A solid wooden tripod with a simple two-man winch is standard gear for digging wells up to 30 to 40 ft (9 to 12 m) deep, although some adaptations have been made. Steel bearings, which had to be imported, have been replaced by locally-manufactured hardwood bearings, soaked in oil. These do not wear the shaft of the winch and can be easily replaced after two years of use. Steel flanges at either end of the winch drum were cut with a cold chisel by a local blacksmith, which saved importing machine-made parts.

The well-digging team also made its own steel shutters in which to cast concrete well-lining rings at the workshops of the Gambia Port Authority. These shutters are a quarter the weight of the manufactured variety and just as accurate. More important, they are easier to handle and help to speed well-lining, which is popular with the well-sinkers as the team is paid by the foot of well dug.

The wells dug by the programme have a 4 ft inner diameter, are hand-dug and lined with concrete down to the water-table. Each well is usually dug to its final depth between May and July when the water-table is normally at its lowest level. It is reckoned that a well constructed in this way, with a depth of 5 ft of water in the caisson tube, should supply a reasonable amount of water for dry-season gardening from November to April.

Changing conditions

Average annual rainfall has been decreasing significantly since 1968. This is shown in Figure 2.14, which records precipitation for Banjul. As a result, ground-water levels were not sufficiently recharged and the GCC's well-digging teams have had to repeatedly retrace their steps and deepen wells (Table 2.1).

Table 2.1

Year	No. of new wells constructed	No. of wells that had to be deepened
1978	14	2
1979	32	4
1980	37	43
1981/82	28	106

These data are drawn from Bob Mann's study,[11] in which he has taken care to ensure that the readings are a valid comparison from one year to another and that the figures do not reflect any significant influence from daily draw-down variations.

At village level, Gunjur village has 12 wells distributed symmetrically so that they serve half an acre each. They are located beside a watercourse. The wells were originally 12 to 15 ft deep, dug through fine collapsing sand. The water level of one of them, for instance, has dropped by 7 ft 6 in. to a depth of 20 ft over two years (Figure 2.15).

Douassu (Figure 2.16) has six wells, in an area that used to be woodland savanna but has now lost its trees. One of these wells, taken as an example, was constructed in June 1979 to a depth of 28 ft 9 in through hard sand and layers of gravel. It has had to be deepened five times in three years, and the sand in the present aquifer is very fluid and unstable. The water-level dropped rapidly during the 1980–1 season, but only a foot in the year up to August 1982, giving a total drop of 7 ft 5 in. over three years.

At Sanyang village (Figure 2.17) there are five wells in a line along the edge of what was a seasonally flooded rice swamp up to 1968. Vegetables are grown there intensively for local consumption. The water-table dropped 2 ft 2 in. over a year in one well, but here at least the wells will not have to be deepened.

Jambur has four wells laid out in a square of side 70 yd, in an upland zone where rice was previously grown and where village women now grow vegetables. Water is now 24 ft down through hard clay and the level dropped 7 ft 6 in. over one year (Figure 2.17).

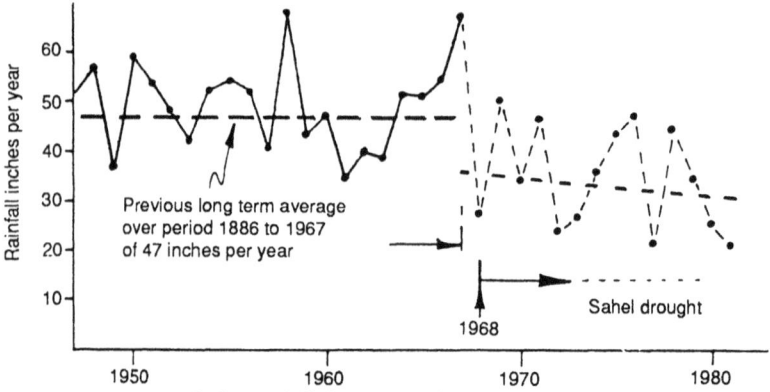

Figure 2.14   *Recorded rainfall for Banjul*

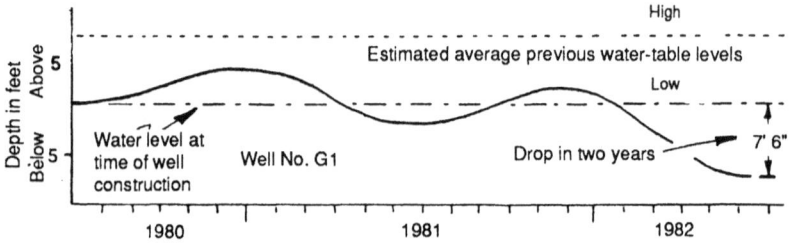

Figure 2.15   *Change in water-table over two years at Gunjur*

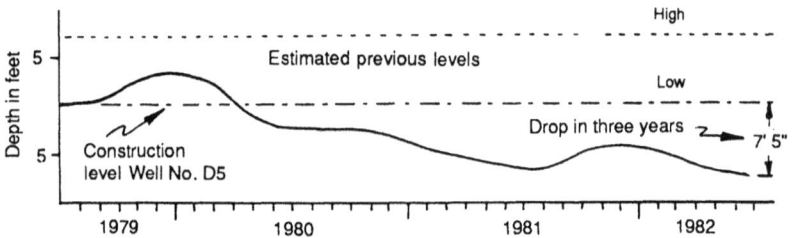

Figure 2.16   *Change in water-table over three years at Douassu*

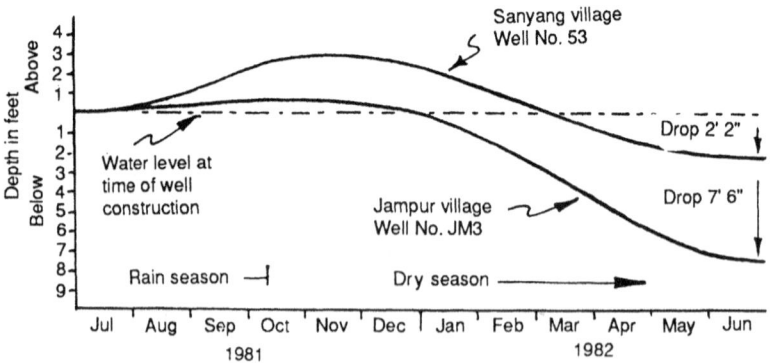

Figure 2.17   *Change in water-table over one year at Sanyang and Jambur*

The human factor

Of course, this is not just a problem consisting of facts and figures: there is a human dimension. People in the Sahel are very poor, and in Jambur it was no easy matter for the village women to raise the modest contribution to the cost of deepening wells. The active women's association had worked for six months in 1982 for a total return of 200 Dalais—less than £50—from their vegetables. This money went to their families and was not even their own. Yet in November 1982 they were having to agree to help pay for deepening wells, so soon after the rainy season when they should have been looking forward to months of water from them. The financial contribution of the villagers is, in turn, only a proportion of the total cost of well-deepening operations, which is funded by the Methodist Church in the UK, the International Co-ordination Committee for Development Projects (ICCO) in The Netherlands and the World Council of Churches Sahel Programme based in Ouagadougou, Upper Volta.

Each village well costs about 1,600 Delasis ($850), and villagers usually pay half of this. But there are villages which have been unable to find the surplus rice to feed the five members of the GCC's well-digging team.

Bob Mann notes that in the Western Division of the Gambia, farmers are no longer confident of growing local varieties of oranges, as the trees have wilted seriously. They are now turning to more drought-resistant tree crops such as mango and cashew. Even the local hardy oil palms are producing progressively fewer bunches each season and many palm trees are dying through pest attack in the crown associated with lower rainfall.

Where vegetation is progressively reduced over large areas, the resulting increase in the level of dust and increase in reflection of solar radiation tends to cause lower or unreliable rainfall by suppressing cloud formation and retarding the normal progress of the summer monsoon systems.

Similar occurrences are reported in nearby countries. Between 1968 and 1974, water-tables in Northern Senegal dropped below tree-root level and resulted in a massive loss of tree cover. This area is only 150 to 200 miles north of the Gambia.

On the rocky Dogon plateau in Southern Mali, between 1981 and 1983 rainfall has been about half the amount needed to recharge ground water reserves. There the White Fathers have pioneered a project which has similarities to the Gambia Christian Council's work in the Gambia. It involves well-digging, small dam construction and village gardening using locally-trained labour and small resources. Villagers organize themselves into teams which are augmented by a trained mason and an explosives miner from the mission: in this area, wells have to be blasted deep into rock strata. The CARITAS—a Christian development organization— team sinks test bores to ensure that hard work does not just result in a dry well.

Where the land, and therefore its people, are this poor, the division between surviving and not surviving is thin. Small-scale efforts such as those described in this article can make the difference.[10]

(*Waterlines* Vol. 2 No. 1, July 1983)

CHAPTER 3
Tube-wells

The first article gives a useful outline of manually constructed small-diameter wells—variously designated as tube-wells, drilled wells,[12] drive point or jetted wells—followed by a description of alternative methods and equipment.

Richard Carter's article outlines the application of jetted tube-wells for ground water development, while the article on Uganda deals with problems of rehabilitating borehole sources in the Luwero Triangle under the general direction of UNICEF. These problems ranged from adapting six-inch diameter boreholes for the installation of the standardized India Mark II pump to adopting more realistic incentive schemes and improving the organization structure.

Finally, Hilary Sunman emphasizes the importance of talking to the people in seeking appropriate technology solutions in Senegal. The government programme involved drilling deep boreholes for village water supplies. Each borehole cost £200,000 to drill and equip; the multi-disciplinary project of 24 sites sought an appropriate solution compatible with these sophisticated headworks.

Reference should also be made to the article in Chapter 7 on the Zimbabwe Blair Research Laboratory's contribution which describes a simple hand-operated rig for drilling tube-wells. It is apparent that shallow tube-wells in suitable locations have the advantage over shallow hand-dug wells if simple, acceptable and easily maintained lifting devices can be provided.[11]

Tube-wells and their construction
Edited by C. K. STAPLETON

The most practical definition of what will be called a tube-well in this article is probably the simplest: 'a tube-well is one which is too small for workers to enter for construction or maintenance'.[12] Such tube-wells will vary in diameter from as little as 25 to 500 mm. In the majority of cases the tools used in their construction will be manually operated, although in some instances a lightweight drilling rig or mast, incorporating a winch powered by a small engine, is used for hoisting the drilling tools, and an engine-driven pump for dewatering the well. Using steel casing as a temporary lining for the tube-well would be kept to a minimum.

Hand-digging of wide-diameter wells (of one metre or more) requires relatively basic tools, whereas tube-well construction requires rather more specialized equipment. Apart from the capital investment in equipment, tube-wells are generally less expensive to construct, partly because less ground formation is removed, which results in much faster penetration down to water-bearing strata. A word of caution is needed here, in that the cost per successfully completed tube-well can escalate because of factors such as loss of tools down the well, time spent recovering the tools, and the ratio of dry wells to successful wells sunk.

The danger of the walls of wells collapsing on workers during construction is avoided. Moreover, a properly constructed tube-well is definitely more sanitary, both from the point of view of a surface water seal and the absence of contamination of the water supply from utensils used to collect water, since a pump is fitted to raise the water. On this latter account, personnel need to be trained in the installation technique and maintenance of pumps, whereas pumps are seldom fitted to large-diameter hand-dug wells. The rate of discharge of water from a tube-well is potentially better than from a dug well because deeper penetration into the aquifer can be achieved. But in low-yielding aquifers, large-diameter wells may be more suitable, especially where there is a big demand for water.

Methods of construction

Methods of constructing tube-wells can be arranged into four groups:

○ Augering, drilling or boring.
○ Percussion.
○ Jetting, well pointing or driving.
○ Sludging.

Augering, also known as drilling or boring, consists of shaving or cutting formation from the bottom of the hole by the rotation of a cylindrical tool with one or more cutting edges. The auger itself is attached to extension rods and a cross-piece used as a handle (tiller) with which to rotate the auger. Several types of auger have been designed for different soil formations. Excavated earth normally feeds upwards and it is contained in the body of the auger until it is emptied, which means that the auger must be removed regularly from the hole, necessitating the uncoupling of the extension rods. These rods can be raised manually from a shallow depth, otherwise a mechanical hoist can be employed on a lightweight drilling rig or mast. This factor is the main limitation on the depth of augered wells.

In the range of auger bits (Figure 3.1), the conical auger bit is similar to the

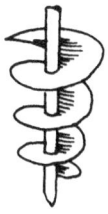
a

d

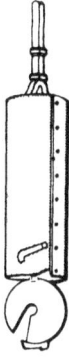
g

b

e

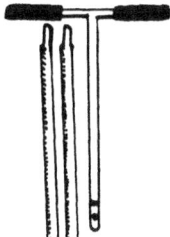
h

c

f

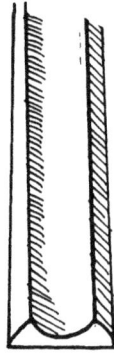
a

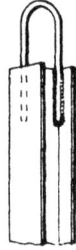
c

b

d

3.1   3.2

Figure 3.1   *Bits for augering tube-wells: (Not to scale) (a) spiral auger, (b) helical auger, (c) continuous flight auger, (d) riverside bit, (e) combination bit, (f) locally-fabricated bailer, (g) cylindrical bucket auger, (h) handle and extension rods.*
Figure 3.2   *Bits for constructing tube-wells by percussion: (a) club-type chisel bit, (b) hollow rod bit with slot, (c) & (d) home-made percussion bit*

spiral point depicted at (3.1a) having a relatively small point which makes it useful in stony, layered formations which preclude the use of a regular auger bit. The formation is 'screwed' loose and must be removed from the hole with another type of auger. These and helical auger bits (3.1b) are used in combination with continuous flight augers (3.1c) to ensure support for the tool string, and assist in maintaining verticality of the hole, and removal of debris.

The riverside auger bit (3.1d) is a tube with two blades welded on at the bottom. It cuts the formation only round its circumference, that is, on its outer edge, leaving the formation which passes inside relatively undisturbed in the form of a core. It is used in hard, dry clay and gravelly soils and in most types of formation below the water-table. A combination auger (3.1e) has two converging blades of a width designed to make it useful in various formations from clay to sand. The bailer (3.1f) is designed to lift sand from below the water-table and to remove loose cuttings. It consists of a cylindrical tube fitted with a simple flap valve at the bottom to admit sand and cuttings in the form of slurry.

The bailer is repeatedly raised and dropped into the bottom of the hole until it is full; then it is removed for emptying. This exercise is conducted at intervals as the drilling progresses. A cylindrical bucket auger (3.1g) is a metal tube with an attachment at the top for the extension rods. The bottom is of helical form with a single cutting edge. It is hinged and latched to facilitate emptying.

Percussion method, as the name suggests, is an up-and-down motion raising specially designed tools 300 to 500 mm then dropping them on to the bottom of the hole to penetrate the soil and thus create a well or borehole. In the case of small diameter and shallow wells, percussion drilling can be undertaken using extension rods and tillers (3.1h) with which to raise and turn the tools manually. Otherwise, with modified tool design, percussion drilling can be carried out with a lightweight drilling rig or mast incorporating a winch powered by a small engine. Percussion is most effective in softer formations, for which there are a variety of specially designed drill bits.

In compacted strata,[13] a club-type chisel-edge bit is used (Figure 3.2a). It is attached to the winch cable and moved repeatedly up and down, adding a little clay slurry to hold the cuttings made by the bit in suspension. When the accumulation of cuttings at the bottom of the hole impedes penetration of the strata, the bit is pulled out of the hole and the bottom of the hole cleaned with a bailer. The frequency of cleaning out the hole is determined from experience by the driller.

Where the strata is loose but not prone to caving in, a hollow rod bit can be used (Figure 3.2b). The circular bottom edge of the bit cuts out a plug of the strata which is gradually forced up the inside of the bit like a core as the bit is dropped into the bottom of the hole repeatedly. Because different strata or formation pack with different densities, the bit may be as little as a third full

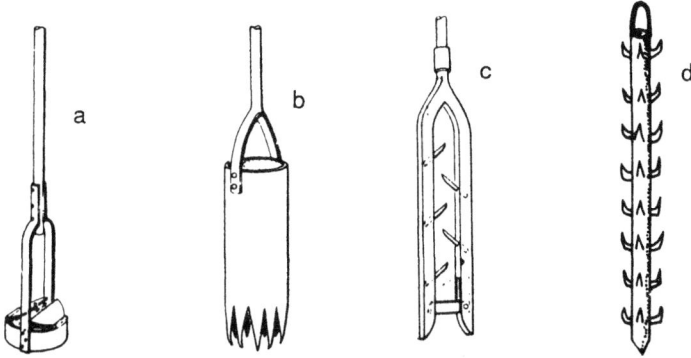

Figure 3.3   'Fishing tools': (a) for recovering pieces of pipe, (b) 'basket' for small objects, (c) latch tool and internal rope spear for recovering tools by their bails, (d) spear for broken ropes or cables

when it needs to be removed and emptied: this operation can best be judged by experience.

In formations which tend to cave in, saturated sand for instance, it will be necessary to insert casing from the top to the bottom of the hole. Penetration can then be effected by bailing out sand from the bottom of the hole and allowing the casing to move down gradually. Special equipment and techniques will be required to drive the casing down, if it does not move down under its own weight.

Percussion bits and bailers are manufactured with a metal loop or bail fixed at the upper end for the purpose of attaching the operating rope or cable. Additionally, the bail facilitates the recovery of the tools, if the cable breaks and leaves the tools in the hole. A tool thus lost is termed a 'fish'. Tools designed to recover these fish from holes follow a general pattern as shown in Figure 3.3. A double flap hinged on a ring of pipe (3.3a) is for recovering pieces of pipe; a basket (3.3b) fabricated from a piece of metal casing with teeth cut into the lower edge which close upon impact with the bottom of the hole to recover small objects; a latch tool internal rope spear (3.3c) has a hinged latch at the bottom for recovering tools by their bails, and spikes with which to hook a broken rope or cable; an external rope spear (3.3d) which has spikes arranged around the outside of a pipe is used to hook a broken rope or cable.

R. G. Koegel[12] suggests that a heavy leaf spring from a large truck or bus makes a good cutting edge for a percussion bit; this cutting edge can be shaped into a chisel profile using a high speed hack-saw blade. This leaf-spring can be fitted into the end of a piece of steel 'I' beam 2 to 3 m long, or two pieces of channel iron back to back, or a piece of pipe flattened at one end to fit closely around the leaf-spring. The leaf-spring should be welded or riveted in place (Figure 3.2c).

Well-point tube-wells differ from other methods described, in that a perforated well screen and casing, with a closed pointed bottom, is used to sink the well, then left in position. This method also can be used to deepen a wide-diameter well, once it has reached the water-table, especially if it is prone to caving in.

Well-points are invariably made of strong metal because of the stresses to which they are subjected. It is possible to fabricate a well-point locally, but commercially manufactured well-points can withstand much greater stress. Above the closed pointed bottom or tip is a screen. This must allow water to enter without becoming clogged and be sufficiently strong to withstand the abrasion of the formation through which it is driven. A common type of well-point screen consists of a special wire, wrapped continuously around a frame so as to leave a slotted open area, through which the water passes (Figure 3.4a). It is known as a continuous slot drive point.

Another common type (Figure 3.4b) consists of a perforated pipe wrapped in a layer of perforated brass sheet. Both layers are soldered to the pipe. Another type (Figure 3.4c) is manufactured by wrapping wire with a trapezoidal cross-section around a set of longitudinal rods. All intersections are then welded. This type of screen has the advantages of a high percentage of its area being open and of being less likely to clog with fine sand because of the slot shape it creates (narrow outside and wider inside).

Two different methods of driving the well-point into the ground can be employed. One method involves raising and dropping repeatedly a weighted 'driver', to hammer the well-point and pipes subsequently connected to it,

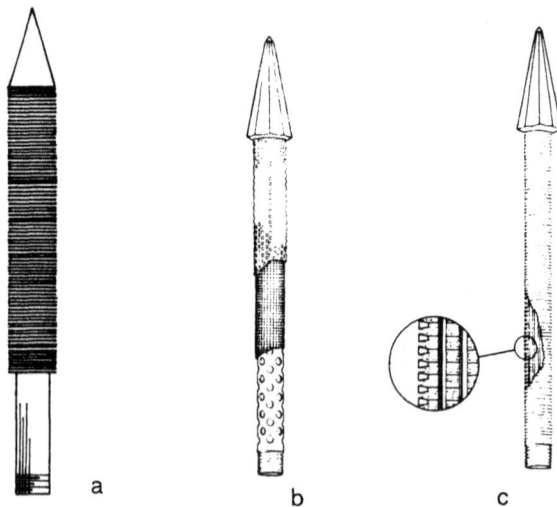

Figure 3.4   *Well-point screens: (a) continuous slot drive point, (b) perforated brass sheet screen, (c) screen made with wire of trapezoidal cross-section*

down to the water-table (Figure 3.5a). The weighted driver is handled manually, striking the top of the pipes at a convenient working height above ground level. A driving cap is screwed on to the threads of the uppermost pipe which is to be hammered by the weighted driver, to protect the threads.

Special couplings are used on the string of pipes attached to the well-point section to allow the ends of the pipes being joined to touch or 'butt up' which then transmits the force of the hammering action throughout the length of the string of pipes and directly on to the well-point. Well-points will not penetrate hard rock and will pass through clay only with difficulty. The other method requires the well-point section to be driven until it protrudes through the bottom of a string of casing positioned at or near the water-table (Figure 3.5b). Some form of seal or packing will be required around the top of the well-point section to seal it to the casing. The well-point section can be driven into position using either a driving weight suspended on a cable or rope, or a driving bar on the end of a string of pipes coupled together to reach above ground level. A lightweight drilling rig or mast incorporating a winch powered by a small engine will be required for this operation.

In 'open hole' jetting techniques, water is pumped down through a hollow drill rod and out through a hole in the jetting bit at the bottom. The greater the force behind the water, the better the cutting action and resultant penetration. A motorized pump is necessary.

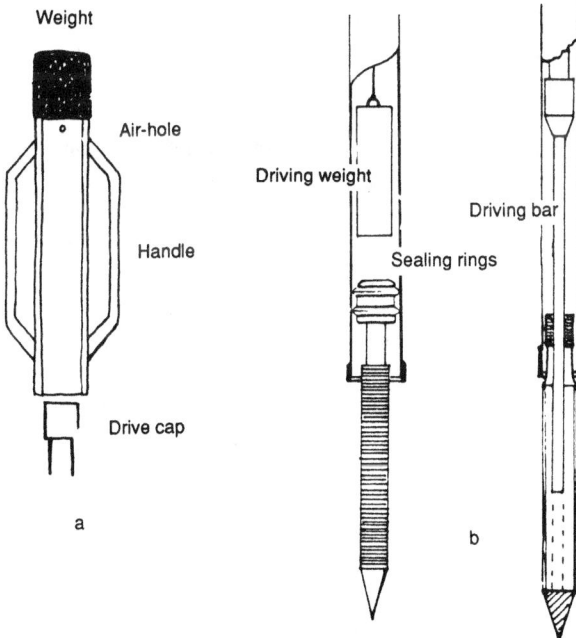

Figure 3.5 *(a) Weighted driver, (b) driving mechanism for well-point*

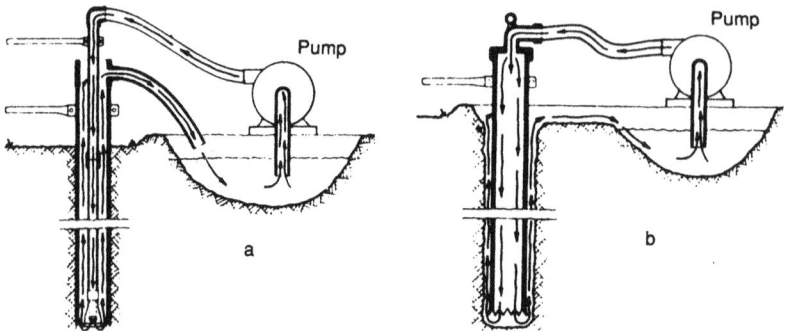

Figure 3.6 *Jetting arrangements: water leaves the tube (a) inside or (b) outside the casing*

In other cases where it is considered advantageous to use casing, water is pumped down the inside of the casing. It returns to the surface loaded with soil particles either inside the ring-shaped space between the jetting tube and the casing (Figure 3.6a) or outside the casing (Figure 3.6b). With the latter method, if jetting is interrupted before the casing has reached the required depth, it may be difficult to restart the process if suspended material settles. If the casing sunk during jetting is temporary, the permanent casing, with screen attached, is lowered inside. The temporary casing is then jacked out of the hole. If the permanent casing is sunk at once, the well screen is lowered inside it and the casing raised far enough to expose the screen. Alternatively, a string of casing with a self-jetting well-point attached may be used. During the course of jetting, the returning circulating water is channelled through a small ditch to a large settling pit. Here it stands long enough to allow the cuttings to settle out before it is pumped back down the drill rod. The volume of the settling pit should be at least three times that of the hole being jetted. It should be shallow (between 0.7 and 1 m deep) and about twice as long in the direction of water flow as it is wide and deep. A settling pit 2 m long, 1 m wide and 1 m deep could be used while jetting a 100 mm-diameter well 85 m deep. Clay mixed in the jetting water improves its action in bringing the drilled cuttings to the surface. Bentonite and mud additives improve the jetting water still further. Clay and these additives tend to coat the walls of the hole and reduce the likelihood of them caving in.

Several methods are combined with jetting to increase the well-point's rate of progress through the soil. Jetting bits are often of a shortened percussion type. Teeth can be cut in the bottom of the casing, which is rotated to loosen the formation. The next article describes a technique for jetting wells with a cheap, reusable well-point developed at the National Institute of Agricultural Engineering, UK. This combines jetting with percussion and rotation.

The soft alluvial soil and high water-table of Bangladesh and parts of India has promoted the development of a low-cost simple method of sinking tube-wells up to 80 m deep without engine power. This is known as the 'sludger' method and could be classified as 'hydraulic percussion' because drilling fluid is used and the tools are moved up and down. A hollow tube or pipe fitted with a check-valve and a bit is raised and dropped into the hole by means of a manually operated cantilever attached to a bamboo gantry. The check valve allows the suspension of cuttings in drilling fluid to pass through on the downstroke. The valve retains them as the pipe is raised. With the next downstroke more fluid and cuttings are forced up the pipe and out of the top.

As the bit and first pipe penetrates, more pipes are added. During jetting, one man sits on top of the bamboo gantry operating the 'flap valve' at the top of the pipe and ensuring that the pipe is sinking vertically. This creates a vacuum in the pipe so that loosened strata is sucked into the bottom. Strata samples are collected and examined every 1.5 m depth. When water-bearing strata are reached the whole length of pipe with bit attached is withdrawn piece by piece, keeping the bore intact. This is replaced by well-screen strainers and pipes or rising main immediately. The well is then developed by cleaning out with a pump or slim bailer to remove sand and other materials. Occasionally, water might have to be surged through the screen by using a weight suspended from a wire rope and then continuously pumping the well with an ordinary handpump for at least 16 hours.

Labour cost per successful well by this method is usually less than US $35. Another $125 covers pipe, well-screens, pump, check valve and concrete for a platform, making a total of about $160 a well (1983 prices).

Well screens

The bottom section of a small-diameter well usually consists of a well screen to allow water from the surrounding aquifer to enter the well. When the screen is in position the particles which make up the aquifer re-arrange themselves as water is extracted from the well so that the nearer the screen, the less fine material there is and water can flow freely into the well. This process of re-arrangement is called the development of the well.

Well screens should have as many perforations as possible to maximize water flow, should be made of material compatible with the chemical and bacteriological characteristics of local ground water, and should be able to withstand the stresses of installation and the hydrostatic pressures of the hole. They can be made of locally-available material (Figure 3.7a) or be commercially manufactured (Figures 3.7b and 3.7c). The cost of commercial well screens and the time needed for delivering them is often the criteria which makes them unsuitable for isolated wells supplying small quantities of water. However, commercial well screens are easy to handle and easily installed and often provide more water for a longer period of time than locally made ones.

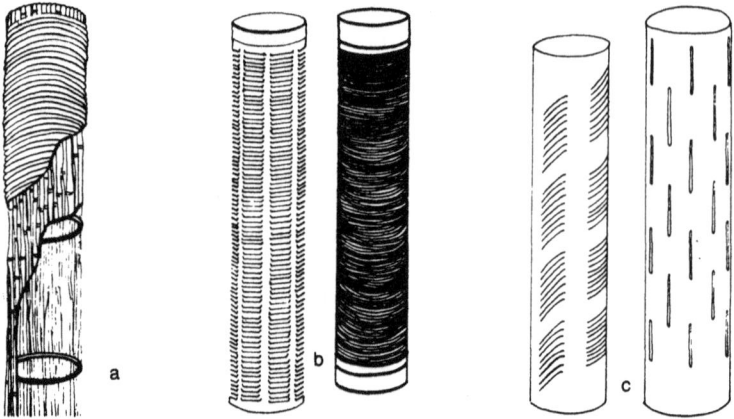

Figure 3.7   *Well screens made of (a) coir and bamboo, (b) louvre-type and continuous slot manufactured screens, (c) plastic pipe, locally made*

Steel, plastic, burnt clay, wood and bamboo have all been used to make well-screens, and each has its own specific characteristics. Steel, or galvanized steel, is strong enough to be driven into position but its lifespan may be very short, perhaps measured in months where the water is aggressive or corrosive. Stainless steel can be used in almost any situation but it is expensive. Plastic pipes and screens, such as PVC, tend to lose their profile under pressure, but holes or slots can easily be drilled into plain plastic pipe to create a screen and it is very light to handle. It is corrosion resistant and is usually cheaper than steel.

There are often facilities for manufacturing burnt clay pipes locally, although sections need couplings to join them together. However, burnt clay is easily broken, and best used where the well has been excavated right to the bottom before the installation of screen and casing. Bamboo and wood may rot and taint the water, although long sections of tree trunks have been used successfully in temporary wells. Screen openings should be cut along the grain of the wood for greater strength. With bamboo, well-screens can be constructed by splitting long pieces lengthwise, arranging them round ring-shaped spacers and binding the whole with rope. Alternatively, narrow lengthwise slits can be cut with a circular saw in plain lengths of bamboo, and the nodes removed. The advantage of this method is that the slits will get smaller as the bamboo swells with saturation in water.

Most well-screens in small-capacity wells are of the order of 1 to 3 m long. The actual length needed depends on the amount of water required and other factors. Thus only a metre of commercial screen might be required where a locally made screen would have to be, say 2 to 3 m long to provide a given amount of water.[14,15,16,17]

Ground-water development using jetted boreholes
RICHARD CARTER

Ground-water development, whether for irrigation or drinking-water supplies, is often desirable, but frequently expensive. Drilling in particular,
especially in remote locations of developing countries, can be very costly.
There are, however, several traditional, relatively labour-intensive and
low-cost drilling techniques which have great potential in the right conditions. These methods generally use the same principle as conventional
drilling rigs, namely fluid circulation, rotation, and/or percussion.

The technique of jetting has, apart from its use in conventional well-
pointing, seen a range of applications in recent years, both in developing and
developed countries. This article describes five such applications, spanning
the fields of small-scale irrigation, drinking-water supply, pumped drainage
and hydrogeological research. There is undoubtedly scope for further
development of the technique to extend its application and benefits.

The method consists of pumping fluid (usually water) down a hand-held
vertical pipe (the jetting pipe) which is allowed to sink into the fluidized soil
so produced. The direct circulation of fluid carries cuttings up the hole to the
surface, while the operators can assist the sinking of the pipe by rotary or

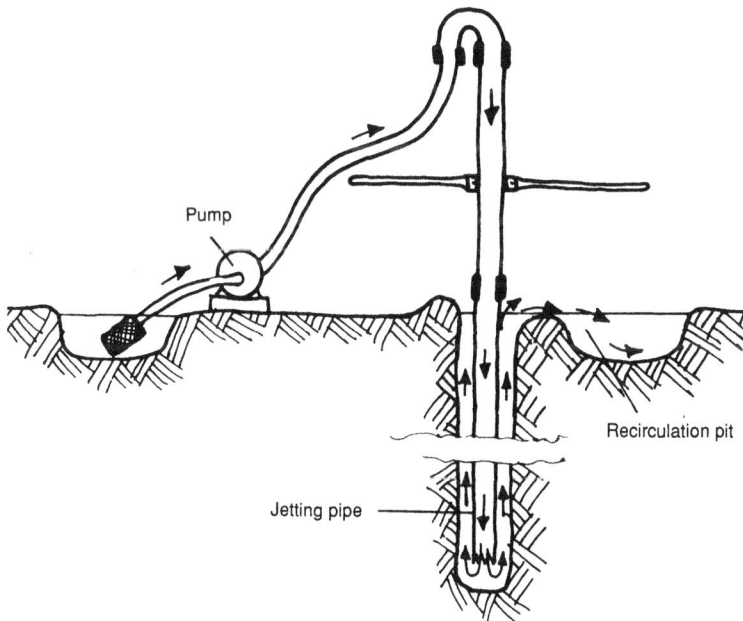

Figure 3.8   *Major components of a simple jetting rig*

percussive actions. Jetting water can be recirculated via a settling pit, but this requires the use of a pump which is tolerant to the passage of solids (Figure 3.8).

Permanent borehole linings can be placed either during jetting by driving a casing or screen of larger diameter than the jetting pipe; or as a separate procedure after the hole has reached the desired depth. In the latter case, either a lining of smaller diameter than the jetting pipe can be inserted before its removal, or, if the ground is relatively stable, the jetting pipe can be removed before the lining is placed.

Jetting is normally carried out with pipe in the size range 50 to 100 mm, and the hole so produced is usually around 150 to 200 mm in diameter. A pump of about 2 to 8 hp (1.5 to 6 kW) is normally adequate for the operation.

Jetting boreholes is an easy and rapid procedure in the right ground conditions, but these conditions are somewhat limited. Unconsolidated silts, sands and fine gravels cause no real difficulties. It is usually possible to penetrate clays, although rather slowly. Coarse gravels are problematic for two reasons; firstly, their high hydraulic conductivities, which often lead to loss of circulation as the drilling water disappears into the aquifer, and secondly because the jetting action can sometimes mobilize particles but fail to lift them, and so they fall back and wedge against the jetting pipe.

The method is unsuitable in hard rock. The main application of the method therefore is for drilling in alluvial deposits; with one exception, the examples which follow reflect this. Drilling depths of up to 30 to 40 m are possible in favourable conditions.

Irrigation in Nigeria

The first application of jetting to be described here has a wide potential. In northern Nigeria there are several major rivers, including the Sokoto, Hadejia-Jama'are and Lake Chad basins. These rivers are markedly seasonal, following a rainfall pattern of roughly a five-month rainy period and a seven-month dry season. The extensive flood plains or *fadamas* of these rivers, often several kilometres wide, experience seasonal flooding and hence recharge of shallow alluvial aquifers, but for the greater part of the year the rivers are confined to relatively narrow channels.

These fertile and well-watered *fadamas* are used for wet season rice cultivation and dry season irrigation. In the latter case water is lifted from either the main river channel or temporary pools and ponds, usually by shadoof. The main vegetable crops are tomatoes, onions and peppers.

In recent years a number of statewide Agricultural Development Programmes have been set up in Nigeria with the objective of improving the agricultural production of small farmers. Although these schemes have concentrated on rain-fed agriculture, in view of its predominance, they have met with remarkable initial results when they have introduced improved practices for *fadama* farmers. The main improvements have been in water lifting, replacing shadoofs with hand-operated diaphragm pumps and motor-driven centrifugal pumps, and in developing alluvial ground-water by use of shallow jetted boreholes.

In the northern parts of Kano State (under the Kano State Agricultural and Rural Development Authority, KNARDA) and Bauchi State (Bauchi State Agricultural Development Programme, BSADP), the *fadamas* are composed of alluvial sequences of clays, silts, sands and gravels. Three variations on the basic jetting technique have been used in these areas.

The first was developed in the early 1980s by consulting engineers Wardrop Associates. It uses a 50 mm jetting pipe, and bentonite drilling mud, enabling a 75 mm PVC casing to be placed in position. The method has been effective, but there are obvious disadvantages as well as benefits to using special drilling muds. The cost and availability of bentonite is a major problem.[18]

The second method used by BSADP[19] involves the driving of a 125 mm casing during jetting. A slotted PVC lining is lowered inside this before removing the casing. Plain water is used with this approach, and it can be recirculated if it is in short supply at the time and place of drilling.

The third approach is that developed by Richard Cansdale for KNARDA.[20] This involves the use of dual jetting pipes—in acrylo-nitrile butidiene-styrene (abs) plastic—and two pumps; one of the jetting pipes has a short (0.5 to 1.0 m) stainless steel 'Johnson'-type well-point on the lower end, and this is left in place as the permanent borehole liner. This technique has only so far been used in river-bed sands and not further back on the flood plain.

For all these jetting methods, local teams have been trained in installation, and so far several hundred low-cost shallow (usually up to 8 to 10 m deep) boreholes have been put down.

Pumping is, in all cases, by suction, since water-tables are usually within 2 m of the ground surface.

The economics of these systems is at present very attractive for small farmers who can afford the initial capital outlay. A borehole and 2 or 3 inch petrol-driven centrifugal pump, together costing the farmer around N 600 to N 700 (about US $1,000) can give him a gross margin of B 3,000 ($4,800, in a single dry season.

The future development of ground-water resources in northern Nigeria by this approach will bring new problems, but also great potential. Competition for a water resource which is not unlimited, and the need for more efficient management on irrigated fields will become important in the future. However, with careful management of resources, both irrigation from shallow boreholes and the actual construction of jetted boreholes could become very important economic activities.

Water supplies in Sri Lanka

The Overseas Division of the National Institute of Agricultural Engineering (NIAE), Silsoe, carried out trials of borehole jetting recently (1982) for small village water supplies in Sri Lanka.[21] The intention was to develop the technique for temporary supply of domestic water needs in areas newly cleared for agricultural development.

Jetting was done with 100 mm steel pipe and usually using water carried to site by bowser. Ground conditions were not particularly favourable for the jetting technique, being mainly soils and rock derived from *in situ* weathering of granites. Surface clays resulted in relatively slow progress, and at greater depths (often 3 to 4.5 m) large weathered angular rock fragments prevented further penetration.

Of 20 holes drilled, seven could be said to be successful, giving yields ranging from less than 1 litre/min to 9 litres/min. The others failed either through encountering shallow unweathered rock or because of the low hydraulic conductivities of the weathered materials penetrated. It should be noted that in these conditions neither conventionally drilled boreholes nor even dug wells in many cases would have had significantly greater success, and they would have involved greater cost and effort.

The main results of the Sri Lankan work carried out by NIAE were to demonstrate the simplicity of the technique, but also to highlight the unfavourable ground conditions.

Drainage in Egypt

As part of an ODA-funded land reclamation project in the Nile Delta, trials were carried out with pumped drainage using jetted boreholes. The project was carried out in conjunction with Hydraulics Research, NIAE and Silsoe College in the early 1980s as postgraduate research. The objective of pumped drainage in the highly saline and alkali soils of the delta was to leach sodium salts from the land so it could be used for irrigated agriculture.

Alkali clay surface soils extend about 3 m below the surface in the project area and are underlain by a thin (0.5 m) sand aquifer. Salinity levels are as much as four times those of natural sea water. The intention was to pump from the confined sand aquifer and so enable vertical flow of surface-applied fresh water through the clays. Twenty-seven jetted boreholes were linked to a single pump to lower the piezometric surface.

The equipment was the same as that used in the NIAE Sri Lankan work and described in Andrew Metianu's article[16] in *Waterlines*. Borehole linings were perforated corrugated plastic field drainage pipe, which has the benefits of easy transport in coils and very low cost.

The main problems encountered with the technique were the suspected 'blinding' of the thin sand aquifer by dispersed clays from above, so leading to low yields, and problems of keeping the pump primed when linking multiple boreholes. Despite these difficulties, some leaching has been achieved in this trial.

'Sludging' in Bangladesh

A variation on the basic jetting technique which enjoys widespread use in Bangladesh's soft alluvial soil is known as 'sludging'.[22]

It allows a three-man team to complete a 50 m deep tubewell in about three hours, and requires 40 mm diameter galvanized iron (GI) pipe, a length of chain, two pipe wrenches and a bamboo scaffold as high as one of the pipe lengths (3 m). Each well costs about US $100 (1979 prices) including the handpump which surmounts it.

First a 600 mm square pit 300 mm deep is dug at the site of the proposed tube-well. The inside of the pit is sealed with cow-dung and it is filled with water. The first length of pipe is placed in one corner of the pit and filled with water by a man who climbs to the top of the bamboo scaffold. He then raises and lowers the pipe, using it as a force pump, creating a vacuum by sealing his hand over the end of the pipe. He ensures that it stays vertical as water and sand cascade from the top.

The other two members of the team give more leverage on the GI pipe with a bamboo pole, pivoted at the scaffold and fixed by a slip-knot to the pipe. The pipe jets its way into the ground as the soil is fluidized. Extra lengths of pipe are added as each one sinks to the level of the top of the pit.

The water from the tube-well is sampled every 1.5 m. With the aid of a simple comparator the driller decides which level and screen size should be used.

Sinking continues about 2 m beyond this point, and then the GI pipe is withdrawn by operating the bamboo lever in the opposite direction. The next phase is the insertion of a 1.8 m long PVC sand trap followed by a 3 m length of slotted PVC screen and enough lengths of PVC pipe to reach up to within 3 m of the ground surface. The lengths are joined with solvent rather than screwed joints; for speed and because the joints are smaller. Finally, a 3 m length of GI pipe brings the well to the surface. The pipe has a 250 mm-long mild steel cross-piece at the top, which is firmly concreted into the pump platform above to anchor the well.

To develop the well (flush out the fine material from the water-bearing layers) an extra temporary length of GI pipe is attached above ground and continuously topped up with water for a few minutes. When it is removed, water gushes from the well for a few minutes and then the handpump can be fitted. It should be operated for at least eight hours before water is drawn for drinking, to ensure that all contamination is flushed out.

A local aggregate of brick chips is used to construct a concrete platform round the handpump.

UNICEF has been funding the sinking of nearly 12,000 km of PVC pipe into Bangladesh's soil, mainly by this method. The sludging of bamboo tube-wells is reported in north-east India, especially the Kosi area of Bihar State.

Research in the UK

The final example relates to further development of Andrew Metianu's (NIAE) equipment at Silsoe College. Henry Bell[23] who carried out this work, extended the depth capability of the NIAE equipment by redesigning it in a light gauge steel of 50 mm diameter. Whereas the 100 mm jetting pipe designed by NIAE has a practical depth limit of around 12 m, the lighter weight pipe has been successfully used to 21 m and could probably reach 30 m before the weight of the drilling column becomes excessive.

As a result of Bell's development work, a network of observation and monitoring boreholes was installed as part of a hydrogeochemical research project near the Sussex coast of southern England. A total of 16 holes were installed ranging from 5 to 21 m in depth. These were lined with 40 mm *abs* plastic, which was sufficient to take water quality samples and monitor water levels. Costs of this programme of jetting averaged out at about £2 per metre, including all mobilization costs and site time, but excluding costs of lining holes.

The holes drilled in the course of this project were all in alluvial deposits ranging from clay to gravel in texture. Problems were encountered in gravels, which effectively prevented progress in some cases, and in which on several occasions circulation of water was lost completely.

The applications of the jetting technique described above have shown the potential of the method for constructing low-cost small-diameter boreholes, especially in alluvial materials. Small-scale irrigation and domestic rural water supplies are the main applications in developing countries, while there would appear to be further scope for use in low-budget research projects in the industrialized world.

(*Waterlines* Vol. 3 No. 3, January 1985)

Tackling water-supply problems in Uganda with REDR
PETER SHAW and ALAN HAYES

The water supply difficulties in the Luwero area of southern Uganda result from a variety of circumstances: a shortage of hard currency to purchase essential materials and spare parts from overseas, following the tripling of oil prices in the 1970s, and political and economic problems before, during and after the liberation war.

The Luwero area or the 'Triangle' covers an area of some 5,000 square miles, bounded by the Hoima-Kampala and the Nakasangola-Kampala roads and an 80 miles radius arc centred on Kampala.

The Triangle is peopled in the main by the Baganda tribe. The Baganda are the tribe of the last King of Uganda, King Freddie, who died in exile in Britain. In their traditional tribal area of Luwero they live by growing coffee and cotton on small but fertile holdings. In the 1960s this area was well served by good bituminized roads, the main villages had electric power, telephone communications and a safe public water supply. Medical services were good and there was a high literacy rate. However, as a result of several years of neglect these services had virtually disappeared by 1981 and civil disturbance in the area had resulted in large numbers of the people being moved into camps situated in or near the larger villages. By early 1984 there were some signs of the people in the camps returning home.

The water supply requirements were twofold:

○ To maintain and improve supplies convenient for the camps.
○ To rehabilitate the sources in the remainder of the area in preparation for the people's return.

Rehabilitation programme

Resources, both human and financial, were available to carry out the rehabilitation programme. Funds were provided via UNICEF and the human resources from the Uganda Government Water Development Department Staff (WDD) and UNICEF, SCF and Oxfam. REDR provided engineers for SCF.

The rehabilitation of water supplies consisted of two quite different operations: work on underground sources and work on spring sources. It was decided, for administrative convenience, that the underground sources would be the responsibility of the SCF engineer and the spring sources the responsibility of Oxfam, with both organizations working under the general direction of UNICEF, although there was some overlap. There was also a difference in the execution of the work. The underground sources were rehabilitated by the WDD teams based at Kampala and Mityana and the protection of the spring sources was carried out by local voluntary labour assisted by local recruited paid skilled labour; the work was co-ordinated by the local administration and supervized by WDD engineers.

The work programme was decided at a weekly liaison meeting by all the interested parties. The people attending the meeting varied depending on the priority each attached to the different projects.

The lines of communication between the WDD were direct from the Engineer to the WDD superintendent and worked well. However, they were the cause of considerable friction among the middle management of WDD. They viewed the secondment of part of their labour force to an outside autonomous body with resentment; understandably, since they had a minute budget for their own projects and their basic monthly salaries were equal to five days' allowances paid to the lowest grade labourer who was fortunate enough to be seconded to the aid agencies.

The borehole teams consisted of about 12 men plus a foreman and a superintendent, together with their rig, a Dando 200 mounted on a Bedford chassis, and a short-wheel-base Land-Rover. To ease access within the Triangle, UNICEF supplied the SCF engineers with a Land-Rover fitted with diplomatic plates. The teams stayed at a safe location as close as possible to the work site.

Improving efficiency

They were paid their basic salaries by the Ugandan Government and various allowances and bonuses by UNICEF which also provided the materials for the works and fuel for the vehicles. SCF provided the engineering back-up and supervision.

Fuel costs were a substantial proportion of the total cost of the works, mainly because the operational bases were a great distance from the work sites. One was at Kampala at the southern apex of the Triangle and the other was at Mityana, half-way along its north-western edge.

Attempts were made to group the works and increase the size of the team. This proved difficult. Politically, it was unacceptable to be seen doing too much work in a particular district at a time. There was a shortage of transport and the security risks were such that the drilling team were reluctant to work in isolated groups without independent transport.

Boreholes in the Triangle are usually cased at 6 in. diameter with a small preparation at 8 in. diameter. The majority had been fitted with the Uganda handpump. This was a piston pump with a bore of 2 in. diameter, operated by vertical rods via a simple lever.

UNICEF, as the financier of a country-wide rural water rehabilitation programme had decided that it would supply the India Mark II pump as a standard for all boreholes requiring a manual pump. The pump had been developed over a number of years for developing countries; it was robust, had the minimum number of working parts and was easy to maintain. Its one disadvantage was that the internal diameter of the pump pedestal meant that a 4 in. diameter adaptor had to be welded to the borehole casing some 18 in. below the finished slab level. If only 6 in. diameter tools were available, not only had the cover slab to be broken up, but the adaptor had also to be removed to clean the borehole. Besides, if 4 in. diameter tools were available then unless the borehole and adaptor were installed reasonably vertically, there was good chance that the drilling jaws would jam at the adaptor.

A pedestal of more than 6 in. nominal internal diameter would have three distinct advantages. There would be few situations where it would be necessary to cut off the casing to install the new pump. Existing boreholes normally have their casing protruding 600 mm above existing ground level. Secondly, it would not usually be necessary to make a watertight joint between the casing and pedestal since the top of the slab could be positioned below the top of the casing. Last, future cleaning operations could be carried out using 6 in. diameter tools without removing the pedestal. The building work needed to construct the pedestal slab, the drainage channel and sump has been greatly simplified and speeded up by the manufacture of purpose-made metal formwork and a simple jig to aid the assembly of the reinforcing steel in WDD's Kampala workshops.

In an endeavour to speed up the work and reduce unit costs, various incentive schemes were introduced based on work carried out to a satisfactory standard. These schemes were not successful since the major proportion of total wages for the borehole teams was the 'night out' allowance. Naturally, every effort was to maximize this payment, with completion very much a secondary objective. To counter this each borehole was given a target number of days for completion and the bonuses for useful work increased. This had a marginal effect only in increasing the output of work. UNICEF therefore proposed a radical change in the way in which bonuses were calculated and paid. Basically, this was to pay a fixed team bonus for each borehole successfully rehabilitated together with a fixed fuel allowance. This was to be introduced after each team had completed three boreholes. It was also proposed to progressively reduce the 'night out' allowance. The scheme was to be administered by the superintendents who would accept responsibility for collecting materials, organizing the work and paying the bonuses. The scheme was introduced in late February 1984.

The problems of working in Uganda are similar to those facing many relief agencies in countries where there is an urgent need to rehabilitate the organizational structure against a complex political background.

The solutions must be individually worked out in each situation. There must be close and sensitive co-operation between donor and receiver organizations so that cultural differences are appreciated and resources are used to best advantage.

(*Waterlines* Vol. 3 No. 2, October 1984)

Talking to the people: a multi-disciplinary approach to drilling boreholes in Senegal

HILARY SUNMAN

'Please make it easier for us to collect water; if we were not exhausted all the time, we could spend some time with our families and get a little pleasure from them.' The hands of the woman who said this to me were permanently crippled and twisted from drawing water from a depth of 50 m. Her sister's hands were covered in thick black callouses from the ropes.

The woman was from a Senegalese village; I spent three months in the country in 1983 working on a feasibility study to install and equip 24 boreholes for rural water supply. The project was funded by the UK's ODA. Balfours, the British firm of consulting engineers, were awarded the contract for design and supervision. Our project was part of the Senegalese Government's programme for drilling deep boreholes throughout the country. We were to consider 12 locations in the pastoralist, groundnut-growing north, and 12 in the rice- and cotton-growing south. Each borehole is to support 2,000 to 5,000 people and 4,000 to 10,000 cattle, and will cost £200,000 to drill and equip. This works out to about £50 per person; the high cost is partly the result of the area's large cattle population. Two-thirds of the water from the boreholes will be used by cattle rather than people.

There is little alternative to drilling deep boreholes fitted with pumps because since the disastrous drought years of the early 1970s, the free water-table has fallen dramatically. Poor rains in subsequent years meant that the shallower aquifers have never been recharged.

Until then, villagers in both the north and south of the country could meet their water needs from traditional wells, drawing water from 20 to 30 m. Now these are no longer adequate, and the deep waters of the Maestrichian aquifer provide the only reliable long-term source for people and their animals.

The north and south of Senegal are very different. In the south, the dominant ethnic groups grow millet and rice for subsistence, and cotton and a little groundnut as a cash crop. In the east of the area, the pastoral Fulani are well-established and cattle-raising is important, although less so than in the north where a Fulani village of 300 people will frequently own over 2,000 head of cattle.

Northern Senegal is the major area where groundnuts are grown, mainly by the settled agricultural Woloff. In the villages of the agriculturalists, round mud-brick thatched huts cluster in timber fenced compounds around a central meeting place. The pastoral villages are dispersed, the same wood fenced compounds scattered over several kilometres, although the villages are still distinct, each with its own chief.

So although the patterns of livelihood are widely different, the villagers of both north and south share two characteristics; they are all very poor, with household cash incomes of between $300 to 500 per year (around $40 per person) and they are preoccupied with one overriding problem—how to find enough water for themselves and their cattle. Our job was to help to answer that question, within the physical and financial constraints the project imposed.

Boreholes are artesian, and water rises to 50 to 60 m below the surface. In parts of the country, parallel-linked wells have been dug and people can draw water manually. But this is a punishing task, and the Senegalese Government wants to spread the benefits of the supply to villages within a radius of 5 km from the borehole itself. This plan means using the expensive paraphernalia of a motorized pump, water-tower and piped distribution network: a scale of installation seemingly at variance with the small communities living largely at subsistence level that the scheme will serve.

The scheme is therefore vulnerable to many of the pitfalls associated with modern technology in rural water supplies. These include inability of local people to maintain motors, shortages of fuel and lack of money, as well as the 'responsibility gap' which can occur when outsiders—'they'—install a system to which local people are unaccustomed. On the physical side, we had to ensure not only that sufficient water would flow through the system (to supply 20 litres/day for humans, 30 litres/day for cattle) but also that the water would be received by the people who needed it at the right location. We were seeking an appropriate technology solution compatible with sophisticated headworks.

So before we developed detailed designs of the systems, we visited the locations of all 24 proposed schemes and talked with villagers in each of the larger settlements within 5 km of the borehole. The purpose of this was fourfold; to identify the populations of people and cattle which would be served by each borehole; to understand their need for water, how much they consume, where they get it from; to obtain their views on the proposed borehole and finally to try and discover whether they would be prepared to take some responsibility for their own water supply, both in operating and maintaining the headworks and outlets, and in making a financial contribution towards the running costs of the systems.

Decentralization

The Senegalese Government has recently introduced a policy of decentralization and the users of public infrastructure facilities—water, health, schools—are encouraged to bear part of the operating costs. In principle it is accepted that this should result in a higher level of involvement and responsibility by the users, but the extent of this has not yet been well-defined by the Government.

The villagers should be able to control the hours of pumping in accordance with their needs, organize their own community budget to purchase diesel fuel and some spare parts, and contribute to the salary of the borehole custodian. He would preferably be a man from the locality, trained by the State organization responsible for boreholes in basic preventive maintenance and operations of the pump and distribution network, who would look after the water-tower and pumping station.

Our field team consisted of an economist, a social anthropologist, and two engineers, and we worked with two Senegalese counterparts from the

Direction de l'Hydraulique, our local client. While the engineers mapped the terrain, examined existing water supplies and identified topographical features which would affect the engineering designs, two teams, each consisting of a social scientist and a local counterpart, carried out interviews lasting for two or three hours in the villages themselves. Despite our fears of being seen as yet another team of foreign experts with clipboards prying into village life, the people were willing to talk about water with us because their need was so great. We found our results invaluable in the later design stages of the project. We seemed to have found an effective formula considering the time limits.

Villagers the world over are suspicious of local government and administration, and Senegalese villagers are no exception; so we kept our approach as informal as possible. We had to talk to the local government offices, to explain the project and to identify villages which would benefit from the scheme, but we always tried to visit the villages themselves unaccompanied by anyone from the administration. Sometimes this was unavoidable, as the local government office often supplied a translator for us, but where possible we preferred to work with a translator from the local livestock or agricultural extension office, who not only knew the area but was known and trusted by the villagers. Although in many villages there would be someone who spoke French, the responsiveness of the villagers was due in large part to the fact that we spoke to them (through interpreters) in their own language.

When we arrived at a village, a motley selection of people in a battered Land-Rover, the first stop was always the Chief's compound. There was no problem in persuading him to gather together a dozen or so village elders to talk to us, as the problem of water is constant and acute. We would establish ourselves under the village tree, or in the Chief's compound and start to talk about the water situation—how the wells are, where they are, whether there was enough water. Part of this phase was to establish confidence.

After visiting only a few villages we realized the urgent need for improved water supplies. Very few of the traditional wells are viable all year round, and the work of drawing water for both human and animal use is a grinding daily toil. By asking detailed questions about the population, and talking about present water needs and the problems of watering and pasturing cattle there was room for some discussion and an increase in confidence. The small group made this easier, and to maintain the informal atmosphere we worked to a check-list rather than a detailed questionnaire. This level of confidence was most important for the next stage of the interview—a discussion of community funding of some operating costs, and community participation in the management of the system. In the north of Senegal where some boreholes have already been drilled and equipped with motorized systems the villagers are accustomed to the benefits and the problems associated with the system—on the one hand the greater ease of collecting water, but on the other the frustrations that arise when the pump breaks down or when there have been no deliveries of diesel fuel from the state agency which deals with distributing it. When this happens, villagers often club together to buy more fuel, collecting it in 200-litre drums carried by horse and cart, but the lack of village-level organization, and hence clearly defined responsibilities, can lead to suspicions about misappropriation of funds and mistrust between villagers and villages. In the south of the country, there are no boreholes yet, and the whole concept of community participation and establishing village-level management committees needed very careful explanation and could take hours of talk to describe.

Villagers' acceptance

Villagers accepted the idea and welcomed taking responsibility for their own water supply in principle. In some cases, there were old rivalries or historic conflicts between villages which would share the same network, so considerable time was spent exploring how potential conflicts could be minimized.

Each village, it was felt, should retain control of its own community water fund until the need to purchase fuel or spare parts arose, and the fund should be kept exclusively for water, rather than form part of a more general community development budget.

The question of the frequency of contribution raised several responses; some argued that it would be best to make an annual contribution, after the sale of the cash crop harvest, whereas others felt that a monthly contribution was easier to control and would ensure year-round operation of the system. The longest discussion always concerned the actual sum of money to be contributed. Both animals and humans would be served by the same system, and as cattle consume 50 per cent more water than humans per day, we felt that the villagers' contributions should reflect this. We were anxious to obtain the villagers' own assessment of how much they could afford and never prompted a response. Interestingly, the level of contribution proposed was remarkably similar in all the villages whether the respondents had any direct experience of boreholes or not, and ranged from about 6 to 12 US cents per person per month and 8 to 18 cents per head of cattle.

In the course of discussions we tried to form some assessment of household cash incomes from the yields and sales of cash crops, and the suggested level of contribution averaged around 2 to 4 per cent of cash incomes, a level which we felt was probably realistic. This level of contribution would also cover between 50 and 60 per cent of operating costs (excluding depreciation).

The villagers' acceptance of the principle of community participation was encouraging, but there is still a significant gap between this and the effective implementation of the system.

We strongly recommended that a technical assistance programme should run in parallel with the construction of the physical works, to assist villagers to set up their own management committees, assess fuel needs, order and store it, to develop simple accounting/auditing systems, and to establish a workable interface with the State organization with which responsibility for the water scheme will be shared. This was the most we could recommend within the project's limits: there were no resources for health, sanitation or nutrition components.

Talking to the people

The final stage of the village research involved a discussion with the village women. They are usually responsible for the collection of water for the home and always responsible for its allocation between different uses, and are hence the only reliable source of information about how much water is actually used, and what sort of distribution network is needed.

The women are not accustomed to interviews, and were reluctant to talk freely in front of their men. The men were often equally reluctant to let us talk with women in their absence, but logical argument normally prevailed. 'We have been discussing men's problems with you, without women present; now we should discuss their problems alone, without you present.' The fact that both the social scientists were women probably helped us here, and the women themselves responded with warmth and interest to our concern for their needs. (This was often expressed in gifts of chickens, which gave us some unexpected logistical problems!)

It was difficult to discuss general issues with women, but they were helpful on detailed questions about how much water they draw daily, (how many buckets or basins), how long it takes them and whether they have to queue, how many basins they use for watering sheep and goats, how much for cooking, for washing and for laundry. We asked these questions of at least three women in each village and obtained remarkably consistent estimates of consumption. In only two villages did average daily consumption exceed 20 litres per person; in most cases, it lay between 11 and 18 litres.

We also tried to discuss health with the women; this was less easy as the connection between water and health is not always perceived. While this did not yield any statistically usable results, the evident high incidence of malaria and diarrhoeal diseases confirmed the link between water supply and rural health patterns. The sheer drudgery and the relentless hard work of water collection came across very strongly; drawing water manually from depths of 30 to 40 m puts an enormous strain on the arms and back. Basins containing 20 litres of water are carried on the head from the well to the homestead, several times a day: a two-woman job, as one must lift the basin on to the other's head and then take it down again. Wells are often surrounded by a quagmire of stagnant water, and I have seen women carrying basins of water up to their thighs in mud.

It might have been possible to design the water schemes from a desk in

Dakar with less field-work, but by spending several hours in a village, talking with users and establishing some sort of relationship, however superficial, with them, we were able to bring a more emotional, subjective perspective to the cold analysis of per capita costs of supply.

From talking to people, we learned where they might get by with their present water supply, and where needs were desperate. Without the field-work we could not have understood the variations between people's life-styles, how this had to influence the recommended designs, or the practicability of a phased development that the villagers themselves could extend at a later date.

Furthermore, the social scientists and engineers worked in parallel, covering the same terrain on the same day. Constant discussion of each place helped to minimize the tensions which can develop in a multidisciplinary team; we all came to understand something of the socio-economic framework for each village scheme. Equally, the social scientists started to appreciate the engineering constraints and possibilities for water supply in the context of people's lives.

In this project, we were designing 'modern technology' systems for rural subsistence communities. The field research programme was invaluable in the attempt to find a practical means of enabling these two worlds to meet, and hence to ensure that despite all the potential difficulties, the substantial capital investment would actually benefit those who really needed it. There is no substitute for simply talking to the people themselves. After the experience of this project, I would find it difficult to overestimate the importance of this.

(*Waterlines* Vol. 2 No. 4, April 1983)

CHAPTER 4
Rain-water harvesting

In 'Rain-water harvesting' Peter Stern sets out the principles and historic background of rain-water collection, together with the problems and advantages of surface water supplies. The article by Arnold Pacey and Adrian Cullis is an extract from their recent publication[24] and describes traditional ways of concentrating rain-water for agriculture, namely runoff farming, so that it can be used before evaporation depletes it unduly. In the introduction to the book the authors discuss the definition of rain-water harvesting: briefly, it is the gathering and storage of water running off surfaces on which rain has fallen directly. It does not include the harvesting of valley flood-water or stream flow, which are typically collected behind dams or by means of diversion weirs. The distinction is between concentrating runoff from within field catchments and distributing an already concentrated flood flow on to a field. Thus in rain-water harvesting the main concern is with small catchment areas or water-sheds and micro-catchment principles, providing runoff from roofs, artificial surfaces at ground level and land surfaces with slopes less than about 150 metres in length.

Derek Ray describes techniques for collecting rain-water based on his research in India. He summarizes the main features and refers to their possible application in drought-stricken Sahel. Although the Indian experience demonstrates that there are few technical obstacles, water-harvesting demands a high level of commitment and co-operation from villagers. There follows an article by Paula Park on the social dimensions of rain-water harvesting and the hazards of imposing a project on a delicately balanced social system.

John Gould outlines the work done in Botswana based on his post-graduate research with the Botswana Technology Centre. He points out that due to the many problems related to rain-water collection from thatch, time and resources would be better spent developing and improving small-scale ground-water tanks and constructing large communal tanks to collect rain-water from public buildings, such as schools and clinics, which have large iron-roof areas. The construction methods and problems experienced with rain-water catchment tanks are also discussed. He considers that the latest tanks developed are probably a more appropriate technology for Botswana today than the original ITDG type. He also refers to a pilot study on combined roof and cement apron catchments which could have applications in isolated arid areas where boreholes are uneconomic. He concludes that rain-water catchment technology has an important role to play throughout Botswana.

Rain-water harvesting

PETER STERN

Since the dawn of civilization humanity has recognized the importance of rainfall as the primary source of water which sustains life. Unlike many of the materials used in the world today, water is a renewable resource. The total quantity of water on the earth is huge and it has been estimated at about one and a half billion cubic kilometres volume. One way of envisaging this quantity is as water to a uniform depth of 3,000 m over the whole surface of the earth. Table 4.1 summarizes the distribution of this water.[25]

About 95 per cent exists as salt water in the oceans and salt seas, and only about one per cent is unfrozen fresh water. But there is continuous movement of fresh water from the oceans, seas and land surfaces into the atmosphere as vapour. From the atmosphere, rain falls on the land, and eventually finds its way back to the oceans.

The volume of water on the move in this way has been estimated as 520,000 cu.km a year, of which some 412,000 cu.km returns to the oceans as

Table 4.1 Approximate distribution of the world's water

Type of water	Per cent of total
Total:	
Salt	95
Fresh	5
Fresh:	
Frozen	4
Liquid	1
Fresh liquid:	
Ground water	0.99
Lakes	0.01
Soil	0.002
Rivers	0.001
Atmospheric	0.001
Biological	0.0005

Table 4.2 World annual water balance (cubic km)

Area	Precipitation (P)	Evaporation (E)	River runoff (P–E)
Land	108,400	71,000	+37,300
Oceans	411,600	448,900	−37,300
World totals	520,000	520,000	0

direct precipitation and 108,000 cu.km falls on the earth's land surfaces (Table 4.2).[26] The water which falls on the land's surface supports all the earth's natural vegetation and rain-fed crops and the annual 37,000 cu.km of river runoff provides the source for humanity's irrigation and domestic needs.

The amount of river runoff which is intercepted and used is not great. At an estimated 3,300 cu.km (Table 4.3)[27] it is only about nine per cent of the total available runoff. Much of the river runoff occurs in areas with high rainfall or in short duration floods so that it cannot be used.

The average annual precipitation on the world's land surfaces is 725 mm but there are very wide geographical variations, ranging from zero in deserts to over 5,000 mm in some tropical areas. More than 600 million people or 14 per cent of the world's population live in arid regions where the average annual rainfall is less than 300 mm. Here the climate is too dry for successful cultivation of crops and generally water is scarce.

In most of these low rainfall areas most of the rain which falls is lost by evaporation. Very little reaches drainage lines and watercourses to become usable water. World-wide, the annual runoff from land surfaces reaching river systems is about 34 per cent of the precipitation (Table 4.2). In the drier parts of the world this percentage is frequently less than 25 per cent and there are many river systems where only three or four per cent of runoff reaches the watercourse.

Evaporation losses can be considerably reduced if the runoff is collected much nearer to the land on which it falls. In other words, a multiple system of small catchments will yield much more water than one large catchment.

Every 100 m of rain falling on a hectare of land amounts to 1,000 cu. m or a million litres—enough domestic water for 100 people for a year if they use an average of 30 litres a day. In practice, it is not possible to collect every drop of rain which falls on land. But even under arid or semi-arid conditions 50 per cent or 60 per cent of the precipitation on a small natural catchment can be collected. If the catchment surface is paved or artificially sealed to prevent the water soaking through, the percentage yield will be even higher.

Table 4.3

Annual world water use	cu.km
Irrigated farming	2,500
Thermal power and industry	425
Hydro power and navigation	180
Domestic	98
Fish farming and recreation	65
Animal husbandry	40
	3,308

Rainfall collection

Two thousand years ago the Nabateans in Israel had developed extensive systems for collecting rainfall from hillsides in the Negev Desert and directing it on to crops in a region where the average annual rainfall was only about 100 mm.

All over the Middle East and North Africa there are rainfall catchment systems up to 2,000 years old. In Jamaica and other parts of the Caribbean, artificial hillside catchments, often paved with concrete, have been used for domestic water supplies since the end of the 19th century. In 1929 a small catchment was being used in a part of Australia with some 300 mm average annual rainfall to provide water for a farm family and its livestock.[28]

But by the middle of the twentieth century collecting rainfall had been virtually forgotten in most countries, although the Sudan had an extensive programme for the construction of earth ponds or *hafirs* for collecting rainfall for rural water supplies.

The advent of cheap synthetic materials suitable for waterproofing natural surfaces revived an interest in rainfall collection. In the 1960s C. W. Lauritzen was experimenting in this field in the United States.[29,30] At about the same time Doxiadis Associates was carrying out an extensive research and development programme in the construction of village rainfall catchment tanks using synthetic materials. The company was working in Kordofan, Western Sudan, on behalf of the Food and Agricultural Organization of the United Nations.[31]

The director and consultant of this programme was the late Michael Ionides who subsequently introduced the technology to the ITDG. This led to an ITDG project in Botswana in 1967–8 financed by Oxfam.[32] The UK Ministry of Overseas Development funded two ITDG projects in 1971. One was a two-year programme for constructing rain-water catchment tanks in Swaziland and the other was a comprehensive research and development programme on rainfall catchment in Jamaica. This also lasted two years and included the construction of a 2,300 cu.km catchment tank in conjunction with the Canadian Aluminium Corporation.

Present problems

The research and development programmes of the late 1960s and early 1970s demonstrated beyond doubt that rainfall collection was still a practical and viable method of water supply in areas where water is scarce. They also showed that traditional methods could be improved by the judicious application of appropriate technology.

So it is puzzling that now, in the 1980s, rainfall catchment systems are not playing a significant part in rural water supply programmes.

In fact, none of the countries where experimental programmes were carried out successfully have incorporated rainfall catchment in their rural development plans. This is partly because little emphasis has been placed on rainfall catchment by the World Bank and UN agencies concerned with water supply programmes. The preference for ground water over surface water as a source for domestic supplies was expressed in a World Bank Paper[33] in 1976 and this has been taken up in development policy.

There are good health reasons for preferring ground water to surface water. Ground water is usually safe to drink without treatment whereas many surface water sources are polluted and the operation and maintenance of treatment systems presents serious problems for many rural communities. However, these problems can be overcome. *Hafir* storages in the Sudan are protected from animal and human pollution and have provided reasonable water supplies for many rural communities for many years.

In the more arid regions of the world potable ground water is not readily available. North and East Africa have ground water, but it is too salty for human consumption. There are extensive areas in Africa, the drier parts of South America, the Indian subcontinent and many islands in the subtropics where ground water can be found but the recharge rate of wells is inadequate to meet demands. In such situations supplementing ground water by surface water is the only possible course, and if communities are remote from permanent streams, rivers or lakes, rainfall collection is the only option available.

Another problem in using ground water is that, except for springs and artesian water, it has to be pumped. Pumping means maintaining and operating machinery and this often leads to almost insuperable problems with fuel supplies, difficulties in providing essential spare parts, repairing the pumps and simply finding the financial resources for maintaining them.

Surface water supplies make the maximum use of gravity and in many situations there may be no need for pumping at all to exploit them.

A simple pulley being used for lifting water — with minimal protection. Mali
(World Bank/Yosef Hadar)

A small-scale water harvesting scheme, showing bunds and two rock spillways (Intermediate Technology/Patrick Mulvany)

Farming with runoff: a weapon against drought?
ARNOLD PACEY and ADRIAN CULLIS

The World Bank has commented that none of its economic statistics 'can convey the human misery spreading in subSaharan Africa.' Since 1970, food production has stagnated in many areas or has increased only slowly, and grain output per capita has shown a steady downward trend. In 1984, 'abnormal' shortages were reported in 24 countries, with famine conditions attributed to drought in several of them.

It is with a considerable sense of urgency, then, that one notes the relevance of rain-water harvesting techniques in certain limited but significant areas of Africa, both for food production and for the conservation of eroding soils. Strikingly, areas in which the prospects for rain-water concentration and runoff farming seem good coincide quite closely with the areas which experienced food shortages in 1983–4.

However, in many of these areas there has been little serious investigation of the potential of runoff farming, that is, farming which makes use of micro-catchments, contour strips, terraces or external catchments to collect rainfall before large losses occur as a result of evaporation. This reflects another of the World Bank's comments, about 'weaknesses of agricultural research.' Information about existing traditions of runoff farming is inadequate nearly everywhere. Sometimes the only well-documented information has been provided by anthropologists and geographers and agriculturalists have made no contribution at all. By contrast, much more research has been done in India, where some very large runoff farming systems exist, but this is insufficiently appreciated elsewhere.

The use of rain-water in runoff farming is only one of a number of approaches to land and water management which together might contribute to a slow recovery of pastoralism, crop production and forestry in drought-prone areas. Its potential varies according to local climate and soils, and also depends on patterns of social organization. Yet the areas where it might make some contribution contain considerable populations, including many of the 30 million people in the African Sahel.

Examples

Because of the inadequacy of research into runoff farming in many parts of the world, most discussions of the techniques focus on the few areas from which detailed studies have been reported—the Negev desert in Israel and the south-western Desert in Israel, where rain-water provided a livelihood for a considerable population more than 2,000 years ago, until about AD 700, and the south-western part of North America. It has been tempting to assume

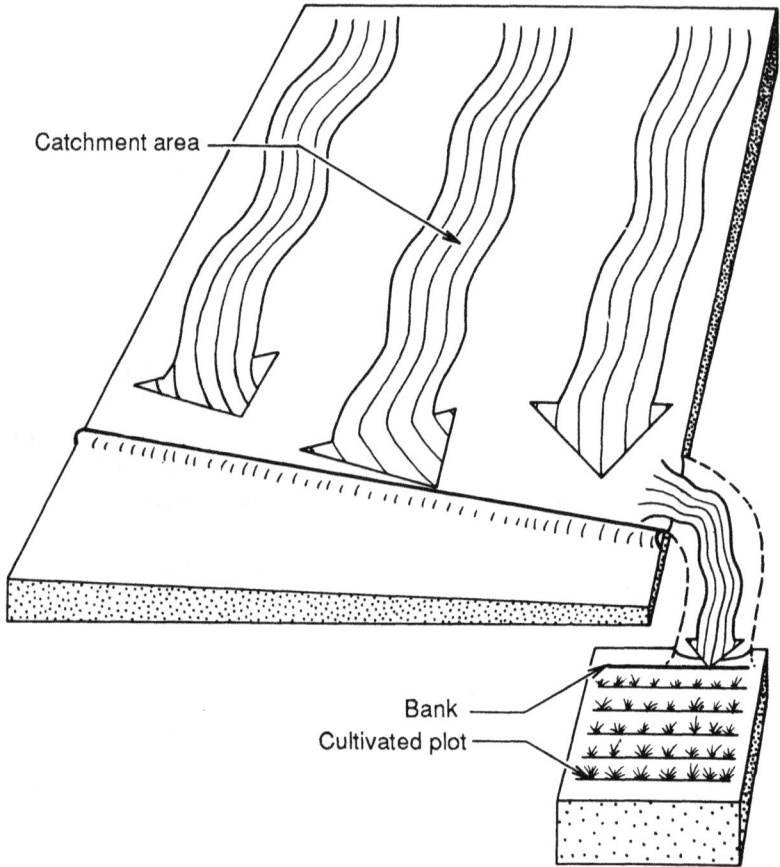

Figure 4.1   *Diagram of the concept of runoff farming*

that the techniques described in these reports offer the best available demonstration of this type of farming.

The Negev example has gained a particular authority not only because of the impressive achievements of desert farming there, and because of the thoroughness of the research work done, but also because of its historical origins. It is a system which has a demonstrable long-term viability.

What is too easily forgotten is that other countries, notably India, have equally venerable traditions of runoff farming, some of which may be more relevant to hydrological conditions in the tropical areas. These are described in Derek Ray's article which follows.

Requirements for runoff farming are very different in regions where rainfall comes in winter, as it does in the Negev and North Africa, as compared with tropical regions where rainfall occurs in summer, at times when evaporation rates are very high.

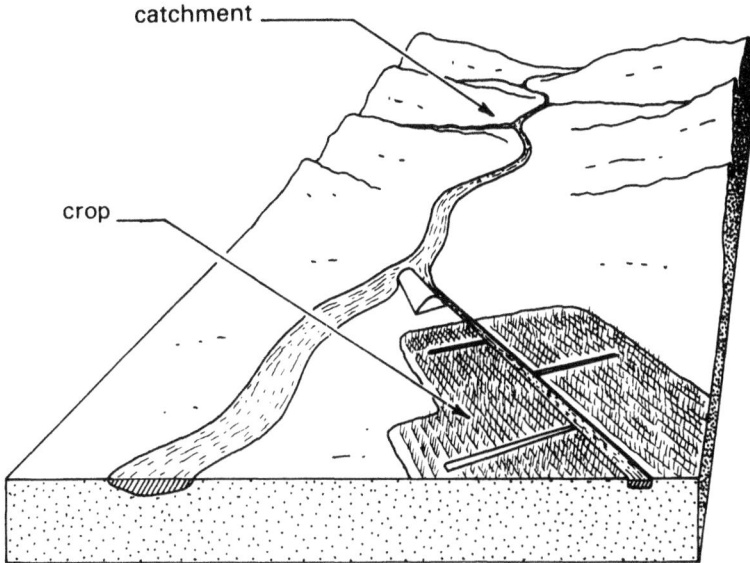

Figure 4.2   *An external catchment. Here spate flow from the river is diverted onto crops*

Regions which seem suitable for runoff farming in the tropics are mostly those with an annual average rainfall of at least 300 mm, and the most suitable are areas with 500 to 600 mm. The latter is a conservative recommendation because of the evidence that average rainfall levels in much of Africa are declining (though interpretation of this is controversial).

However, annual rainfall is not the most important criterion. What matters more is the balance of rainfall and evaporation during the growing season, which is rather favourable in the Negev. By contrast, in areas where rainfall occurs in summer, the evaporation rates during the rainy season are very high, and the crops' water needs are correspondingly greater.

A runoff farming system designed for a crop with a 100-day growing season will usually need several storms producing significant amounts of runoff spaced at regular intervals within the 100-day period if the crop is to do well. In the Negev, a couple of storms during the cool winter growing season can produce sufficient soil moisture to support a crop on a runoff farm. In tropical areas with summer rainfall and where evaporation is high, there is no question of such sparse rains being sufficient.

One limitation of most of the techniques on which detailed research has been done is that because crops are grown during the season when rainfall is expected, it is necessary to avoid collecting too much rain-water on cultivated plots because inundation and waterlogging can kill growing plants, especially seedlings. Thus, in American experiments, arrangements have sometimes been made for excess runoff to be diverted away from cultivated

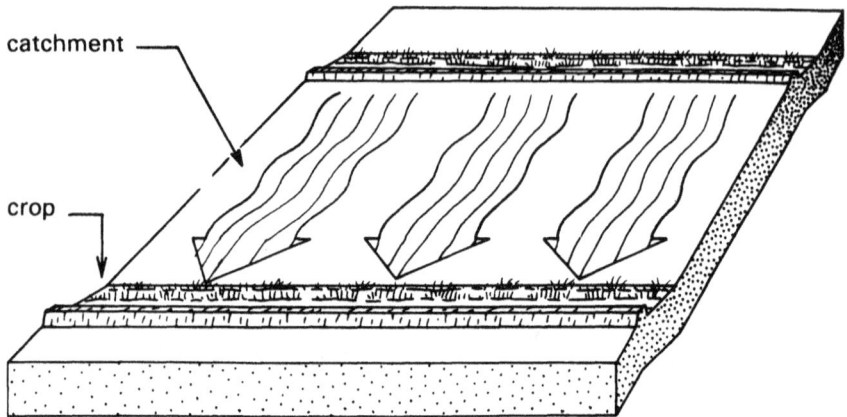

Figure 4.3   *Schematic diagram of contour strips, a type of within-field catchment*

plots, and in the Negev most plots are equipped with spillways of such height that excessive depths of water on the cropped area are avoided.

In regions with limited rainfall in a hot summer season, it is necessary to store more water in the soil, hence postponing the planting of the crop until after the rainy season is past. One such strategy involves building high bunds or banks along contours so that strips of land can be inundated to a depth of as much as a metre. This water slowly infiltrates the soil or evaporates, and a crop is planted as the water subsides. By this time, the season of highest temperatures may be over, so the crop is able to grow under conditions where evaporative demand is relatively modest.

Contour bunds

The technique is used in Sudan, on plains to the east of the Nile where there are large areas of clay soil and gentle slopes. Here embankments are made 'to intercept sheet-wash runoff following heavy storms.' Quick-maturing millet is planted immediately the water left by a storm has subsided. 'The crop grows and matures in 80 days, using the moisture that has been induced to infiltrate the soil behind the bunds', according to one writer.

In North and South Yemen, a similar approach to water storage in the soil is used but in connection with flood-water harvesting rather than rain-water. Indeed, the rainfall from which the floods originate occurs mainly in a nearby mountain area, not in the immediate environs of the cultivated land. It flows in torrents down steep *wadis*, and where these discharge on to flatter land, the water is diverted from its natural channel by dams or barrages, and is led via canals to inundate large areas of land. There the water is ponded to a considerable depth behind large bunds, sometimes 2 to 3 m in height. Within 10 or 15 days the flooding has subsided and crops can be planted.

Similar techniques are used in other tropical, arid or semi-arid areas where the rains come in summer, including parts of southern Pakistan (where systems of this kind are known as *sailabas* or *kuskabas*), and northern India (which has *khadins* and *ahars*). In some of these places the source of water is rainfall on a nearby catchment, as in Sudan, but in others, flood-water is used, as in Yemen.

The introduction of improved systems of runoff farming cannot, of course, depend entirely on knowledge of traditional systems. It will also be important to collect all the data possible on rainfall and runoff volumes. It will be necessary, for instance, to design bunds and spillways on the basis of conventional agricultural engineering experience. Contour bunds have to be laid out to ensure their accurate alignment with the contour. Improved methods of runoff farming will require the interaction of modern and traditional ideas.

(Waterlines Vol. 4 No. 4, April 1986)

Water harvesting in India
DEREK RAY

Technologies for water harvesting and rain-water collection used in runoff farming in India are of various kinds, but particularly notable are inundation tanks (called *khadin* in Rajastan), percolation tanks (often associated with Maharashtra) and village tanks (long established in South India and Sri Lanka and now being introduced into areas of north India such as the Siwalik hills).

Several features of these tanks are noteworthy. First, they are appropriate investments for Indian villages because they use local labour rather than capital in construction, require and use traditional rain-water collecting skills and can be readily managed by a village self-help organization. Initial capital requirements need not be high; for example, Rs 5,000 per hectare irrigated seems feasible in the Siwalik hills. This can be readily offset against the extra revenue received from growing two crops or making one crop much more reliable. The investment ought to be able to repay its costs from agriculture alone.

Complementary benefits

Thus the second feature of water harvesting is the bright prospects for increased profits from farming. However, the tanks of South India do not seem to be fulfilling their potential for profit, with tank beds often overfilled with silt, while villagers' water management skills are frustrated by over-

CWD—G

bureaucratic authorities. Measures to improve the profitability of South Indian tanks should emphasize ownership by smaller groups and more local control over use and maintenance of the water. The introduction of tanks to the Siwalik hills is following this line of approach. Those who actually farm the land beneath the tank bund pay for and supervise the release of water and maintenance of the catchment area, the bund and the channels.

This leads to the third feature of water harvesting, the need to have a pool of village skills, talent and capital to draw on. Local control and freedom from bureaucracy is all very well but it makes outside finance more difficult to obtain and pushes farmers back to relying on their own capital and skills. A village needs seed capital, perhaps livestock which can be sold or used as collateral, or relatives in town who are prepared to invest in the village. The villagers also need at least some literate farmers who can look after making arrangements, book-keeping and running the water association. This is more likely to be possible with villages in India than in many parts of Africa.

A question for those concerned with introducing water harvesting to villages in the Sahel is how far the technology can be adopted without the villagers already being skilled in co-operating over the use and maintenance of facilities. By its nature, water harvesting requires the agreement and co-operation of a number of farmers, and holding a group together requires skills and mental resources. Developing and training group leaders in such skills must have as great a priority as training in the techniques of water harvesting.

The fourth feature of water harvesting is the wide range of complementary benefits for villagers and the environment. As noted, increased farming profits alone should justify water harvesting.

However, the system encourages (and usually requires) the planting of trees in catchment areas as well as the control of grazing. New sources of income linked to trees include fruit, timber and fuelwood from the forest; and hay, rope and baskets woven from grasses planted on catchment slopes which are too steep for growing trees, and are now protected from livestock. These products offer income and employment for families whose land is not near enough to irrigate their crops with the collected rain-water. The trees and grass on the catchment stem erosion, increase the biomass in the area and significantly improve the water-holding capacity of the land.

For some villages it makes sense to rotate crops with grass leys which can be used to feed cows (and in India buffaloes) or goats for milk production. This also increases the complementary benefits of water harvesting because the tethered livestock (for their access to the catchment area must be restricted) provide new sources of income and employment, offer improved nutrition for farm families and have the added advantages of producing dung and being available for draught power and transport.

Summing up, water harvesting and collecting technologies in India are appropriate, profitable for farming, make full use of village capital and skills and benefit the land-poor and the environment. At the same time, they demand a high level of commitment and co-operation from villagers.

We are presently witnessing a tremendous expansion of projects based on rain-water harvesting or collecting in Sahelian countries. The critical factor that decides whether these activities are successful or not will surely be the willingness of villagers to submit to the discipline of community effort and their willingness to share the benefits and continuing costs of maintenance and management. The Indian experience demonstrates that there are few technical obstacles in the way of water harvesting. The problems to be overcome are social, political and economic.[34]

(*Waterlines* Vol. 4 No. 4, April 1986)

Social dimensions of harvesting rain-water in Turkana
PAULA PARK

In 1980, an epidemic of pleuro-pneumonia in north-western Kenya, coupled with an intensification in armed livestock raiding, devastated the Turkana people's herds, leaving them with neither a source of food nor the money to buy it. In response to the crisis, the World Food Programme, Oxfam, the European Economic Community and other donors set up the Turkana Rehabilitation Project (TRP) with the Kenyan Government. The aim was to provide food relief for more than 70,000 people.

The TRP is still in action, although food aid is going to fewer people. The Turkana now work on a series of projects, designed to increase their self-reliance and develop their arid land, in exchange for food.

Among these projects are some for water harvesting—capturing rainfall from *wadis* and natural depressions, and redirecting it to allow cultivation of sorghum or improved livestock fodder. Imported by experts from Yemen and Israel, water harvesting techniques once seemed the perfect panacea for drought.

Basic water harvesting techniques

Unfortunately, projects were launched without a clear understanding of the social structure within which they would have to be implemented and maintained.

The TRP uses three basic techniques for harvesting water: building bunds to trap runoff as it flows down slopes, using bunds to divert spate floods from *wadis* for irrigation and building micro-catchments.

○ A level trapezium-shaped piece of land where water tends to accumulate naturally is enclosed with bunds on three sides. The uphill side is left open to allow water to flow in from higher land, carrying humus to fertilize trees and plots of sorghum.

○ The spate floods which course down *wadis* can be diverted by means of bunds to natural depressions, where the water can be used to irrigate crops. This requires large areas of land, and therefore large numbers of people are needed to work on spate irrigation schemes.

○ A micro-catchment is a technique for concentrating water from an area enclosed by earth bunds so that it can irrigate a small pit constructed at its lowest point. The pit may contain a single tree. Micro-catchments are possibly the easiest of the three techniques to build, but require co-operation between people to protect the trees.

These techniques all use manual labour in construction, and it was originally thought that they required little equipment or expertise.

The first setback was technical. According to a consultant who has designed water harvesting schemes in Yemen and Ethiopia, some of the TRP's were poorly constructed in the first place. Some bunds were so weak that goats could trample them down, while some were not built to follow the land's contours accurately. His first task as consultant to the project was to instruct site managers in the building of earth bunds and catchments which would work.

But while efforts are being made to iron out wrinkles in the technology, the social systems, customs and desires of the Turkana themselves have not yet played a significant role in a development scheme which was designed to help them.

Rainfall is scarce and erratic in Turkana. Annual averages range from between below 250 mm in the lowlands to 450 mm on the higher land. There are good soils but also vast stretches of barren land. Only the toughest grasses, shrubs and trees can survive on the grasslands. The Turkana have adapted to this by keeping mixed herds of goats, sheep, camels and cows. They can divide up their herds and drive them to areas where the fodder is most suitable. Cattle consume mostly grass, while goats feed on shrubs and the lower branches of young acacia trees. This leaves the middle branches of mature trees for the camels to browse on. When the fodder in one area is used up, the herd is moved to another area and large patches of pasture are preserved by custom for the dry season.

The nomadic herds are the key to human life in Turkana. Besides providing milk, which makes up 70 per cent of the diet of pastoral Turkana people, livestock is used for dowry, in negotiating land rights and to hire extra labour. Only those who were not suited to nomadism, usually women and the old, would traditionally settle and plant sorghum near rivers. If an able-bodied man began to cultivate land, he would be considered weak and incompetent by other pastoralists.

Food for work

The TRP countered hundreds of years of Turkana tradition by employing Turkana on food-for-work schemes to build rain-water harvesting structures for sorghum production, and it is therefore not surprising that many Turkana have reacted half-heartedly to the TRP scheme. Chief Kuchil of Kakuma explains: 'We have three problems—raiding, livestock diseases and obtaining drinking water for our herds . . . the TRP has not helped us with any of these.'

The food-for-work programme was designed to help poor families without animals, but some pastoralists who are successful have been able to offload members of their families on to the project. They sometimes take advantage of the food supplied to build up their own herds, and if a woman is able to stay near a trading centre, there is the added advantage of being able to send children to school. For destitute families, however, the 6 kg of food they receive each week can do no more than feed them. The TRP's new policy of stressing the importance of growing good fodder for animals, as opposed to growing grain, only helps those Turkana who already have animals, not poor families who are dependent on food for work.

There are also problems with land tenure. The Turkana system of land tenure seems communal and flexible to outsiders. However, there are specific rights over critical resources, which the TRP has fallen foul of, on occasion. Some rights to land are earned through labouring, but some are ascribed to a certain family or group. Farmers who have been assigned to land by the TRP have sometimes been forced to hand over their crop to the richer pastoralist who customarily uses the land.

The core of the confusion lies in a lack of communication between the TRP and the Turkana people. 'No one has looked at traditional water harvesting and examined its constraints,' explains Adrian Cullis, an Intermediate Technology rain-water harvesting specialist who runs an Oxfam scheme working on small-scale water harvesting techniques in Turkana. 'We do not know whether land, labour, seeds or water are constraints, we haven't looked at the problems of weeding, and we cannot be absolutely sure what the need is for improved water harvesting.'

Chief Kuchil and other Turkana complain that no one has ever asked them what their needs and problems are. 'When the project started,' recalls Chief Kuchil, 'I was not asked about ways to make people self-reliant. I was asked to help settle people in relief camps, and then to tell them to work hard on the *shambas*.' Recently, the TRP has held meetings with local people, but according to some of the participants at meetings in Kakuma, they were lectured about the importance of trees and water harvesting, not involved in discussions about problems and solutions.

'Development has been imposed on the Turkana,' claims an Oxfam report. There are, indeed, good roads in Turkana, and impressive new grain stores for the TRP. In some areas, trees seem to grow from dry sand. But the destitute Turkana whom the schemes were designed to help are still poor.

In fact, there are fears that the TRP has led the Turkana backwards rather than forwards. The project has concentrated people into camps. Nomads are attracted to the sites to trade, and bring some of their animals with them, which contributes to the overgrazing. The concentrations of population even make raiding easier. 'In the past,' said one old man, 'other tribes only stole our cattle. Now they want pans and cooking supplies to sell.' Another fear is that the destitute Turkana settled in the camps are beginning to depend on maize as their sole source of food. This can lead to protein deficiencies and food-related diseases.

Even with all these problems, it is important to note that the water harvesting schemes which were properly constructed, especially the small-scale ones, will stand for some time, with maintenance. The Turkana *are* using them. After good rains last year, plants are growing on the earth bunds, and this will help to bind the soil.

Some TRP co-ordinators are struggling hard to create a trusting relationship between themselves and the Turkana, but this will take time. They feel it would help if they understood more about the social system which has enabled the Turkana to survive for thousands of years.

(*Waterlines* Vol. 4 No. 4, April 1986)

Rain-water catchment systems in Botswana
JOHN GOULD

Botswana is located in the heart of the Southern African Plateau, and straddles the Tropic of Capricorn between 18° and 27° south of the equator. It has a continental and semi-arid climate, and a mean elevation of 1,000 m above sea-level. Although the altitude has a moderating effect on the summer temperatures, the January mean being around 26° C in much of the country, it does little to enhance rainfall due to the flat nature of the terrain.

Rainfall in Botswana is both erratic and unevenly distributed. Mean annual totals range from more than 700 mm to the north-west to less than 200 mm in the south-west. On the eastern side of the country, where 80 per cent of Botswana's one million population live, average rainfall is generally between 450 and 550 mm per annum. Although the annual distribution of rainfall is very clearly defined, with 90 per cent of rain falling between November and April, variations from year to year can be considerable.

The majority of the population of Botswana still live in grass-roofed dwellings, although the number of people owning at least one iron-roofed building is increasing rapidly. This, along with the construction of modern schools, clinics and other government buildings in rural areas, is giving greater potential for the use of roof catchment as a supplementary water supply at the point of consumption.

Although the low and erratic rainfall in Botswana means that large catchment areas and storage capacities will be required if a reasonable rain-water supply is to be provided with any reliability, there are two factors specific to Botswana which make rain-water catchment an attractive supplementary water source for the future. First is the peculiar triangular migration system, whereby many Botswana have three homes: a village home, a cattle post and a 'lands' area where crops are cultivated. Second is the huge land area of the country—561,000 sq km—relative to the small and predominantly rural population (941,000 according to the 1981 census). Thus Botswana has a land area more than twice that of Britain, yet a population density of less than two people per square kilometre.

Together, these factors result in many people spending at least part of the year in remote and isolated localities. Despite a very ambitious drilling programme to try to exploit the huge Kalahari sands aquifer, covering most of the country, it is beyond the realms of possibility that ground water could supply the needs of every scattered household within the foreseeable future. Rain-water catchment, however, may offer just that possibility. But, due to the absence of iron roofs in more isolated localities, it is necessary to examine the possibilities of catching rain-water from ground or grass roof surfaces.

Problems with thatch

The biggest drawback in the collection of rain-water from thatched roofs is that the water becomes turbid and discoloured. As a result, it is regarded as dirty and unsuitable for most purposes. In a survey of 150 households in three villages in the north-east of Botswana, 99 had only grass-roofed buildings, and of these water was collected from the thatch in just nine cases. At only one household did the owner admit to drinking the rain-water. This was normally collected in an informal way by placing buckets, basins or oil drums under the eaves. The perception of runoff water from thatch as generally being an unsuitable source has also been confirmed by research in Lesotho.[35]

One of the recommendations of the recently conducted Water Points Survey[36] in eastern Botswana, was to examine the feasibility of manufacturing low-cost rain-water catchment tanks for use on thatched rondavels. There are two common types of thatching in Botswana, a loose traditional thatch and a more modern, often metal capped, tight thatch. The former is highly unsuitable for rain-water catchment due to the uneven nature of the eaves. The latter, although better, still requires curved guttering which is difficult to manufacture and fit to the buildings.

Due to the many problems related to rain-water collection from thatch it is the writer's opinion that time and resources would be better spent developing and improving small-scale ground catchment tanks already widely in use, and constructing large communal tanks at schools, clinics and other public buildings which have large iron-roof areas. The latter could use locally made bricks and labour and would provide useful clean supplementary water, in addition to acting as examples to the community. On the basis of calculations using a 58 year series of rainfall data from Francistown, it has been determined that the most appropriate volume for a catchment tank is equivalent to the area of the catchment surface in square metres multiplied by 0.2 m.

ALDEP tanks

The Ministry of Agriculture have provided grants and loans to farmers throughout Botswana to build underground rain-water catchment tanks through the Arable Lands Development Programme (ALDEP). These tanks, devleoped in the late 1970s, have two basic designs; a dome brick and plaster tank for areas of loose soil, and a chicken wire and plaster tank for areas with more consolidated soils. The tanks, normally with volumes of 10 cu.m. to 20 cu.m., collect rain-water from traditional mud- and dung-plastered threshing floors with areas of approximately 100 sq.m.

The original rationale of constructing the tanks was to provide water for draught animals and human consumption during the first early light rains. This was in order that ploughing could begin as soon as the main rains arrived, thus, hopefully, leading to increased crop yields.[37] In practice, however, water in the tanks is used predominantly for domestic purposes, especially during drought conditions when ploughing cannot proceed. In many cases the drought has resulted in all the rain-water in the tanks being used up.

However, many farmers own, or have access to, donkey carts and have collected water from distant boreholes in oil-drums for storage in their tanks—which are therefore a very valuable facility. Apart from being able to reap benefit from the tanks in drier periods this is also very important for keeping the tanks in good working order, because there is a serious danger of cracking if they are allowed to dry out completely.

Livestock damage

Another problem is that the corrugated iron covers of the plaster and chicken wire tanks can be damaged by livestock. The cover is essential to prevent evaporation and to stop dirt entering the tank. There have been a number of cases of cattle damaging these covers, and in one case a cow actually fell into a tank and had to be slaughtered there, as there was no way to haul it out. Many farmers are now protecting the tanks and catchment aprons by surrounding them with thorn fences.

Although, so far at least, most of the tanks have been found to be technically sound, perhaps the biggest concern revolves around the question of water quality.

Although the people using the water generally perceive it as being good, bacteriological analyses have produced some disturbing results. In five tanks tested by the Department of Water Affairs, three contained coliform bacteria in quantities too numerous to count, and all had faecal coliform counts ranging from between 15 and 1,000 in a 100 ml sample, making the water most unsuitable for human consumption. The Ministry of Agriculture is aware of this problem and has through its extension staff, advised all tank owners to boil their water before consuming it.

However, out of nearly 20 tanks visited in a random survey, not a single case of boiling drinking water was encountered. With so many tanks already in use and this technology apparently the only method available to provide water at the point of consumption in remote areas, it is extremely important that water quality should be improved. A pot chlorinator may prove to be a simpler and more convenient method for destroying pathogens than boiling.

Lessons from the past

The concept of catching rain-water from the ground surface and storing it in subsurface tanks is not new to Botswana. Research in the 1960s culminated in a joint pilot project by ITDG and Oxfam in 1969. The aim was to train primary teachers from 12 schools to build low cost, excavated tanks using only sand, mud, wire, polythene, a small amount of cement and a large quantity of labour.

The idea was to excavate a sloping-sided trapezoidal tank and line it with alternating layers of black polythene sheeting and mud. This is turn was reinforced with 'sausages' made up of sections of thin-walled polythene tubing filled with a 9:1 sand:cement mixture and tied off at each end. The sausage 'skins' were pricked and the sausages soaked in water before use, so that they set hard.

A couple of the earlier tanks contained 'beehive-shaped' structures fashioned from these sausages, to reduce the evaporation of water and to support a well-head. In these cases, the interstices between clusters of 'beehives' were filled with sand. The publication of a detailed report on the project,[37] which publicized this technology and assessment report[38] three years after have contributed to two conflicting misconceptions about the project.

On the one hand is the idea that the technology has been widely adopted in Botswana and that subsurface catchment tanks are a common sight throughout the country. This misleading impression is due to the inclusion of the ITDG beehive tank design in many popular texts, including some for school use. A limited number of tanks were constructed, and even fewer of the beehive type.

On the other hand there are some people who see the ITDG pilot project as a total failure. This point of view may, in many ways, be just as far from reality as the first. Although it is true that only seven per cent of the 12 schools participating in the project actually built tanks, and only two of these were still functioning three years later, a pilot project is by definition designed to expose both the strengths and weaknesses of a given technology.

In addition, there may be non-physical benefits from any project which should be taken into account during an assessment. These may include the extent to which replication may have occurred elsewhere, or the influence the project may have had on later developments of the technology. The ITDG project in Botswana certainly led to some replication of the technology, both within the country and in Zimbabwe and Swaziland. In 1981, a primary school headmistress in the village of Morwa near Gaborone had a cement lined excavated catchment tank constructed for irrigating a school garden. The tank was paid for from school funds. In addition to such developments there has been a growing general awareness of the utility and practicality of subsurface tanks for rain-water catchment from ground surfaces in semi-arid environments.

The fact that at least four tanks dating to as far back as 1969 are still known to be functioning in Botswana and Zimbabwe proves, at least, that if carefully constructed and maintained, the method is technically sound. It is difficult to ascertain whether the ALDEP tank programme was directly influenced by the ITDG project, but it seems inevitable that there must have been some indirect influence.

Link with community

If the project did fail in any respect it was, according to Pacey,[38] because it was unable to build up sufficient momentum to lead to more widespread construction of the tanks. This may have been partly due to the fact that the tanks were built to irrigate school gardens which, in many cases, did not really satisfy a felt need in the community. The labour requirements may have been unrealistically high as a result, especially considering that voluntary labour was demanded.

Despite these drawbacks the lack of follow-up after the pilot project may have been the crucial factor in preventing this particular innovation from gaining popularity.

It is probably too late to re-introduce such labour-intensive, low-cost tanks in Botswana, as the nation has gone from rags to potential riches in the last 15 years with the discovery of diamonds. Although the rural areas still require much basic infrastructure, more resources are available today to provide it, given the prevailing political climate.

The ALDEP catchment tank project has thus developed partly in response to lessons from the past, with labour requirements having been
reduced, while the 'felt needs' of the people are more closely satisfied. Thus,
although more expensive, the ALDEP tanks are probably a more appropriate technology for the Botswana of the 1980s than the ITDG type.

Prospects for the future

It seems likely that rain-water catchment systems will be used increasingly
throughout Botswana during the next decade in localities where, for one
reason or another, the government is unable to provide a permanent and
reliable alternative supply. This includes both small remote settlements and
also larger settlements where fresh ground water may be unavailable.

A good example of this latter case is found in the village of Nata. This
village, on the edge of the Makgadigadi Salt Pan, 200 km north-east of
Francistown, has no fresh ground-water sources within 40 km. At the
present time the vast majority of the 1,850 population share with cattle a
highly polluted saline river as their main water source.

A bowser (water tanker) has been temporarily provided under the
national Drought Relief Programme to bring 5,000 litres of fresh water daily
from a borehole 43 km away. This water has not been reserved as a drinking-
water supply and normally runs out before more than a fraction of the
community has been satisfied. Most of the villagers are thus forced to drink
contaminated river water and suffer the resultant consequences to their
health.

Due to technical and financial constraints it seems unlikely that borehole
water will be piped to Nata for at least three or four years. Even then, the
supply may not be reliable.

Feasibility study

A feasibility study has been conducted to find out the possibilities for
providing at least drinking water through rain-water catchment, in addition
to a supply for more general use at the school and clinic. The results of this
study have revealed that it would be possible to supply the drinking water
requirements of the village entirely through rain-water catchment with a
level of reliability of at least 95 per cent.

Although it was calculated that the runoff from all the corrugated iron
roofs in Nata would be far in excess of the present bowser supply, the
logistical problems of providing a rationed communal drinking water supply
from dozens of scattered tanks would be immense. For this reason, the
possibility of constructing one or two rain-water catchment surfaces and
combining these with roof catchment from a few of the larger roofs is being

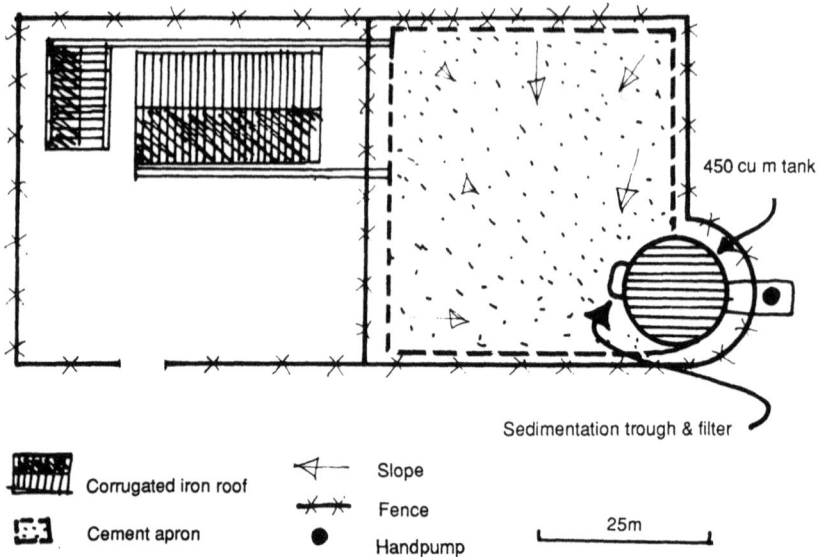

Figure 4.4 *Proposed roof and rain-water harvester at the Botswana Agricultural Marketing Board warehouse in Nata*

considered. Although the initial capital costs of the project would be high, these could be reduced if local labour and materials were exploited to the full as part of a Government Labour Based Relief Project. Once constructed, the running costs for the supply would be low, in contrast to the high recurrent costs of the present bowser supply, and the scheme would be able to pay for itself within two to three years.

Figure 4.4 shows a diagram of the larger of the two rain-water catchments required in the project. It uses a combined roof and cement apron of 2,700 sq.m and feeds a 450 cu.m tank. As far as the writer is aware, there is no other combined catchment of this type in use in Southern Africa. If constructed it would be a prototype for this technology, which could have applications in many isolated localities in semi-arid areas of Africa.

Most of the future developments of rain-water catchment in Botswana are likely to be concentrated in small isolated rural settlements where it is uneconomic to provide a borehole supply. Even in larger settlements, rain-water catchment systems could play an important role in the future as a reserve supply, for periods when the piped supply is out of action. Roof catchment tanks may also help to fill in gaps in future piped supplies, by providing an improved water source for scattered settlements on the edges of villages. It would be extremely expensive to pipe water to these.

Bacteriological analysis of the quality of water in covered roof catchment tanks has shown it to be generally pure and quite fit for human consumption. Yet another factor favouring rain-water as a supplementary water source in rural Botswana is that people generally prefer the taste of sweet rain-water to that of the often slightly saline borehole supplies. Even in urban areas people sometimes drink water from catchment tanks in preference to water from nearby stand-pipes. Despite the relative cheapness of the urban water supplies, a catchment tank can still provide enough water to pay for itself within 15 to 20 years. The long-term future benefits of rain-water tanks, even to supplement urban supplies, has been recognized by the Botswana Technology Centre which is currently trying to encourage the Government to introduce tax relief for people who invest in tanks.

In remote rural locations, ground catchment tanks may well help to provide water during the coming decade, when other nearby sources are lacking. An expanded ALDEP tank programme could help cater for this by training more builders, although attention is required to sort out problems of water quality associated with these tanks.

To what extent rain-water catchment systems are adopted in future remains to be seen. Nevertheless one thing is certain: this technology has the potential to play an important role in providing small-scale water supplies in both rural and urban localities throughout Botswana.

It is disappointing that the World Bank and many United Nations and other leading agencies are putting so little emphasis on rain-water catchment during the IDWSSD[39] as the technology is promising for both arid and humid localities in many countries.

(Waterlines Vol. 2 No. 4, April 1984)

CHAPTER 5
Water Conservation

Chapter 4 dealt with rain-water harvesting from within small catchments on micro-catchment principles. This chapter will deal with water conservation in a variety of catchments and structures, both surface and subsurface, for collection, diversion and ground-water recharge.

In the first two articles Eric Nissen-Peterson refers to rock catchment dams and to sand subsurface dams, based on his work with self-help groups in East Africa.[40] In his article on gully-plugging in Gujarat, T. S. Randhawa emphasizes that this is an appropriate and simple technical method not only to achieve ground-water recharge, but also to assist in increasing the capacity for storing and spreading water, reducing soil erosion and flattening slopes for cultivation.

The article on simple diversion weirs by Tim Stephens deals with simple weirs up to a maximum height of two metres; nevertheless, experienced technical advice on siting, design and construction should still be sought. The final article by John Fowler on the design and construction of small earth dams is subject to the same caveat.

Water from rocks
ERIK NISSEN-PETERSEN

The biblical patriarch, Moses, provided water for his thirsty people from a rock in the desert. Until a few years ago, it seemed unlikely that we could do the same in our age. However, it is now possible to rely on rocks and mountains as water catchments, even in arid and semi-arid zones.

Moses' modern successors in Kenya are DANIDA, the Ministry of Agriculture and several thousands of Kamba people. Despite drought and famine, the Kamba are providing a free and voluntary labour-force in the biggest rain-harvesting project ever seen in this part of the world. The project is called the Mutomo Soil and Water Conservation Project and it is situated in the semi-arid Southern Division of Kitui District in eastern Kenya.

The aim of the project is to improve the living standards of the 80,000 inhabitants and their livestock, without damage to their vulnerable environment, where the main problems are lack of water and erosion of topsoil. The techniques for achieving these ambitious objectives are simple, low-cost and labour-intensive. The people carry out the work themselves under the guidance of a team of technicians from Kenya, Denmark, Sweden and the USA. This article will deal with the section of the project which is concerned with the catchment of rain-water from rocks and mountains.

Options

Experience has shown that rain harvesting systems are more reliable than a system of boreholes and pipelines, provided that the design comprises a balanced combination of four components, namely:

○ A rain catchment area of suitable size, surface area and slope.
○ Gravity delivery of rain-water runoff from catchment area to reservoir.
○ A reservoir of the correct capacity and design.
○ Gravity delivery of water from reservoir to consumers.

It might be considered that rainfall data should play an important role in the design process, but this is not the case in an ecological zone such as this where violent thunderstorms can contribute up to 90 per cent of the total precipitation or where the annual rainfall is sometimes only 10 per cent of the average. Experience has therefore indicated that rainfall calculations should be based instead on a maximum hourly precipitation of 100 mm.

The basic rule in calculating rain-water runoff is that 100 mm of rain on a 100 sq.m surface with 100 per cent runoff will yield 10,000 litres of water.

The runoff velocity is estimated according to the surface and the slope of the catchment area. A rocky impermeable surface of a mountain or a rock outcrop, either above or below ground-level, is therefore an excellent area for harvesting rain-water because it can yield nearly 100 per cent runoff.

All rocks and mountains slope in one direction or another, diverting rain-water via distinct routes into specific areas. Runoff routes can be further directed into desired areas by building slightly sloping lines of flat stones set vertically in mortar on the rock. These gutters have two functions: to catch rainwater runoff from the catchment area and to send the water by gravity to the storage reservoir.

When considering which option to choose, the following factors should be borne in mind:

○ The rural community which is going to carry out the water project on a self-help basis must really want it.
○ The construction work should require a level of craftsmanship and supervision that is available in the project area.
○ The natural features and depressions of the rocks and mountains should be fully exploited to reduce the cost of materials and labour.

○ Local materials should be used whenever possible.
○ The reservoir must be at a lower level than the catchment area to allow the runoff to flow in by gravity.
○ The reservoir should also be at a higher level than the consumers' tapping point to take advantage of the force of gravity.
○ The volume of the reservoir should correspond with the volume of the runoff from the catchment area in an average rainy season.
○ The reservoir should preferably be big enough to hold sufficient water to last from one rainy season to the next.

Types of catchment

Having reached an acceptable compromise between the factors mentioned above, the design of the catchment can be worked out. The following types of rock catchment have been constructed under the Mutomo Project:

Natural rock catchment. A depression in a rock covered with soil, stones and vegetation was excavated by hand to form a reservoir and stone gutters were built around the catchment area.

Gravity rock catchment. A stone masonry wall 5 m high was built on a shelf on the side of a mountain. The dam wall was prevented from sliding and overturning by the pressure of the stored water behind it and its own weight. Stone gutters were used to feed it, as with all rock catchments.

Reinforced rock catchment. This was similar to gravity catchment, but was reinforced with iron rods concreted into drilled holes in the rock floor and sides. The reinforcement allowed a thinner stone masonry wall to be built.

Arch rock catchment. A curved wall of concrete blocks was built between two steep rocks less than 20 m apart. It was anchored to the rock sides by iron rods embedded in drilled holes.

Multi-arch rock catchment. A series of arch walls were supported by buttresses of stone masonry anchored to the floor with iron rods.

Earth rock catchment. An embankment of excavated soil was constructed near the base of a mountain. To prevent seepage between the soil and the rock floor, the embankment was given a stone masonry core. As with other types of earth dam, the discharge of overflow is crucial to maximize the lifetime of the dam.

Subsurface rock catchment. Overlying soil was removed from a large rock which lay below the ground surface. The dam wall was built using the excavated soil over a stone masonry wall.

The following are also used in conjunction with rock catchments:

Shallow wells are sunk into water-bearing pockets near the bases of suitable mountains, fed by accumulated runoff. The wells are built of curved concrete blocks or concrete culverts made on-site.

Sand dams. Stone masonry walls are built across a seasonal river-bed. The wall can protrude up to 4 m above the level of the sand in the river-bed and the wall rests on the bedrock under the sand. The wall can be built as a gravity rock catchment or between rocky banks on the arch principle. Each flow of water down the river will deposit a layer of coarse sand which eventually reaches the level of the top of the dam wall. Water is stored in the sand deposit and in the banks of the river-bed upstream. This type of reservoir is much less subject to evaporation and pollution than surface reservoirs of water.

A subsurface dam is a similar structure built across a seasonal river-bed, but it does not protrude above the sand in the river-bed. The dam wall can consist of stone masonry or impermeable soil, and is built into the floor and banks of an impermeable river-bed.

Water-points and sanitation

The arrangements for community water-points are determined by the type of catchment. Stored water in a rock catchment above ground-level is piped by gravity via a simple siphon system to a point within 200 m of the reservoir. The water-point consists of a push-button tap erected on a concrete slab.

Water stored in a rock catchment below ground-level is lifted out by a bucket attached to a rope and pulley, while water stored in sand deposits is lifted out from a shallow well with a bucket, rope and windlass. Surface water in earth dams is used mainly for livestock. If water is needed for domestic purposes, a well is sunk downstream of the dam and water is drawn from there.

The community which will use the water project decides where a water-point should be situated and who should have access to it.

In an area where water has been scarce for several lifetimes, the quality of water has only secondary priority. It is surprising, therefore, but also encouraging, that many people attend the sanitation classes provided and there seems to be no doubt that the larger the volume of water available, the more people become concerned with the cleanliness of the water they use for domestic purposes.

Simple and fairly effective efforts are being made to keep the water sources clean. Rock catchment areas are cleansed of soil and dirt, and fenced with thorny bushes so that people and animals cannot contaminate the runoff water.

Wells are liable to contamination even when they are covered. Sealed wells with handpumps are preferable, but these cannot yet be installed in our area.

CWD–H

Although the rains were only 25 per cent of the average precipitation during the initial 17 month project period, it has been shown that rain-water catchment in semi-arid zones can be successful.

One way of quantifying success is to look at the response of the local inhabitants, who are contributing free labour and free local materials for the water projects. When the project started, there were less than 100 people who offered their co-operation; now more than 10,000 have organized themselves into self-help groups and are actively working on 105 water projects.

Another way of measuring the success of the rain-water harvesting aspect of the project is that a separate project, the Mutomo Water Tank Project, had to be initiated a year ago to meet the demand for roof, road and ground-water tanks. Although it has no financial assistance from any organization, this project has now completed about 70 water tanks with a total capacity of holding about 3,000 cu.m of rain-water.

The list that follows highlights the aspects which have been of vital importance in achieving so much in this rain-water harvesting project in such a short time:

○ There is a clearly defined need for water.
○ *Mwethya* or self-help groups have been a part of the Kamba culture for a long time. People are therefore used to working on community principles.
○ The designs used in these rain catchment projects are easily understood and everybody can help in building and maintenance.
○ All staff employed by the project are local people from within the project area, except for two expatriates. They are therefore committed to improve living standards in their area.
○ A management unit, consisting of the five most senior technicians on the project, is in control of funds, vehicles and employment.[5,17,40,41]

(*Waterlines* Vol. 3 No. 3, January 1985)

Water from sand

ERIK NISSEN-PETERSEN

In the semi-arid and arid zones of the world, water has been found in sand since the first thirsty creature scooped in a dry river-bed and found drinkable water seeping into his excavation. Green vegetation growing along dried-up watercourses is also a sign that there is water somewhere in the sand or soil below the river-bed. For an experienced person who knows the local vegetation and landscape, it is fairly easy to tell almost exactly the depth of the water-table and the salinity of the water.

Larger deposits of stored water underground can be found by studying satellite photos on which green vegetation growing on fresh water shows up in red. Green vegetation growing on saline water gives a bluish colour. This method of locating underground water sources is, however, relatively expensive and not very appropriate for the kind of small-scale water projects to be described in this article.

Natural subsurface dams

The key to understanding why some parts of a seasonal watercourse can hold water for a long time while others cannot lies in the geological structure below the sand and the coarseness of the sand particles themselves.

In the project area in southern Kitui in eastern Kenya, most of these underground reservoirs, or natural subsurface dams, are created by one or more bedrocks lying across a river bed, acting as a barrier for the annual flood water (Figure 5.1). Surface water is delayed at these points, for long enough to infiltrate into the sand and river-banks. Water flowing downstream within the sand also gets trapped at these barriers and cannot easily pass. The period of time for which water can be retained in the sand depends on the depth of the sand, the degree of permeability of the river-floor and the sides of the reservoir below the sand, and the coarseness of the sand particles. Coarse sand can hold up to 35 per cent of its own volume of water; fine sand much less.

Natural subsurface dams have their drawbacks, however. First, the annual floods tend to destroy the wells that people dig in the sand to reach the water, so that they have to be redug each year after the floods. Second, many people and animals have lost their lives when the unlined walls of these excavations collapsed on them, and third, climbing down to the water-table with dirty feet and containers allows various diseases to be transmitted.

To eliminate these problems, the project has sunk permanent concrete wells into the old unlined excavations. New sites for wells can also be found by hand-augering, then power-driving iron rods into the ground to support the walls.

Assisting nature

Unfortunately, there are not enough natural subsurface reservoirs for the ever-increasing demand for water for domestic use, livestock and seepage irrigation. Fortunately, it is neither difficult nor expensive to copy and improve on nature in this field of enterprise.

Man-made barriers in valleys and river-beds have been known for a long time; the oldest known to the author is in the Negev Desert in Israel. This scheme is some 3,000 years old and provided the Nabateans with water for a variety of purposes, including cultivating wheat.

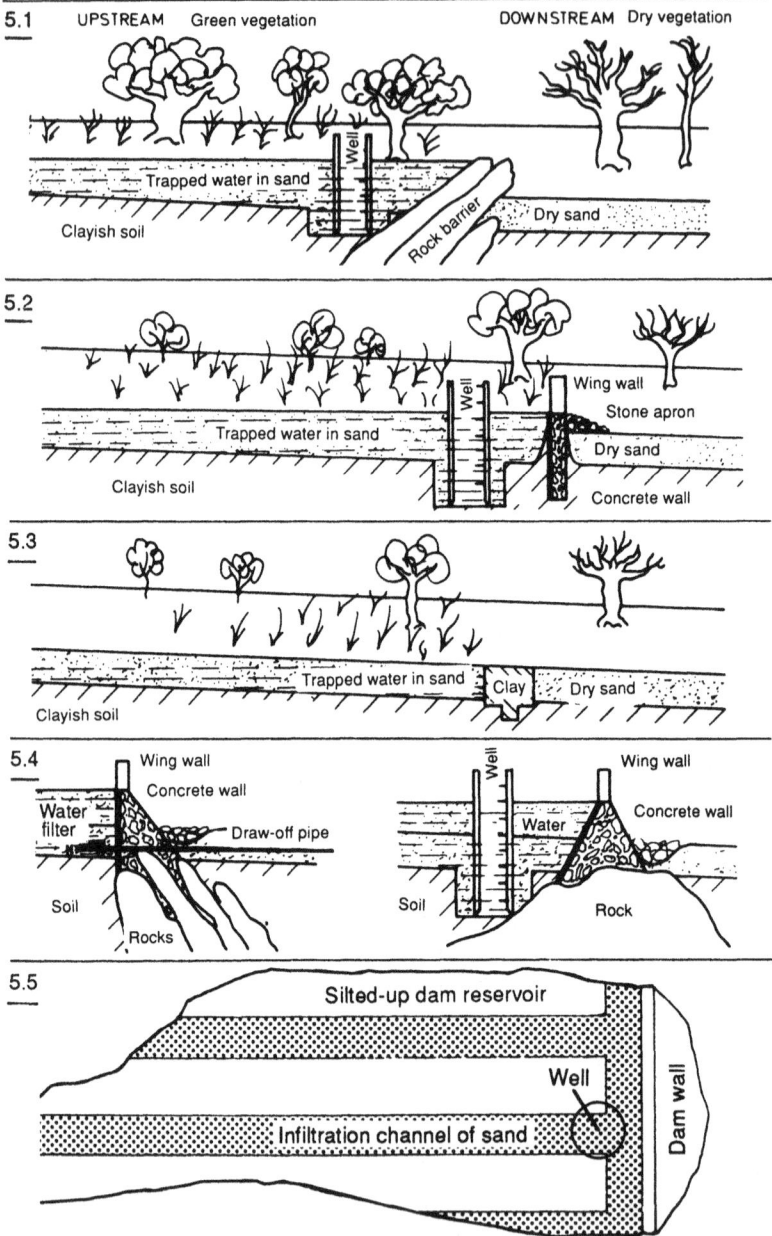

Figure 5.1 *Natural subsurface dam with a shallow well.* 5.2 *Subsurface dam of concrete with a shallow well.* 5.3 *Subsurface dam of clay.* 5.4 *Sand dam with pipe (left) and well (right).* 5.5 *T-dam (seen from above)*

Nowadays, many soil and water conservation projects in Africa have taken up old designs and modified them to include techniques using concrete, stone masonry and soil. Such techniques have been proved suitable for self-help groups who combat soil erosion and retain rain-water in the soil and river-beds.

A natural rock barrier may have a gap in it or slope too heavily to one side, allowing water to escape. In such a place a stone masonry wall can be built on the rock up to the sand in the river-bed. The ends of the wall must be keyed into the river-banks, if these are of soil. Also a wing wall of masonry must be built into the banks to protect them against flash erosion.

This type of masonry wall can also be built successfully across a river-bed in rivers without rocks, provided the river basin has an impermeable floor and sides into which the wall can be keyed (Figure 5.2).

If money is in short supply or stones and cement are not easily available, a wall of compacted soil, 1.5 m thick, can be built. Clay is the best material for this purpose (Figure 5.3), but it is not easily found in east Africa. As an alternative, a mixture of red laterite soil and black cotton soil can be mixed in a dry 50:50 ratio, then compacted with water.

Several of these inexpensive barriers should be built upstream of any subsurface reservoir, to allow as much water as possible to accumulate upstream of the main reservoir. If a bigger subsurface water reservoir is needed, it might be worth considering a sand dam (Figure 5.4), which is similar to a concrete subsurface dam. The difference is that a sand dam can be constructed to a maximum of 5 m above the level of a river-bed. This will make a much bigger reservoir which becomes filled with water, and hopefully coarse sand, by the annual floods.

A pipe to draw off water can be installed in the wall at the level of the old river-bed, allowing water to flow by gravity to a position downstream of the reservoir.

The pressure of the deposited sand and water in the reservoir can be taken up by an arch wall constructed between two solid rock outcrops on the river-banks, or, in most cases, by a concrete or rock masonry wall which is kept in place by its own weight, a so-called gravity wall. The formula for this design is width = height − 30 cm, the crest being 30 cm wide. In both designs, wing walls must ensure that flood water cannot damage the riverbanks or bypass the sand dam.

T-dams

A T-dam is a way of rehabilitating a reservoir which is silted up with such fine soil particles that its capacity to hold water is substantially reduced (Figure 5.5).

In order to improve the infiltration rate of flood water into the silted-up reservoir, several T-shaped channels are dug into the silt reservoir and filled with sand. A shallow well is sunk at the junction of the T-shaped channels, which should be at the deepest point of the basin. Often, the water in the surface basin is dirty and unhygienic, while water from the well will appear clean.

Earth dams are usually classified as surface reservoirs, but since a great deal of water is held in the banks and bottom of the reservoir, that part will be considered as a subsurface dam in this article. The water stored underground can be drawn from a shallow well situated downstream of the earth embankment.

Advantages

Evaporation only takes place from the upper 50 cm of a sand reservoir, and only when the water level is within 75 cm of the surface. Comparing this with the more than 200 cm annual evaporation from an open water surface, a sand reservoir saves a substantial volume of water from evaporating into the atmosphere. Moreover, water-breeding insects, for instance disease-carrying mosquitoes and snails, cannot live in a subsurface reservoir. Snakes and wild animals are not attracted by the water stored underground, and pollution by people and domestic animals is also limited. The water is only accessible from a well, which can be locked when not in use.

Silting reduces the capacity of a surface reservoir, but increases the capacity of a subsurface dam. From an agricultural point of view, a subsurface reservoir stores water in the soil longer than a surface reservoir, giving a farmer with land on the banks of a reservoir a longer growing season. Such a reservoir is suitable for growing fruit trees and multi-purpose trees for fodder, fuel, or as a wind-break.

It might be expected that a raised water-table might add salinity to the soil over the years. Practical experience has shown nothing of the kind over a 10-year period. Indeed, the salinity of water stored in one subsurface dam has fallen to a drinkable level over a period of six years.[5,40,42]

(*Waterlines* Vol. 4 No. 3, January 1986)

Assisting ground-water recharge by gully-plugging

T. S. Randhawa

Programmes for the conservation and scientific use of ground-water resources are currently receiving serious attention in developing countries like India. Food production can be doubled and quadrupled with hybrid seeds and fertilizers, but the case of water is different. The total supply is limited while the demand is constantly increasing with population growth.

Northern India has rivers which flow all the year round and an extensive network of irrigation canals. Excessive canal irrigation without proper drainage has led to the waterlogging of vast areas. Further west is the Great Indian Desert, after which comes Gujarat (partly arid) which has few rivers and streams and is predominantly dependent on ground-water. Ground-water levels are falling dangerously to the extent that in coastal areas sea water is seeping in and rendering agricultural land and wells too salty to use. In other areas of Gujarat, wells are seasonally running dry with increasing frequency.

These are illustrations of the two extremes of the problem in the state. The latter is considered to be more serious because not only is agriculture affected but villagers sometimes experience a serious shortage of drinking water. In the drought of 1982–3 some villagers had to be supplied with drinking water from tankers. In such areas, methods to assist ground-water conservation and recharge can help. A combination of three solutions can be used:

○ Conservation of ground-water.
○ Ground-water recharge and storage.
○ Surface storage of rain-water.

Conservation

Some State Ground-water Boards have circulated profiles of ground-water use for different areas of their state. Where utilization is high, say 80 per cent, credit institutions and government agencies have been cautioned not to finance any further tube-wells or dug-well schemes.

In deciding between the second two options, it may be possible to decide in favour of one by using a cost-benefit analysis. Is it necessary to recharge ground-water? Why not store water on the surface and use it from there? Can some comparison of cost be made between evaporation losses due to surface storage and the expense incurred in constructing such structures as gully-plugs to aid in the recharging of ground-water followed by pumping the water for use?

The best method to use largely depends on the source of water. Where water is available perennially (from snow-fed rivers) surface storage and distribution is the option which is being practised, as well as ground-water use.

However, where areas are dependent on the monsoons for their year's supply, ground-water recharge and storage is the best alternative. The main reason is that a tremendous surface storage capacity would be required if the summer monsoon rains are to be collected and stored on the surface for use during the year. Further, a new network of village canals would have to be built. There is an existing network of village wells which are used as distribution outlets for ground-water and existing ground-water storage capacity is being utilized instead of spending money on constructing new dams for storing water. There would also be large losses from dams due to evaporation.

Ground-water recharge projects are inexpensive compared to major dam projects. And, of course, in the coastal areas where sea water is seeping in because of a reduced ground-water level, the only option is to recharge the ground-water and push back the encroaching sea water.

In areas where ground water is used, small- to medium-size dams do exist, but they supply water for irrigation to limited areas only. An advantage of gully-plugs (micro-dams) is that the flow of runoff is slowed down which helps in reducing soil erosion. This would apply if the water was going to waste, to the sea. Even if it was ultimately going to be collected by a dam or a weir, micro-dams would reduce silting there. On the whole, dams and micro-dams are complementary, in configurations depending on the specific geographical considerations.

The technique of gully-plugging goes hand in hand with contour bunding and terracing. It can be part of a comprehensive watershed development scheme which would include levelling gully beds and land shaping, the construction of farm ponds and field channels, and pasture land development and afforestation. The ultimate step could be the application by the farmers in an area of a combination of appropriate farming techniques, including livestock development, with access to credit facilities.

Development costs

Consider, for example, a study carried out on one watershed in the Panchmahal district of Gujarat in western India. Table 5.1 is a breakdown of costs involved for the various watershed development techniques. The total watershed development area is 990 hectares and the average cost of land treatment is Rs 1,535/hectare. This will require the co-ordination of various

Table 5.1   Costs of watershed development

Method	Area (hectares)	Cost (Rs/hectare)
Afforestation	100	1,500
Pasture development	19	1,160
Field channels	172	300
Contour bunding	350	500
Terracing	206	2,500
Gully-plugging and levelling of gully bed	143	4,200

Table 5.2 Data on gully-plugging in the Panchmahal Project, Gujarat

Total area under gulley	143	hectares
Total length of gulley	9,689	m
Average width of gully	20	m
Average gradient of gully bed	3	per cent
Horizontal distance between 2 plugs	20	m
Total number of plugs requred	484	
Average section of plugs	6.35	sq m
Total length of plugs in the watershed area	9,680	m
Estimated earth work	61,525	cu m
Average cutting for easing gully bed	0.45	m
Area of gully bed which needs easing levelling	40	hectares
Estimated earth work for cutting, filling, levelling gully bed	90,000	cu m
Rate of earth work	4	Rs per cu m
Total estimated cost for gully plugging and levelling of gully bed	606,100	Rs
Cost/hectare	4,238	Rs

programmes, including the District Rural Development Agency, the Tribal Area Development Agency, the District Local Board and the River Valley Project.

Assuming that the money expended in this development is to be re-covered from the farmers at 10 per cent interest, the benefit-to-cost ratio has been worked out to 1.4:1. The unit of land can be the entire watershed itself, if manageable, or a subwatershed. Some state governments (like Gujarat) have taken a policy decision to implement soil conservation work over an entire watershed.

Table 5.2 shows data on gully-plugging in the Panchmahal Project.

Apart from recharging the ground water, gully-plugging and easing the gradients of the gully bed also help to stabilize the beds, flatten them for cultivation, and increase their capacity to store and spread water.

Gully-plugging (and other watershed development techniques) are appropriate and simple in the technical sense for achieving the objective of ground-water recharge. They are suited to various rural development schemes operating in developing countries in general and India in particular. Schemes of this type in India involve the Integrated Rural Development Programmes, the National Rural Employment Programme and the Rural Landless Labour Employment Guarantee Programme. All these schemes envisage labour-intensive work organized by the District Development

Officers, the material component being limited to 33 per cent of the planned work estimate. The process of gully-plugging and watershed development is highly labour intensive and ideally suited for adoption under both these schemes and programmes like the Desert Development Programme and Drought-prone Areas Programme. The technique is being increasingly used.

Referring again to Tables 5.1 and 5.2, the estimate for gully-plugging in the Panchmahal Project was based, in round figures, on a total gully length of 9,700 m with plugs at 20 m intervals. The estimated earthworks for these plugs was some 60,000 cubic metres. A further 90,000 cubic metres of earthwork was estimated for levelling the gully bed over 40 hectares. At Rs 4 per cubic metre, this gave a total cost of some Rs 600,000 or Rs 4,200 per hectare.

Awareness

Rural people are now more aware of the need for water management and conservation. As a good example, one village has 26 irrigation wells and at any one time some will be dry, under repair or disused, while some farmers will have no wells at all. A well is an expensive proposition (costing from Rs 20,000) and when water is pumped from it, it will reduce the water level and output of the nearby wells.

In this particular village of about 100 families, all the farmers have come together and formed a co-operative irrigation society. The output from all the wells has been connected by a network of underground pipes. Permission to irrigate land is given by the executive officer of the society and the units of electricity used for pumping the water are recorded. The farmer is then billed by the society. This may equally apply to a farmer who has a well and has given its services to the society or used it for irrigating his own land as to a farmer who does not own a well. In the former case the farmer has the advantage that should his well run dry or be under repair he will receive water from another well in the grid. Similarly, because his well will be supplying water to the grid, the cost of all repairs to the well and the pumping machinery will be borne by the society.

This irrigation society has been working since 1981 and has been making a steady profit. Up to now its accumulated assets include a tractor which it hires out to farmers. It is a remarkable example of the co-operative use of water by private farmers.

(Waterlines Vol. 3 No. 2, October 1984)

Simple weirs for diverting water

TIM STEPHENS

Simple weirs up to a maximum height of 2 m are ideal structures for small-scale agriculture and domestic water supply where more complex designs are not practical because of cost, remoteness of the site and lack of qualified personnel. Experienced technical advice on siting, design and construction should be sought. Cheap and easy to construct, such weirs are not usually used to store water because of their limited capacity, and often play a more important role in raising and diverting flows.

A solid rock foundation for the weir is essential if it is to be low in cost. Weirs built on soft foundations require complex and expensive works. The rock should be hard, impervious to water, free from major cracks and fissures and, ideally, stretch from one side of the watercourse to the other. Where the rock is not solid for the full width—although it must be at least as wide as the spillway that will be built into the weir—flanking walls or simple earth embankments can be used to support it (Figures 5.6, 5.7 and 5.8).

The flanking walls should be well-keyed into the foundations. If the water-flows it has to withstand are likely to warrant it, the walls should be stone-pitched or concreted upstream and have a minimum freeboard of 0.75 m (preferably 1.0 m to 1.25 m) from the top of the flanking wall to the crest of the weir. The weir spillway does not have to be built in a straight line but can follow an irregular course if this is necessary to make use of the best rock. If a solid rock foundation is not available for the weir overflow section, a gravity weir should not be considered.

Design and construction

An assessment of expected peak floods should be made. If hydrological data is not available, an estimate should be made based on information gathered from local people and common knowledge of the climate to calculate the spillway length. Where the climate is extremely variable or the estimate is uncertain, greater lengths of freeboard and spillway should be allowed to minimize risks.

Once a figure for the peak possible flood has been reached, the maximum depth of overflow to be allowed for can be calculated using the formula where:

$$Q = CLH^{3/2}$$

Q = Design (peak) flood in cubic metres/second
C = Co-efficient (1.7 normally satisfactory for estimates)
L = Weir crest (spillway) length in metres
H = Depth of water, in metres, over the crest at flood flow Q.

5.6

Weir

Solid rock foundation

5.7

Earth
retaining wall

River-bank

Concrete key

Weir

Extend into
good foundation

Solid rock foundation falls
away one side

5.8

Earth
retaining wall

Retaining walls

Earth
flanking wall

River-bank

Concrete
key

Weir

Solid rock foundation
falls away both sides

Earth flanking walls can be replaced with concrete/masonry if site conditions allow it

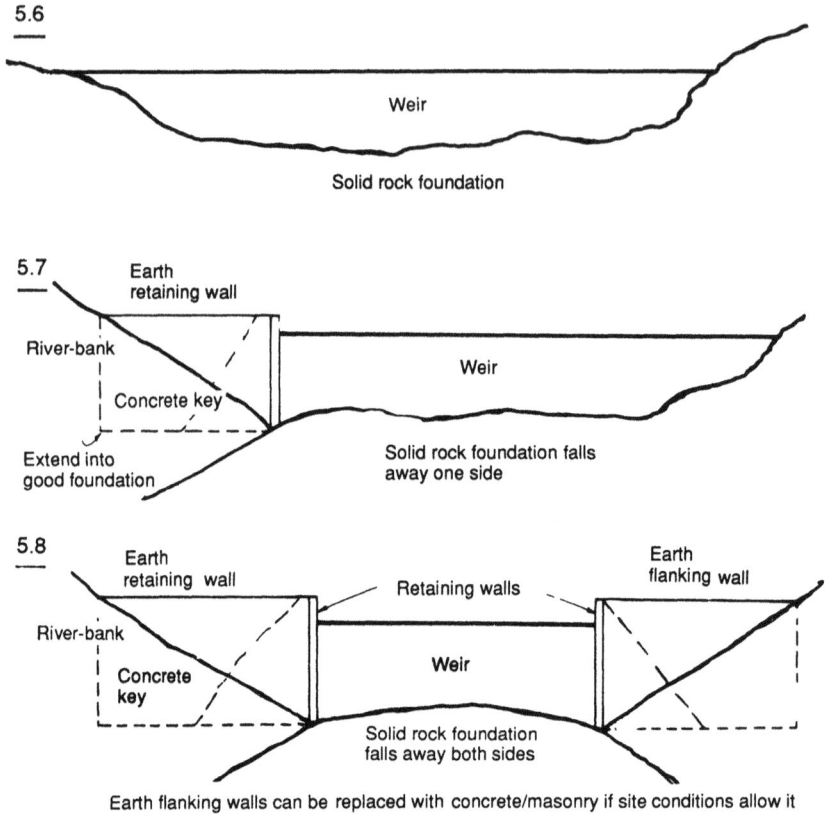

Figure 5.6   *Cross-section of a watercourse showing an ideal rock base. 5.7 Cross-section of a watercourse showing the use of one flanking wall where the rock base falls away to one side. 5.8 Cross-section of a watercourse where two flanking walls are necessary*

It may be necessary to compromise between the spillway length and depth of overflow. The depth of water over the crest at maximum flood flow should never exceed 1.8 m on a 2 m weir. Wherever there are flanking walls, the net freeboard must exceed the depth of the design overflow by a minimum of 0.5 m.

The site, availability of materials and likely construction time and labour available usually determine whether the weir is to be made of concrete, masonry or a combination of the two. Figure 5.9 gives examples of cross-sections of weirs made of various materials and it should be noted that all have the following design parameters in common:

○ A solid rock base.
○ The upstream face of the weir is vertical.

○ Minimum crest widths of 0.35 m for walls up to 1.0 m high, 0.4 m for walls 1.0 to 1.5 m high and 0.45 m for 1.5 m to 2.0 m high. Where the overflow depth is expected to be high, a minimum crest width of 1.0 m is advised regardless of the height of the wall.
○ The downstream face is 'battered' or uniformly stepped so that at any point, base width equals crest width plus two-thirds of the height.

Methods for constructing three types of weir now follow. Making a weir out of concrete cast in a shuttering will result in a neat and structurally sound wall, but requires good materials and quite skilled labour. The shuttering can be timber, stone or brick.

For mixing concrete, clean water which is free from impurities is essential. Clean medium-to-fine sand and good 20 to 40 mm diameter stone aggregate should be mixed at a cement to sand to stone ratio of 1:2.5:3.5. All ratios are by weight and where volume batching of aggregates is adopted the normal precautions should be taken.

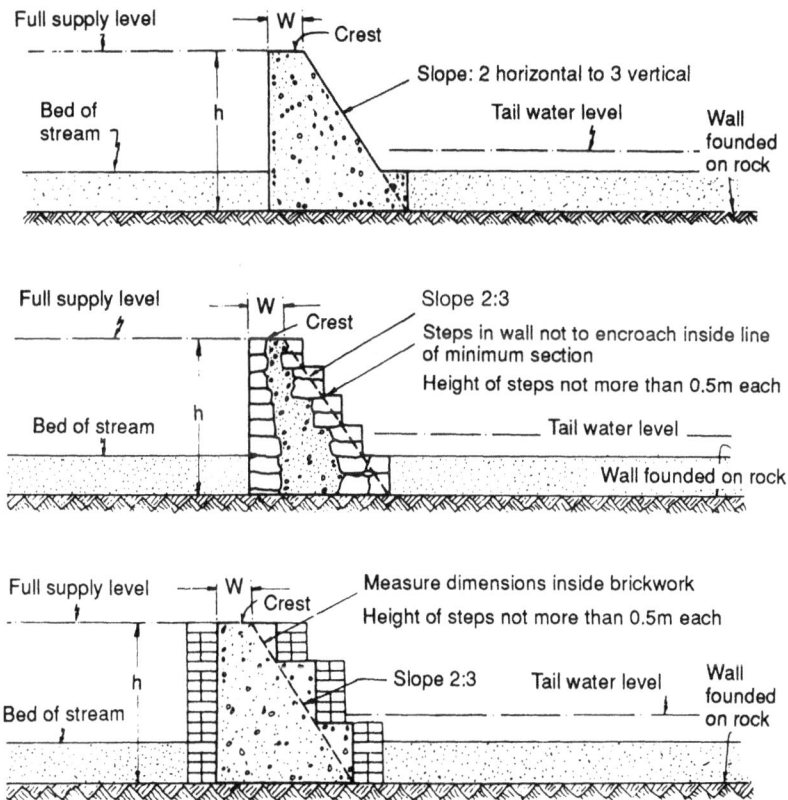

Figure 5.9 *Cross-sections of weirs made of concrete (top), masonry or masonry/concrete (middle) and brick/concrete (bottom)*

The concrete can be made with a cement to sand to stone ratio of 1:3:5 with 'plums' incorporated into the concrete. A plum is a solid, cleaned stone, no greater than one third of the thickness of the wall and surrounded by at least 50 mm of concrete. Tapping a plum into the wet concrete will prevent air pockets beneath it and provide a useful key for the next bed of concrete.

The concrete should be kept moist and shaded for more than seven and preferably 28 days, to allow it to develop the necessary structural strength.

If steel or timber shuttering is used, it must be clean, oiled, correctly assembled (so that it prevents fine material leaking through), braced and propped, and high enough for the amount of concrete being used. If the weir is constructed in sections, these must be keyed into each other and water-proofed. Brick or stone shuttering is often more convenient, especially for a one-off project, and the shuttering is left in place after construction. However, the brickwork or stonework is not considered part of the design and the width of the base, between the inner sides of the formwork, must still equal the crest width plus two-thirds of the height, as above.

Each layer of compacted concrete poured into the formwork should not be more than 0.5 m thick. If brick or stone shuttering has been used it is advisable to plaster the inner faces of the shuttering, particularly if poor quality brick has been used.

Less complicated to construct than concrete, masonry weirs require less skill. Nonetheless, standards of building must still be quite high and good quality, dressed or well-shaped stone must be used. It is important that a good bond is achieved between each successive layer of masonry using fresh mortar consisting of 1 part cement:5 parts sand.

If brickwork is used to build a weir without other materials, it must be of high quality, that is, from factory-made bricks. Alternatively, cement blocks of a similar standard may be substituted. In both cases, the upstream face of the weir and its crest must be plastered and each step on the downstream face should not be more than 225 mm high. All bricks must be soaked in water before they are used.

Guidelines

○ All loose rock, dirt and organic material should be removed from rock base.

○ The rock surface should be chipped and roughened to remove weathered layers and to provide a key for the base of the wall.

○ Immediately before construction, the surface of the rock must be swept and washed, and before placing the masonry, brickwork or concrete on the base or a previously constructed layer, a slurry of ratio 1 part cement:3 parts sand of a creamy consistency and at least 10 mm deep, should be laid to provide the necessary bonding.

If the weir has to be built where high overflow levels or flash floods are unavoidable and is immediately upstream from a steep drop or slope, some consideration must be given to anchoring the weir to reduce the risk of it sliding or overturning.

A 150 to 200 mm-deep key with a minimum width of 200 mm should be cut into the rock base if rock-cutting equipment is available. The first layer of concrete or masonry will include this key to strengthen bonding to the base. Where cutting is not possible, anchorage can be provided by drilling holes 400 mm deep and embedding steel bars in them with grout. The wall can be built around these. They can be linked by reinforcing bars, wire or fence mesh.

Retaining walls should be constructed of the same material as the weir with good keys to the foundation, flanking walls or sides of the channel. If necessary, the concrete key should be taken down to solid rock.

An outlet is usually necessary to permit normal flows to pass the weir and allow diversion of water for irrigation. Perhaps most important, an outlet at the base of the weir can be used for lowering the water level upstream in emergencies or for inspection and maintenance of the wall.

For an outlet to release normal flow, all that is required is a pipe through the wall, as long as it is at the right height and of a suitable diameter. Diversion outlets can take the form of a pipe or a sluice gate at an elevation that will allow water to flow into a canal or similar distribution system by gravity.

Any pipe through the wall should be installed at the time of construction and have one or more flanges projecting to prevent water seeping round the outside of the pipe. A gate valve should be installed at the downstream side of the weir and an energy dissipator may be required at the outlet. Peak flows should be allowed to pass over the crest to one side of the outlet to protect it from the flood water.

If properly constructed, an annual inspection followed by remedial works, usually at the end of the main flood period, is enough to minimize the risk of the weir being damaged.

Maintenance

Any cracks or plaster which has flaked off should be repaired as soon as possible.

Severe erosion by silt or gravel suspended in the water may require the construction of an outlet which will pass all but peak floods. Additional protection may be required for the crest and downstream face of the weir.

Seepage under or around the weir is not usually serious. Where measures are taken to reduce it, they must be on the upstream side. Attempts to block the downstream side of the weir could lead to dangerous pressure building up beneath the weir, tending to lift it. Lining the basin immediately upstream of the wall with puddled clay, or ploughing and compacting it for instance by allowing cattle to trample it, may help limit seepage losses.

The overflow section must be kept clear of any obstruction. Fencing along the crest is not recommended, otherwise debris could accumulate and reduce capacity. All flanking walls must be kept in their original condition and any erosion around them avoided.

DO

○ Use clean water and fresh cement for mixing concrete and mortar.
○ Lay the concrete and mortar as soon as possible after mixing.
○ Ensure that the foundation is clean and any cracks are sealed when laying the first layer of concrete.
○ Key every layer of concrete to the next one by grooves, rock outcropping and slurry wash.
○ Tap every plum into place and ensure that no stone makes contact with another or with the masonry or brick shuttering.
○ Flange any outlet and install it in the wall at the time of construction.
○ Maintain the weir in its original condition.

DON'T

○ Use any foundation other than solid rock for this type of weir.
○ Reduce concrete quality to cut costs. Where stone aggregate is not available, a cement:sand mixture of 1:5 can be used instead.
○ Allow concrete to dry too quickly.[43]   (*Waterlines* Vol. 4 No. 4, April 1986)

The design and construction of small earth dams
JOHN P. FOWLER

Dams or reservoirs are widely used to preserve surplus rainfall. They can be constructed with a variety of materials and in many different ways. Usually it is reckoned to be a highly technical and expensive job, but this need not necessarily be so. However, it must be remembered that a body of water is a potential danger if the dam breaks and therefore experienced technical advice should be obtained on all aspects of design and construction.

From experience in building small earth dams in Kenya, where hand-tools and wheelbarrows are used effectively, one can get better consolidation using bare feet and hand-rammers, than from a bulldozer's giant tracks—and even better are the feet of cattle or donkeys! Oxen with dam-scoops can be used to enormous advantage.

Earth *is* a suitable material with which to contain water, but it must be the *right sort* of earth and this might take some time to find as samples from alternative sites must be compared. A simple form of comparison is to rub a sample of subsoil between the hands, then wet a small amount of it in one palm and spread it over thinly, letting it dry before trying to brush it off (see Guidelines for more detail on soils). Another comparison test is to make a ball of soil from each site, place them in moving water and observe the disintegration of each ball.

Choosing the site

The most favourable site for a dam is usually where high ridges on either side drop fairly steeply into a valley. The wall should be built preferably where the valley narrows and the storage area is as wide and as long as possible. (See Figure 5.10.) The 'borrow area' is the area from which the earth is removed for building the wall. It should also increase the holding capacity of the dam.

The spillways are extremely important and should be carefully designed to take away the maximum of likely flood water (see Guidelines for more details). When a suitable site is found, consider where the flood water will go once the dam is full.

Earth walls are usually about five feet higher than high water-level. Water must *never* flow over an earth dam wall, as it does in the case of a concrete weir; the principles are entirely different.

Having found a good site in a suitable place, check carefully that there is no pervious sand or gravel layer on the sides of the valley or under its floor by

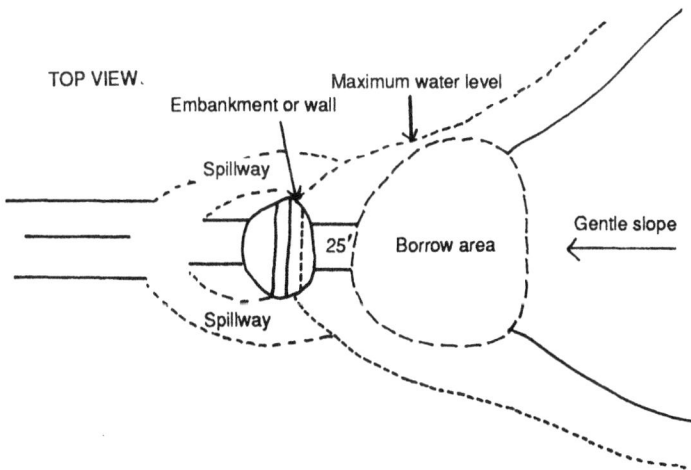

Figure 5.10 *An ideal site*

CWD—I

SIDE VIEW - SECTIONAL

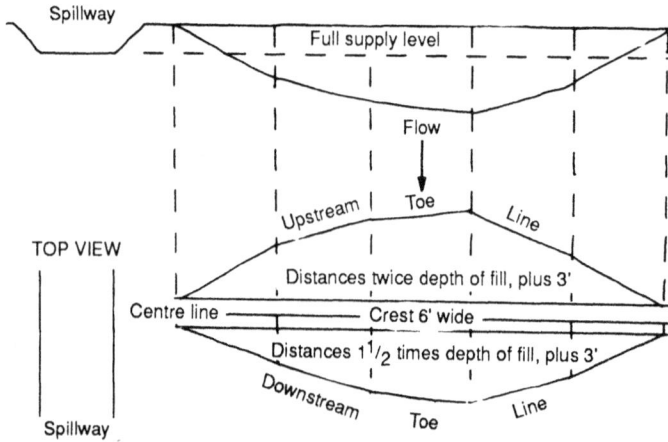

Figure 5.11   *Setting out of upstream and downstream toe lines for dam wall*

digging a test pit. Take note of the catchment area and bear in mind the need for an adequate spillway. The greater the catchment area, the bigger the spillway needs to be, so it may be better to have a dam near the head of the valley.

Test that the soil is adequate for the type of wall you want to build: the homogenous embankment is the easiest (Figure 5.12). Make sure that all the necessary tools, finance and labour are available, and choose the right time of the year.

Construction

First, clear the site of trees, bushes, grass and roots. Collect topsoil and pile it in a heap out of the way, then peg out site as indicated in Figure 5.11. Rip up the whole area on to which the embankment is to be built and dig small ditches parallel to the foundation trench, to help prevent the wall slipping. In a swampy area it is wise to make French drains to carry water away from the foundation ditch, to below the downstream toe-line. These will help to prevent the lower part of the wall becoming waterlogged, especially if no rock toe is incorporated. Remove all sand and gravel to the lower side of the foundation ditch: any stones can be heaped up at the toe (Figures 5.11 and 5.12). Dig the foundation ditch down to a hard impervious 'seat' throwing the earth on the lower side of the valley below the site and spreading it out in thin layers, consolidating it well.

Extend the ditch sideways as far as possible and 'key' in to the valley sides.

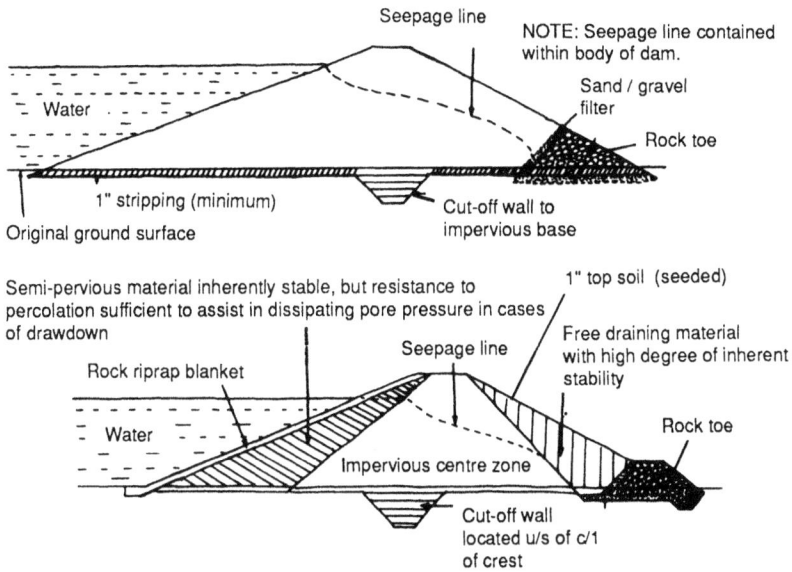

Figure 5.12   *Homogenous embankment with rock toe*

Choose the best earth/clay and spread it in thin layers in the foundation ditch and consolidate it very well, using water if necessary. This is called a puddle-core and in some cases a puddle wall (or clay hearting) is extended above it, as the wall proceeds upwards, thus giving the embankment (wall) a clay core. This may be necessary in bigger dams or where the earth is semi-pervious (Figure 5.12).

When the ditch is filled, start building up the upper side, layer by layer, right across the whole site from side to side and from back to front, consolidating each layer of 3 to 6 ins. as you go. This work seems never ending to begin with, but speeds up as the wall gets narrower. The earth should be free from clods, large stones, roots, etc., and should be well watered if it is dry (see Guidelines).

Bevel the valley sides if they are steep so as to obtain a good bonding of the embankment to side slopes. Work on the spillway(s) can be done at the same time as the embankment is being built, as excavation is involved and that material is then used for the embankment. As the embankment nears completion, it is often extended sideways to form the side wall(s) of the spillway(s). The top or crest of the embankment should slope slightly towards the upstream side so as to facilitate drainage. The top and lower side should be spread with top-soil and planted with grass, if possible. Otherwise it can all be covered with a thick layer of pebbles/stone to stop erosion. This is especially needed on the upper (water) side to prevent damage from small waves that lap against the wall.

The bottom of the spillway(s) may need to be paved with stone and the sides protected in the same way from erosion. The 'outfall' area needs particular attention—this should be well below the embankment.

It is possible to place a pipe in position when or before you begin to build the wall. However, this can bring problems and a syphon pipe exit is probably easier to deal with. PVC piping is ideal; water can begin to flow by pumping it up from below the wall.

A cattle trough can be built at a convenient place below; also a standpipe for drinking water for human consumption. The whole dam, or only the wall, can be protected, with a fence, to keep out livestock.

The embankment may be useful for carrying a road, in which case the crest must be made wide enough (minimum 10 feet). Care is needed so as not to obstruct the spillway and erosion must be controlled.

Dimensions

The length of the embankment depends on the distance between the sides of the valley or depression. The height is governed by the nature of the site, the required capacity of the dam and the finance available.

The width is proportional to the height. A 10-foot wall will have a minimum of 40 feet at the base and 5 feet at the top. A minimum of 4 × the height makes rough calculations very easy, thus making a 2:1 slope on the water side and a 1½:1 slope on the lower side, with a crest width of ½ height. If the soil available is of poor or doubtful quality for the job, increase the proportions to 3:1 and 2:1 up to a maximum of 6 × height. (Remember, this increases the work and therefore the expense.) These larger proportions are also recommended for embankments over 20 feet high. However, 20 feet should be the maximum height for an 'amateur' attempt as there are many finer points that an engineer would look into carefully before constructing a larger dam.

The simplest way to calculate the capacity of the dam is to multiply the surface area by ¼ of the maximum depth of the water, then multiply by 6¼ gallons. So, if the surface area is 48,000 sq ft × 5 ft. (¼ of 20′) × 6¼ = 1,500,000 gallons.

For the volume of earth in the embankment multiply the cross-sectional area of the embankment at the deepest point by the top length of the wall (6 ft + 76 ft ÷ 2 × 20 ft = 820 sq ft). Divide by 2 where the valley slopes are gentle or by 3 where the slopes are steep. Thus, for a wall that is about 20 ft. high and 40 ft. long with a gentle valley slope: volume = 820 sq ft × 400 ÷ 2 = 164,000 cu ft.

It is worth relating the size (volume) of the embankment to the storage capacity of the dam; this will vary enormously with the different sites, and will be an important factor to consider when choosing your site.

The cut-off wall, or clay core, is built in the foundation ditch, which varies enormously according to the site. However, it should be a minimum of 4 ft. across the base with well-sloping sides.

Other considerations

There is a small stream running in the valley you want to dam. Either wait for the dry season when it dries up, or divert it, or build the embankment on each side of the stream and have an all-out effort to close the gap (not as easy as it sounds and it can lead to seepage later). Alternatively, culverts can be laid which will later be blocked up. Great care should be taken to prevent seepage.

A small amount of seepage is to be expected (as indicated in Figures 5.11 and 5.12), thus a rock toe is highly recommended. If severe seepage occurs, it may be due to piping. This is particularly serious if soil particles are seen in the water; every effort must be made to block it, preferably on the water side of the embankment. When tree roots rot, piping can occur. A small amount of water can be lost through seepage into lower strata under the dam. The loss of up to 1 in. in a week should not be considered unreasonable.

Evaporation is considerable in hot, dry areas, when up to ½ in. of water is lost every day. So, the larger the surface area of the dam, the greater the loss of water. Thus a large, shallow dam will dry up sooner than a smaller, deeper dam.

Silt is a hazard, especially in the arid areas, and is an important factor to consider when choosing a site. It may be possible to build silt-traps upstream from the dam. Overgrazing of the catchment area should be avoided if at all possible. It must also be remembered that the presence of water will bring more livestock into the area of the dam.

There are probably fairly strict government regulations that pertain to the building of dams and these should be adhered to. Although it may not be easy to discover who knows about them—persevere! Grants and subsidies may exist to help you. There may also be a government Dam Construction Unit or Advisory Service.

Don't become 'fixed' on the dam idea. Consider other potential sources of water: boreholes; wells; protected springs; steam jets and pipelines; then carry out a cost-benefit analysis. Subsurface dams are another, often natural, source of water. Barriers can be constructed across seasonal rivers, below the surface of the sand bed. The sand will hold water to the extent of about a quarter of its volume.

A bulldozer, if used alone, is not a very suitable machine for dam building—a scraper is far better. Used with care, a dozer can build a dam to contain up to 6 ft. of water. Poor consolidation is the problem.

This article has dealt with the details of choosing a suitable site, and constructing the embankment which creates the dam. The embankment and spillway design is all-important and can be summarized as follows:

○ Embankments must be stable under all conditions of saturation and loading.
○ The foundations should have adequate bearing capacity.
○ Embankments should be sufficiently watertight and the percolation of water through, under and around the sides should not exceed safe limits.
○ Sufficient spillway capacity should be provided to maximum estimated floods, while maintaining a dry freeboard of at least 2 ft. between the maximum reservoir water-level and embankment crest level.
○ Anti-erosion and other protective measures, particularly in the spillway, should be adequate to ensure long-term stability and safety, with a minimum of maintainance.

Long, low dams are safer and cheaper than high dams, but evaporation is relatively high in shallow reservoirs.

Guidelines

Engineers talk of soil mechanics and soils are analysed and tested to give an indication of their 'engineering characteristics', but don't lose heart! For the homogenous embankment you need a fairly coarse graded soil containing 20 to 40 per cent silt and clay. If you have a sample of well-sieved soil in a clear glass jar, shake it up with water and let it settle; you will see the bands of different materials—sand, silt, clay. A spoonful of cooking salt will facilitate the process. Sometimes soils can be mixed to achieve the desired proportions.

For a variety of reasons, avoid using the following types of soil: sodiac soils are very unstable; calcitic clays—they are stable but porous; humic soils are porous and become unstable; schists and shales can slip when wet; heavy clays can crack and cause piping and fine silts are unsuitable on their own.

Pore pressure is a factor to be reckoned with, especially if a dam is to be emptied quickly. Pore pressure disequilibrium can lead to earth slips.

A wider variety of soils can be used for the construction of zoned embankments, but more careful supervision is required. Soil will always settle even in the best consolidated walls. Allow 1 in. in every foot for this.

With spillways and catchments the spillway(s) basically has to take the place of the former stream-bed, and should be of a similar capacity. However, it will probably have to be wider, so as to keep the high flood level as low as possible, remembering the minimum freeboard required (5 ft. above floor of spillway, or less if the spillway is exceptionally wide). The larger the catchment area, the bigger the spillway(s) should be. There are various other factors including the annual average rainfall, the intensity of storms and the rate of run-off.

Drop in water level during transition to
hypercritical flow

LONGITUDINAL SECTION

Water surface in outlet channel

Max. flood water in reservoir

H

Concrete cill

Anti-erosion cutoff
walls as required

H = difference between the spillway cill
and water level in the reservoir

Spillway cill in line
with embankment crest

Gradient not less than 1 in 75
to ensure that hypercritical flow develops.
Max gradient depends on hardness of
spillway floor and sides as required

Slopes upwards from entrance
to spillway cill on gradient of
about 1 in 50

Crossfall

Outlet channel

Crossfall

Inlet channel

Funnel shaped entrance to
reduce head losses

Spillway outlet discharges well clear of
downstream toe of embankment

A

Embankment
Plan

CROSS SECTION A - A

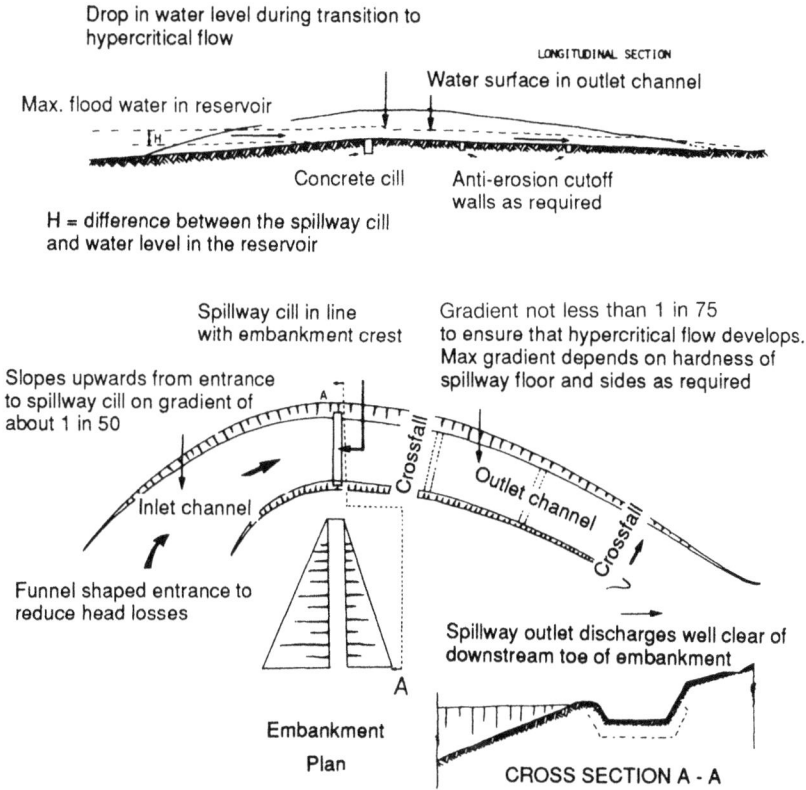

Figure 5.13   *Typical details of spillway*

The rate of runoff is a critical factor which is influenced by relief (percentage of slope), soil infiltration, surface storage (materials, ponds) and effective plant cover. To illustrate this, a 1,000 acre catchment area which slopes gently and has good plant cover needs a 40 ft. wide spillway whereas a 1,000 acre, poorly vegetated, hilly area needs a 100 ft.-wide spillway. Various formulae and graphs can be obtained to help the calculations.

The spillway slope should be 1:75 and often has a sill construction of rock, brick or concrete across its width, in line with the embankment crest. This leads to a hypercritical flow which ensures that there is no 'backing up' of water in the dam (Figure 5.13).

If a suitable site is found in a rocky area, a conventional concrete weir *or* a rock dam with a concrete or clay core should be considered. Alternatively, an impervious layer of earth/clay can be built on the upper face (Figure

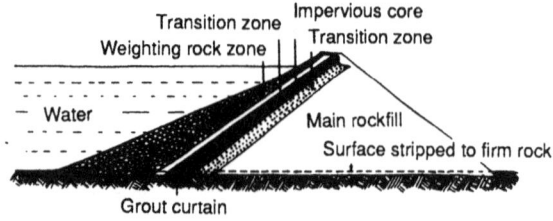

Figure 5.14   *Rock-fill embankment*

5.14). For a small dam it may even be worth trying a layer of butyl rubber, as concrete is liable to crack and thus spoil the dam.

Note that there is a definite relationship between the moisture content of a soil and the maximum density which can be obtained by compaction. For example, using the Proctor test, the maximum density of a particular soil sample was proved to be obtained when the moisture content was 13.5 per cent. The density was less when the soil was both drier than this, and wetter.[43]

(*Appropriate Technology* Vol. 3 No. 4, February 1977)

CHAPTER 6
Pumping Alternatives

Selecting the right pump is of prime importance. So many factors need to be taken into account: local conditions, spares, skills, organization, finance and, above all, the needs of the people. Choice is extensive. This chapter provides some guide-lines together with a few examples ranging from low to high technology, each a relevant option for particular locations.

The article by the ITDG Water Panel appears to be the first attempt to provide guide-lines to facilitate the choice of a pump properly matched to the water source and prime mover. At the time of writing, the Panel realized that the article was far from perfect, but it was hoped that constructive comments and criticism would lead to a more detailed report. Although this has not happened, a state-of-the-art-survey has been published by IT Publications on human- and animal-powered pumps.[44]

Traditional pumps should be carefully considered. The example included here is the chain and washer pump, which previewed Simon Watt's 1976 book on this technology, now unfortunately out of print. IT Publications hope it may be reprinted in the near future.

The remainder of the chapter looks at pumps powered by renewable energy. The article on the hydraulic ram describes a simple automatic device which uses the power of falling water to force a small portion to a greater height. Here again it is hoped that a book on this subject can be published to replace the original, now out of print. The article on windpumps describes the installation of two Kijito pumps manufactured by Bobs Harries Engineering Ltd in Kenya for the village of Kaikor in the Turkana Desert. Solar pumps are another alternative based on renewable energy, with great potential. The final article describes their application to the Oxfam water supply for six refugee camps in north-western Somalia, as an alternative to petrol- or diesel-driven pumps.

Each of these methods of pumping water has specific applications but in most cases the handpump option would be the first choice, subject to reliability. The important work undertaken on the testing and development of handpumps is the subject of the next chapter.

Water for rural communities: the choice between pumping methods

By the ITDG WATER PANEL

Faced with the rising cost of fuel for running conventional engine-driven pump sets together with the notorious difficulties of supply, spare parts and maintenance, it is hardly surprising that an increasing number of project holders are considering alternative pumping methods. The choice is vast, ranging from traditional human-powered devices to modern solar-powered pumps, but problems arise when it comes to selecting the method best-suited to a particular need, as no guide-lines to selection are available. This article aims to highlight the main factors to consider when choosing a pump for a specific duty, which basically involves:

○ Finding out the precise use of the pump that is specifying the operating requirements.
○ Deciding how it is going to be worked, namely specifying the prime mover.
○ Choosing the most suitable pump available, bearing in mind such inseparable factors as the tools, spare parts and skills needed to maintain the installation, and the organization and finance required for its satisfactory long-term operation.

Capacity

The capacity of a pump is the quantity of water that it is required to deliver in a given time. An indication of the water requirements for various purposes is given in Table 6.1 and these guidelines can be used to calculate a first estimate of the total quantity of water needed each day. It should be noted that in addition to being approximate, these figures are elastic to varying degrees. For instance, the more convenient the supply, the more water will be used—a fact that raises the important point that improved water supplies should be accompanied by appropriate sanitation and drainage measures. In addition to natural increases in population during the lifetime of the pump, an improved water supply will probably attract people and animals from other areas and allowances should be made for this, too. Water losses from leakages, wastage or unauthorized withdrawal must also be provided for. Where a pump is being used for irrigation, the method of delivery and scheduling of the water must be taken into account; Stern[45] and the FAO[46] provide helpful examples.

The rough estimate of the daily water demand can be easily confirmed simply by observing and checking local practices. The capacity of the pump(s) can then be calculated by dividing the total demand by the number

Table 6.1 Approximate water requirement for various purposes

Use	Daily requirement
Domestic	
minimum for survival	5 l/person
water carried home from distant communal supply	10 l/person
water carried home from nearby communal supply	30 l/person
one tap in each house	50 l/person
multiple tap connections	200 l/person
Livestock	
cattle	35 l/head
horses, mules and donkeys	20 l/head
sheep and goats	5 l/head
poultry	25 l/100
pigs	15 l/head
Irrigation	
including conveyance and field application	5 to 10 mm or
losses	50 to 100m³ha

of hours of daily operation. For example, if the total quantity of water required each day is 100,000 litres and one pump is to be selected for 5 hours operation each day, then the required pump capacity will be 20,000 l/hr. If 10 hours or 20 hours daily operation is feasible, then smaller capacity equipment can be chosen—10,000 and 5,000 l/hr respectively. However, with these lower rates of pumping, additional water storage will be necessary unless there is a continuous off-peak demand, from irrigation for example, which exactly matches the pump's capacity.

The physical layout of the water source will influence the choice of pump and Table 6.2 gives some indication of suitable combinations. Site modification is sometimes necessary to enable pumps to be used with particular sources (indicated by the key ● in the table). If the water source is a well, initial pumping tests should be performed to determine the yield characteristics of the aquifer. Standard graphs are available for a complete interpretation of the data obtained from the pump tests, but much information can be gained by simply observing the drawdown (change in water level) when pumping at a constant rate for several days. If the yield is low, a high-capacity pump will be unsuitable and a lower-capacity pump should be chosen: if more water is needed then the installation of smaller pumps on several wells should be considered.

Table 6.2 Pumps used in different water sources

Pump	flowing water very low	flowing water low	flowing water high	open water very low	open water low	open water high	open well low	open well high	tube-well low	tube-well high	Prime mover
Water scoop/swing bucket/*dhone*	★			★							human
Rope and bucket/*mohte*	★	★		●	●		★	★			human; animal
Shadoof (counterpoise lift)	★	★		●	●	★	★	★			human
Archimedean screw	★			★		★					human; wind; diesel; electricity
Ladder pump	★			★							human; wind; diesel; electricity
Chain and washer pump							★	★			human; animal; wind
Persian wheel (chain of pots)							★	★			animal; diesel; electricity
Water wheel	●	●									water
Handpump											
pump body at ground level							★	★	★		human; wind
pump body below ground							★		★	★	human; sun; wind; diesel
Hydraulic ram		●	●		●	●					water
Water											
river		●	●	●	●						water
tidal											water
Centrifugal (single and multi-stage)											
horizontal		★	★	★	●		★	●	★	★	diesel; sun; electricity
vertical/submersible turbine		★	●	●	●		★	★	★	★	diesel; sun; wind; electricity
Propeller/axial	★			★							diesel; electricity

KEY: ● = Site modification sometimes necessary

Head (see Footnote A)

One of the most important points concerning the water source is whether the water level is within the practical limit or 'lift capability' of the pump. Most pumps which rely on suction for their operation cannot lift water higher than about 6 m and any attempts to suck water from greater depths will result in cavitation (boiling under low pressure) possibly causing considerable damage and making pumping impossible. The practical solution in this situation is to position the pump below ground so that it is closer to the water level or even submerged. Table 6.2 shows the lift capability of different pumps, where *'low lift'* indicates that the water is not too far down to suck to the surface. The depth from which water can be sucked without causing damage varies with the type of pump and the altitude of the installation. If a choice of pump exists, it is usually best to select a pump which requires the minimum NPSH (net positive suction head) at its inlet; a figure that can be obtained from the manufacturer. This procedure will help to avoid an unnecessary decrease in the practical suction head by choosing unsuitable equipment (see Footnote B).

Seasonal variations in the water level must also be taken into account when choosing the pump. Priming problems may be experienced with centrifugal pumps even when the NPSH is greater than the minimum

Footnote A - Calculating the hand force

Handpumps supplied locally may not be accompanied by any further information as to the head for which they are most suitable. However, most of them are based on the same principle and it is possible by examining the pump to calculate the hand force required:

$$F = b \frac{(5.5L + S - H)d^2 + Hc^2}{9a} - W \frac{a-b}{2a}$$

where H is overall head (m)
L is length of pump rod (m)
S is suction head (m) — negative if pump body is submerged
a is maximum distance between user's hand and fulcrum (cm)
b is distance between fulcrum and pump rod (cm)
c is internal diameter of pump cylinder (cm)
d is diameter of pump rod (cm)
W is weight of pump handle when removed from pump (kg)
and F is hand force required (kg). F should be about 15 to 20 kg if the pump is suited to the head in question, allowing children above this weight to operate it if the handle is high enough for them to hang on.

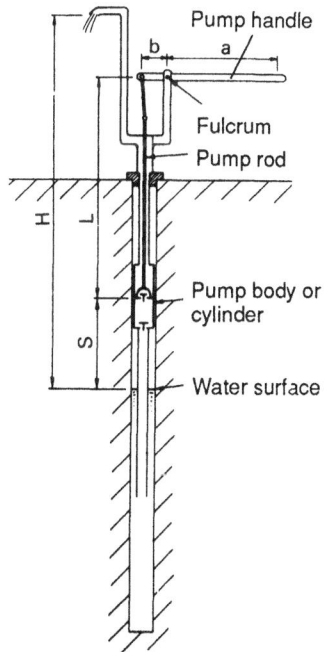

specified by the maker, either because of minute leaks allowing air into the suction pipework which are impossible to detect, or because of gases dissolved in the water coming out of solution.

Apart from the distinction between low and high lift, which determines where the pump should be mounted, it is also necessary to know the exact magnitude of the head in order to calculate the power required to pump the desired amount of water and to estimate the cost of doing so. It is the head during pumping which determines the power requirement. When water is pumped very slowly, the relevant head for power calculation is simply the difference in level between the outlet (typically the pump spout) and the water surface. At higher capacities, the head may increase because of friction caused by the water flowing through the pipework or because the water level is lowered: a tube-well pump delivering through a hose-pipe will suffer from both these effects whereas a shadoof in open water will experience neither.

If the water level in a well falls significantly at the required pumping rate, even though the yield may be adequate, consideration should be given to the use of smaller pumps on two or more dispersed wells in order to ensure pumping through a lower head. In such cases, the power required and associated capital and running costs of using several smaller pumps—either in parallel to deliver the required quantity of water or in series to meet the required head—should be compared with the single pump option.

Water quality

The presence of silt, sand or grit in high concentrations can be a major problem in certain instances: when the source is flowing water; during the development of a new well; in water holes stirred up by animals or receiving run-off from the land. Sediment in the water will wear down moving parts of the pump; this affects certain pump tyres more than others. In general, pumps in which the water is moved by one component sliding against another, such as a piston in a cylinder, are more susceptible, whereas centrifugal pumps and diaphragm pumps, which use a flexible chamber, are less affected. However, sand or grit can indirectly damage centrifugal pumps by preventing the foot valve—fitted at the bottom of the suction pipe—from

---

Footnote B—Calculating suction head

The allowable/practical suction head can be calculated by deducting the NPSH required by the pump from the atmospheric pressure level. Atmospheric pressure expressed as a head of water is approximately 10 m at sea level and reduces by about 10 per cent for every rise of 1,000 m in altitude. An indicative minimum NPSH for hand pumps is 3 m and for centrifugal pumps 4 m or more, meaning that at sea level they can suck water up respectively 7 m and 6 m or less. The relevant head for power calculation is the height of the pump body above the water surface *during pumping*.

seating properly. This will cause the pump to empty overnight and run dry on start-up, a situation that should never be allowed unless the manufacturer states otherwise. To overcome this problem, a priming tank may be mounted on the inlet side of the pump so that its casing is always full of water before starting up. Alternatively, a self-priming pump may be used.

Salty or brackish water will corrode metal (particularly ferrous) parts more rapidly than fresh water and in these instances pumps with wetted parts of plastic or wood will be useful. Traditional pump materials are brass, bronze or gun-metal, which are all expensive alloys nowadays. Where domestic water supplies are drawn from open wells by rope and bucket, the risk of contamination is high. Some common measures taken to improve well hygiene include chlorination and the fitting of handpumps so that the well can be sealed. Self-tipping bucket systems have been reported but the authors have never heard of any significant applications.

Output and costs

It will often appear, at first, that there is quite a choice of possible prime movers. Table 6.3 gives an indication of the output to be expected from each and the corresponding capital and running costs, whilst Table 6.2 shows the possible combination of pump, prime mover and water source. Particular attention should be paid to the units used. The useful power output in terms of water lifted is given in kilojoules (kJ) per hour per unit of prime-mover size. To obtain the required power output in kJ per hour, multiply the number of litres required per hour by the number of metres through which the water has to be lifted (the head) and divide by 100. Thus, one litre lifted through 100 m, 10 litres lifted through 10 m, or 25 litres through 4 m, are all equivalent to one kJ of energy.

Table 6.3 gives some of the information needed to calculate financial and economic costs. Other necessary data will vary from place to place and will have to be checked locally. In the case of draught animals, for example, the following facts should be determined: what they will be doing when they are not pumping; who will be paying for them at these times; how much of their food will have to be purchased, and so on. Unless all the relevant factors can be evaluated in financial terms, it is better not to attempt an economic and financial analysis but rather to get the feel of the locality and rely on the judgement of local residents in order to reach the right choice of pump and prime mover.

In Table 6.3, capital costs are given in US dollars for indicative purposes where a sufficiently representative international value is known. These should always be checked against local prices or quotations which will be much more accurate. Locally-made items are often much cheaper although quality is variable. Running costs are given in units of fuel per megajoule (MJ) of water lifted, where 1 MJ is 1,000 kJ. Throughout this article kJ and

Table 6.3 Indicative performance of various prime movers*

Prime mover	Type of pump	Output (i.e. water lifted)	Capital cost	Running cost
Human	Handpump	1.3 kJ/hour/kg body wt	$500 to 800 or local	0.5 kg rice/MJ water lifted + 0.012 kg rice/day/kg body wt
Animal	Persian wheel	1.7 kJ/hr/kg body wt	local	1.3 kg hay/MJ water lifted + 0.013 kg/hay/day/kg body wt (or 3.5 times these amounts of green fodder) + attendent
Wind	Reciprocating	300 kJ/day/(m² rotor area) (m/s average wind speed)³	$250/(m² rotor area) or local	None
Diesel	Centrifugal	700 kJ/hour/rated kW (but not available below 3 rated kW)	$600 rated kW** or local	0.6 litres diesel/MJ water lifted
Electricity	Centrifugal	400 kJ/hour/rated kW	$0.1 to 0.3 rated W** or local	2.5 kWh/MJ water lifted
Sun	Photovoltaic	Sunny day — 800 kJ/day/m² panel Cloudy day — 0 to 200 kJ/day/m² panel (1 m panel rated at about 80 W)	$2500/m² panel	None

Example: Comparison of animal and sun power for raising 300m³ a day through a height of 5 m.

Power output = 300 m³/day × 1000 l/m³ × 5m × ¹/₁₀₀ kJ/l = 15000 kJ/day = 15 MJ/day

Animal: Say four bullocks are available — total weight 1600 kg.

No. of hours pumping per day $\dfrac{15000 \text{ kJ/day}}{1.7 \text{ kJ/hour/kg} \times 1600 \text{ kg}}$ = 5.5 hours/day

Running cost = 1.3 kg hay/MJ × 15 MJ/day + 0.013 kg hay/day/kg × 1600 kg = 40 kg hay/day or 140 kg green fodder/day.

Sun: Panel area = $\dfrac{1500 \text{ kJ/day}}{300 \text{ kJ/day/m}^2 \text{ panel}}$ = 50 m² panel

Capital cost = \$2500/m² panel × 50m² panel = **\$125,000.**

Notes

* This table is designed to give a rough idea of the performance of prime movers. In some cases, however, such as that of water-powered lifting devices, it has not been possible to qualify the data.

** The CIF cost of items ordered abroad and flown in.

MJ refer to water lifted as defined above, and should not be confused with the energy content of the fuel or with the energy required to operate the pump. For example, whilst running costs for diesel pumps are, on average and very approximately, 0.6 litres diesel per MJ water lifted, 0.6 litres of diesel give up to 25 MJ of energy when burned, of which 24 MJ are lost as heat in engine, pump and pipe.

The final choice of pump with regard to cost must take into account the people who will be using the water. For example, the cheapest method of raising water in a particular situation might appear to be an open-well pump. However, if the locality already has tube-wells it will probably be cheaper to use these and choose a different method of pumping water rather than dig new open wells. On the other hand, if the locality has no wells to start with, pumping costs should be considered when deciding on the type of well to provide. This exercise will involve comparing capital and recurrent costs of the alternatives of water source and pump combinations. However, the views of those using the water are more important than a numerical answer.

Water for domestic uses should be of high quality, necessitating protection of the source against pollution, and this may preclude the use of pumps such as the rope and bucket which are traditionally used with unprotected sources. Although a much higher economic value is sometimes placed on water for domestic uses compared with water for irrigation, it is still important to choose the cheapest method of pumping consistent with proper water quality. The careless choice of a more expensive method of pumping will either result in less water being pumped due to higher running costs or in fewer units being installed due to greater capital costs, both with adverse effects to the users.

Future prospects

Table 6.3 has been limited to pumps that are currently available. However, some promising alternatives are being developed and several new ideas are under investigation. It seems likely that solar photovoltaic pumps will be considerably cheaper in the future as new techniques become available for producing the photovoltaic panels and as the volume of production increases. Pedal-driven pumps offer the possibility of increasing a person's output by perhaps 50 to 100 per cent, thereby reducing the recurrent costs of pumping compared with handpumps, and reducing the time spent pumping water. In certain situations, this would help to maintain or even shift the balance in favour of human pumping, thereby providing employment.

The power densities available in river currents represent another source of energy that man has ingeniously harnessed over the centuries. Although development activities continue in an attempt to improve the power abstracting capability of these machines, a major constraint to their widespread application is the enormous seasonal variation in flow of many watercourses: both floods and drought will present severe problems for the satisfactory operation of the pumping system.

Attention is also being given to alternative fuels derived from biomass for running internal-combustion engines. In time, some of these will be competitive with automotive fuels, but their development is dependent on the use of agricultural land that might otherwise be producing food—a potentially explosive situation.

These new methods all require substantial investment in research and development in order to arrive at good workable designs, but ultimately their acceptability in the field will be governed by reliability, durability and 'maintainability'. However, at this point, the authors consider that because of the necessary processing costs, none of these alternatives can compete with firewood for stationary applications, except by default. Firewood and crop residues are by far the most common and were, until quite recently, the cheapest source of energy in many countries. Reliable biomass-burning pumps could be a great success under favourable conditions and could do a great deal more to encourage reafforestation projects than improved wood-stoves projects.

Availability

Even though there may be only a limited choice of pump available locally, it may be best to opt for one of these rather than introduce a new type. In particular, a newly introduced pump is likely to suffer from a lack of spare parts and little maintenance expertise, and also may not find immediate favour with the users. Large projects involving hundreds or thousands of pumps will normally have to organize a supply of spare parts and trained logistical and maintenance personnel: this is something that has not always been done in the past. In these cases, it may well pay to choose a new type of pump when acceptability trials have shown clear advantages. Such trials should last long enough for the users to overcome any unease due to the novelty. In the case of small projects, there may not be the means to purchase trial pumps, in which case a detailed study of relevant activities in the surrounding or similar area is recommended.

Before choosing a pump, it is essential to establish the requirements for its successful operation. These include factors such as the tools, spares and skills required to keep the equipment running and the organizational and financial arrangements needed to guarantee satisfactory lifetime performance. Some pumps are more tolerant to wear or misuse than others—they have a wider performance band—and are therefore easier to maintain. Most of the traditional devices fall into this category and may well be worth considering in situations where more sophisticated pumping machinery could cause more problems than it solves.

A tour of adjacent areas will probably reveal many pumps out of action for various reasons and it is no use installing more pumps that cannot be maintained in working order. Various approaches have been tried, depending on the proportion of the equipment that is locally made or can be locally maintained. Pacey[47] is essential reading. To identify pumps which do not require externally-assisted maintenance in perpetuity, the United Nations launched the Village-Level Operation and Maintenance (VLOM) Pump Development Programme, with the prospect of very big orders for any manufacturer who can successfully devise such a pump. The Consumers' Association[48] gives details of performance, endurance and user tests conducted in the laboratory on 24 commercially-available hand pumps. A follow-up field-testing programme is now underway with support from the United Nations Development Programme.[51]

(Appropriate Technology Vol. 9 No. 1, June 1982)

The chain and washer pump

SIMON WATT

The chain and washer pump, sometimes called the paternoster pump because of its resemblance to a string of rosary beads, is a pumping device that has been known and used for many centuries both in China and Europe. It works by the action of the chain and washers which are pulled in a continuous loop up inside a closely fitting pipe over a geared chain wheel (Figure 6.1). Water is carried up between each washer from the mouth of the submerged pipe, and discharged at the top of the pipe into a trough.

The maximum practical lift for this sort of pump is about 15 to 20 m and several chain and washer assemblies can be fitted on the same axle. The chain and washer pump is large and bulky and can be described as a high mass/low power ratio pump. This means that each component of the device is not under great load or highly stressed, allowing relatively soft materials such as wooden or rope chains and oiled wood bearings to be used.

The pump was widely used in Europe from the 16th century onwards to drain mine workings. It was preferred to the piston suction pump because of its low cost, ease of construction and reliability. The pipe was usually built from iron-bound timber planking, and the washers were made from balls of leather-covered horsehair. The balls were fairly flexible and made a good fit inside the pipe even if the diameter of the pipe varied. The leather-bound ball washers were often replaced with bundles of rags which were cheaper and, although less efficient, served the same purpose in lifting the water up the pipe.

The leather or cloth balls are now replaced with discs made from wood or iron plates, and the discs are often fitted with a rubber seal to reduce water

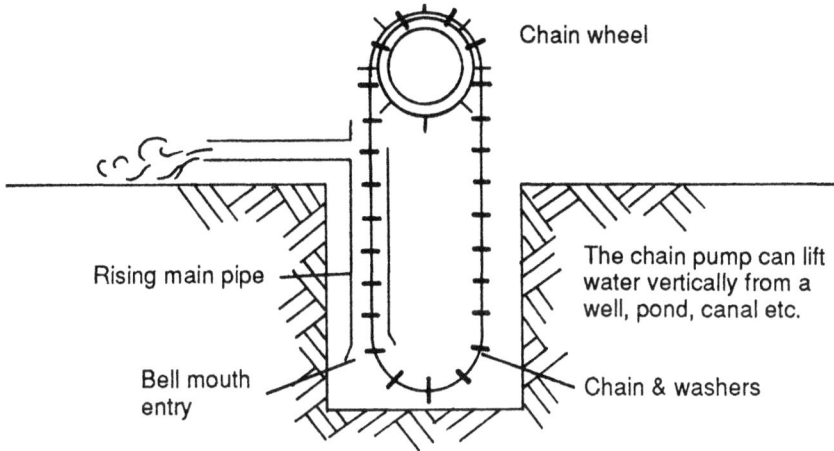

Chain wheel

Rising main pipe

The chain pump can lift water vertically from a well, pond, canal etc.

Bell mouth entry

Chain & washers

Figure 6.1   *General arrangement*

leakage down past the discs.

Chain pumps have many advantages over other types of pumping device. They are robust and can be made from local materials to low construction tolerances by local craftsmen; they are slow moving and the corrosion, wear, or failure of one part will not usually prevent the pump from working. The pumps can manage water containing silt and other solids, and they can be easily maintained and serviced. As they are slow-moving devices, they can be powered by man, animals, wind power, or slow-turning internal combustion engines, with the minimum of gearing or high performance bearings. Their reliability is such that they were used up until the second half of the 19th century as bilge pumps for the ships of the British Royal Navy.

Principles of operation

The robust chain and washer pump with its high mass low power ratio contrasts with the more modern and widely used smaller centrifugal pumps, which have a low mass/high power ratio. With the chain pump, therefore, the sturdy slow-moving components do not need great skill and tolerance in manufacture, nor skilled maintenance. The centrifugal pump, on the other hand, is relatively small, and has to concentrate the pumping effort through the faster moving, smaller components that need to be made from stronger materials, with very accurate workmanship. To make them work at all, expensive gearing has to be used. This gearing, if it is not to waste most of the pumping energy during transmission, must be accurately made and maintained.

Perhaps the greatest advantages of the chain and washer pump for rural areas are the slow speed of rotation and the steady unvarying rate of working

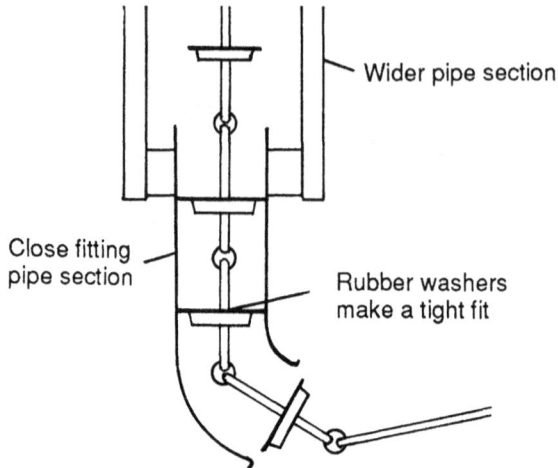

Figure 6.2   *Alternative improved seal*

that are completely compatible with the speeds at which men, animals, wind machines and slow-speed diesel engines can work. The continuous loop of linked chain and washers is pulled up the rising main pipe, carrying water with it between the washers. Unless the washers are a reasonably tight and accurate fit, water will leak back down the pipe, and the pump will not work at all efficiently. However, the 'cascade' of washers will probably limit the leakage to acceptable amounts. An alternative design has an accurately made and close-fitting section of pipe at the submerged lower end of the pipe (Figure 6.2). The rubber sealed washers make a tight fit in this section of pipe (which may be steel or plastic), and fit only loosely in the wider section of pipe above. The washers do the work of lifting in the close-fitting section, reducing leakage to a minimum; in the looser and cheaper section of pipe above they do no lifting work, but they also do not wear themselves out against the sides of the pipe in friction.

This is a most useful innovation. It might be possible to manufacture the washers and the lower pipe section in a workshop, then distribute them to local areas to be built into the locally made body of the pump. Other innovations include a bell mouth entry at the bottom of the pipe to guide the washers into the pipe, and a non-return ratchet on the chain wheel to prevent the chain from running backwards under the weight of water in the pipe.

The rising main pipe

This pipe holds the water between the chain washers as it is being lifted up to the surface. It must be smooth inside to prevent leakage past the washers, and to reduce wear on the washers as they rub against it. It must be robust, watertight, cheap and easily made or replaced. The pipe is hung down into the water from the surface. It has only to support its own weight and to stay steady as the chain passes through. It does *not* have to carry the weight of water inside the pipe.

Many different materials can be used to make the pipe, including timber, bamboo, iron, water-pipe, plastic, asbestos, and the shape can either be square or circular. However, the difficulties of making sure that square washers enter the square pipe at the correct angle make the square section a poor choice; it is normally used where the only material that can readily be used is timber planking. The internal diameter of the pipes does not generally exceed 10 cm.

We have already mentioned the innovation of using a close-fitting short section of smooth, accurately made pipe at the lower submerged end of the rising main, which prevents leakage past the washers. This may be made of plastic, smooth iron, or a carved hardwood resistant to decay. It may be fitted at the end of a cheaper, loose-fitting pipe, which may then be of any shape and made from any material so long as it is watertight. At least two washers must be passing through the lower section at any one time.

Some rising main pipes that are commercially manufactured have iron pipes flanged at the top and bottom so that the pipe may be lengthened deeper into the water. Iron piping is, of course, very much heavier than the equivalent plastic or timber pipe, and will need supporting on solid ground under the water. Bell mouth entry sections are usually fitted to the bottom end of the rising main pipe to guide the chain and washers into the pipe. These are made of timber or more often, galvanized iron sheeting.

The chain and washers

The original leather and horsehair or rag balls that were used as washers in the early chain pumps moulded themselves to the varying shape of the rising main pipe, reducing leakage to a minimum, but had high friction losses as they were pulled up the pipe. They would wear away quickly and probably rot in the water after a few months.

The washers that are mostly used today are wood or steel discs cut accurately to fit exactly into the rising main pipe. They must have a short section of solid chain passing through them to hold them in the correct position both as they enter the pipe and pass up the pipe. The washers must be supported both below and above on the chain link to carry the weight of water and take the full load on the chain as it is turned on the cogged teeth of the chain wheel.

The careful and accurate construction of the washers will reduce water losses and wear, but will increase costs and a balance must be made between the increased costs of this component and increased efficiency. It is perhaps

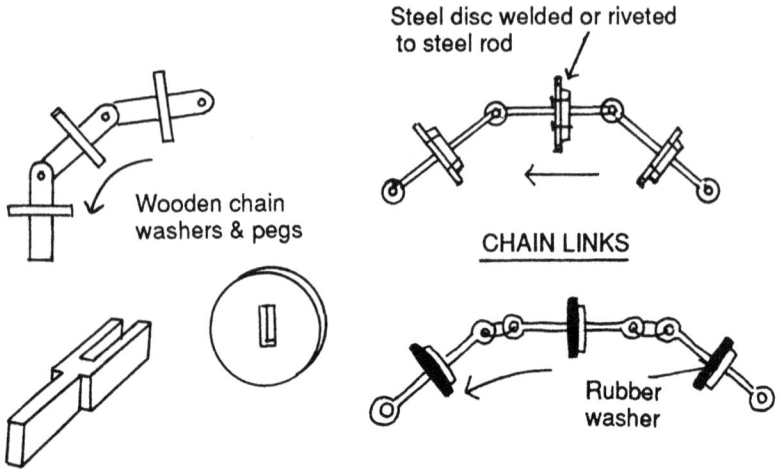

Figure 6.3   *Chain links*

worth the extra expense of fitting the washers with rubber seals. The chain is made from pegs, shaped wooden rods, rope or 5 mm diameter steel chain links (Figure 6.3).

The links must support both the weight of the loop that hangs from the chain wheel, and the weight of water in the rising main pipe. In a typical pipe of 10 cm internal diameter, the weight of water supported over a 20 m lift would be about 150 kg. With a smaller pipe of 7 cm internal diameter, and a 10 m lift, the weight of water supported would be 50 kg. Deep wells and large pipes, therefore, need strong metal chains; wooden or rope chains should only be used for the shorter lifts.

Nylon and rubber balls are a useful possibility for the chain and washers, but the chain would need to be made carefully to fit exactly on the cogged teeth of the chain wheel. There would also be difficulties if the nylon rope stretched under load, as the discs or balls would not then coincide with the chain wheel.

Structure and bearings

The framework that supports the chain and washers, rising main pipe and chain wheel must also be braced against the power source applied to it. This may be a hand crank, or a geared driving arm powered by oxen or horses. The solid timber framework of most of the examples demonstrates the size of structure needed.

Some chain pumps are built using the back axle and differential assembly of a motor vehicle as a transmission gear to take the power from an

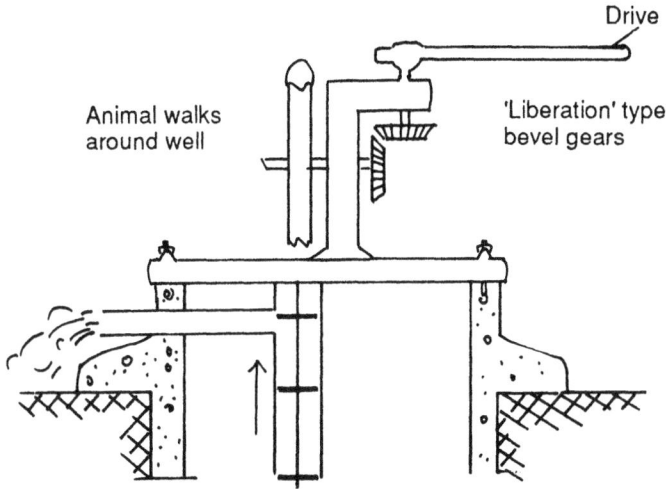

Figure 6.4 *Chain pump mounted over well*

animal-drawn driving arm on to the pump axle. Special bevel cast-iron gears are used on the 'Liberation' type pump (Figure 6.4), pegged timber gears are widely used in Asia.

The bearings that support the chain wheel axle will provide most of the frictional resistance of the pump, and much of the power loss will occur here. There is a dilemma in choosing the bearings for devices that are to be used in rural areas; they may be expensive, high performance, sealed bearings that will have to be completely replaced when they are worn out, or oiled wood-block bearings which are not designed to keep out the dust and sand, but can be cheaply renewed when they are worn. Wood block bearings, if they are carefully made, prepared, and greased, are very suitable for the slow-moving chain and washer pumps; wood bearings could not, of course, be used in high-speed pumping devices.

Chain wheel

Various designs of the chain wheel can be made. They range from cut-down wooden cartwheels to especially prepared cast iron wheels. The wheels support the chain at a radius of between 20 to 30 cm and must be robustly made to support the weight of the chain and pumped water in the rising main pipe. They are slow turning, and do not have to be dynamically balanced. The size is such that they can be made from cast iron in one small casting; a larger casting requires considerable skills and equipment.

The chain wheel is mounted in the centre of the axle shaft, which must be strong enough to support the complete pumping assembly. The axle may be made from wood, steel rod or pipe, but the ends must be made exactly circular to fit into the wood bearings. If a steel axle is used, the wood block bearing will wear away before the steel, and the axle will continue in good condition almost indefinitely.

Occasionally, as many as five chain wheels are fitted into a single axle, each chain wheel with its own chain and rising main pipe. The loops of chain and washers may then be added as they are needed to provide a crude but effective form of gearing.

(*Appropriate Technology* Vol. 3 No. 1, May 1976)

The Hydraulic Ram

SIMON WATT

There is no cheaper method of raising water than the hydraulic ram, and there is no other device that needs so little attention once installed. It could be much more widely used than it is at present.

It is a simple device, invented in the early 1800s. The power from falling water is used to force a small portion of the water to a height higher than the source. All propositions relating to the pumping of water involve four principle considerations: the vertical height the water has to be raised; the total distance it has to travel; the size of piping used for both suction and delivery and the rate at which it is required to raise the water.

The vertical distance the water has to be elevated is called the static head. The resistance offered to the flow of water by the suction and delivery pipes is called the friction head. This must be added to the static head to determine the total pressure against which the pump has to work. Given these particulars, it is a fairly simple matter to determine the size of pump and the horsepower of the engine required to work it.

How it works

The hydraulic ram does not require an engine or external power, and it has only two working parts. It provides its own power to force water to a higher level. The simplicity of the ram is often mentioned—but it is simple and efficient only when it is suited to the job. The only maintenance required is to clear rubbish away from the strainer on the intake and to replace the clack and non-return or delivery valve rubbers when they wear.

Only a small proportion of the water that runs into the ram will be pumped. If 2,000 gallons are to be raised each day, then between seven and 14 times that quantity must be fed into the supply pipe from the water source. The height to which water will be raised depends on the head, or fall, into the ram, and also on the length and size of pipe that leads the water into the pump. This pipe is called the drive pump. A small amount of water with plenty of fall will pump as much water as a greater amount with only a little fall.

The size and length of the drive-pipe must be in proportion to the head against which the ram has to work. The water may come from a spring on a hillside or from a river. It must be led into a position from which it can pass through a relatively short supply pipe to the ram, at a fairly steep angle (about 30 degrees from horizontal).

If a very long pipe is needed it would be better to feed the water into a tank or cistern, so placed that a drive pipe of suitable length can be used. Bends or curves in the drive pipe should be avoided and the velocity of the water in the pipe must not be restricted in any way. A good strainer is essential on the drive pipe at the source of supply to keep out rubbish. A 'sniffle' or air-valve should be fitted in the pipe close to the ram to prevent the air dome becoming waterlogged and to maintain a constant air volume.

As water runs down through the drive-pipe it goes faster and faster until it forces the impulse valve (or clack) to close suddenly. The weight of the moving water suddenly stopped creates a very high pressure and forces some of water past the non-return or delivery valve and into the air chamber, compressing the air more and more until the energy of the moving water is spent. This compressed air acts as a spring and forces the water in a steady stream up the delivery pipe to the storage tank.

The hydraulic ram is most efficient when the volume of the air chamber is equal to the volume of the discharge-pipe, therefore the larger rams are best suited for long-distance pipes, if there is enough water to operate them. Any fall from 3 to 100 feet can be employed, but generally the more working fall you obtain, the less the ram will cost and the less drive-water it will need to raise it.

A small ram built recently had a small amount of water to run it, with plenty of fall but not very much lift. The working fall was 20 ft., the lift above ram 44 ft., and 8.4 gallons drive water per minute was used. This delivered 1.6 gal/min or 100 gal/hr., that is 2,400 gallons per day.

Building a ram

First build the clack valve (Figure 6.5). If no metal lathe is available, a machine shop will do the work for a small price. Chuck a 3 in. × 1 in. pipe-bushing in the lathe and turn the inside smooth, where the clack strikes. Turn out the threads and eliminate any sharp edges. Drill two ¼ in. holes near the end of a piece of strap iron ¼ in. × 1½ in. × 3 in. and, using it as a template, drill and tap holes in the top of the pipe-brushing. Grind off the galvanizing, then bolt the clack-spring support solidly to the bushing and

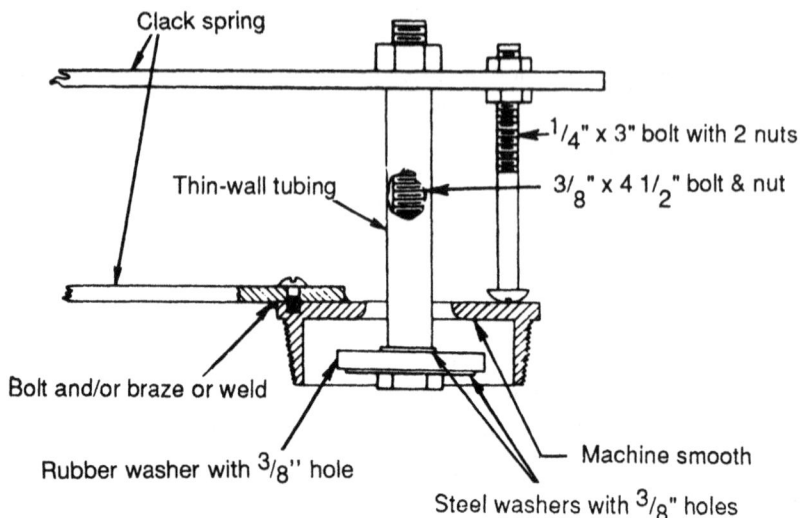

Clack spring

$^1/_4$" x 3" bolt with 2 nuts

Thin-wall tubing

$3/_8$" x 4 $1/_2$" bolt & nut

Bolt and/or braze or weld

Rubber washer with $3/_8$" hole

Machine smooth

Steel washers with $3/_8$" holes

Figure 6.5 *Hydraulic ram clack valve*

braze it. Bend a 36 in. iron strap, 1½ in. × ⅛ in. around a 2 in. pipe to make the clack spring. Drill two ½ in. holes through the end and also through both the support and two short pieces to make up the pad as shown in the drawing. Cut pieces of rubber inner tube and assemble the sandwich: this vibration from breaking off the support prevents the pipe-bushing. A brace can be added for additional support but is not absolutely necessary.

The clack valve itself is made up of a rubber disc and metal washer ⅜ in. smaller than the inside of the bushing and assembled on a ⅜ in. by 4½ in. bolt. The best rubber is from an old tractor tyre—it shows no wear at all after eight months' use. It can be cut on a band-saw and sanded flat and even used on a disc sander with coarse paper. A similar one is used for the check valve. Slip a washer over the bolt and short length of thin-wall steel tube (¾ in. outside diameter conduit) with the ends filed exactly square, then through a hole in the clack spring. Adjust by bending so the rubber clack strikes true and does not rub on the sides of the bushing.

Drill a hole for a carriage bolt to adjust the stroke of the spring; also a pair of holes about 3 in. from the round end of the spring for a tension bolt. If the bottom hole is filed square to fit the underside of the bolt, it will not turn when adjustments are made.

The check valve (Figure 6.6) is similar in construction, but a ½ in. by 2 in. galvanized bolt is used. Machine the lip true where the valve rests but do not cut it down further than necessary. This gives clearance for the water to pass. Drill two holes on each side of the middle for a 4 in. common nail to pass just above the valve metal washer, to keep it in place. Leave enough clearance so

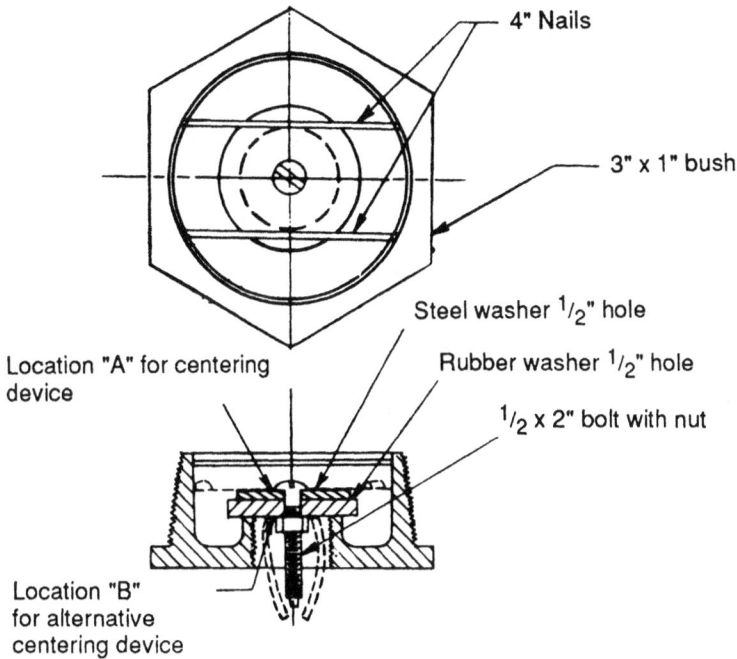

Figure 6.6 *Hydraulic ram: check valve. The centering device prevents the moving assembly from slipping to the side (off-centre)*

the valve can open just about $1/16$ in. Spread the bolt with a centre punch just below the nut, so the nut can't work loose. Cut the nails off and file threads across their ends so the bushing will screw into the tee above it.

Just one other small job before assembly: drill a $1/16$ in. hole in the centre of the 1 in. nipple just below the check valve and bend a piece of copper wire to the shape of a cotter-pin and insert it from the inside of the nipple with long-nosed pliers. Spread the outside ends. This copper wire restricts the jet of water coming out, yet moves enough to keep the hole clean.

The air chamber can be a 2 ft. length of 3 in. pipe, threaded on both ends with a cap on the top end. The top end can have a plate welded over it. It must be airtight at great pressure. The inside of the pipe can be coated with asphalt paint to protect it from rust and to seal any small leaks in the weld. Let it dry in the sun while assembling the rest of the ram.

Assembly

Use plenty of good grade pipe-joint compound, both on inside and outside threads. Screw components together firmly but not excessively tightly and leave them in the correct position for the installation. Set the ram reasonably

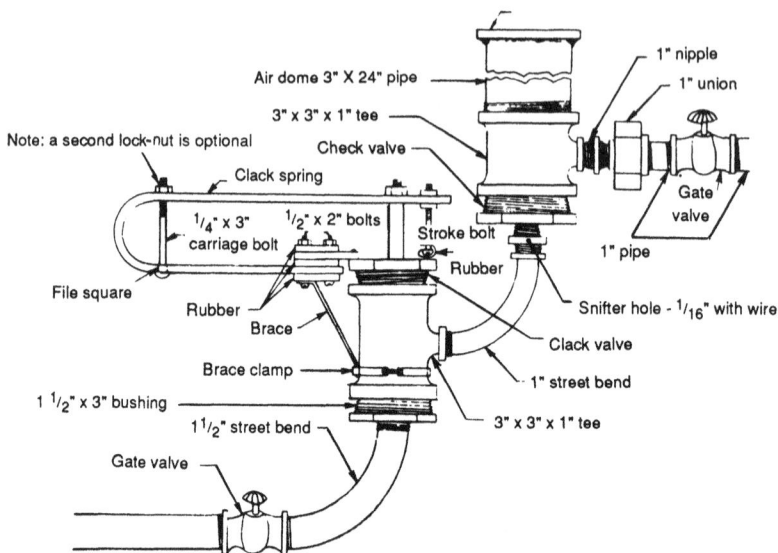

Figure 6.7   *Hydraulic ram—complete assembly*

level, but nothing is demanding in this respect. The air-valve must be immediately below the air dome so the bubbles will rise into it. Clack and check valves must be free from binding and touch evenly all around. The tractor-tyre rubber with some fabric on the back seems to be of just the right toughness and resilience to last a long time.

Whilst it is often recommended that the ram is mounted in concrete to withstand vibration caused by the pounding of the impetus valve it is not absolutely necessary. In fact it is a convenience to be able to shut off the two valves, loosen the unions, and take the ram to the repair shop for cleaning and painting. Painting does not assist it to operate but it looks better when visitors see it. The cost of a home-built ram can be about one-tenth of the manufactured cost.

A piece of rubber stretched over the head of the stroke bolt quietens the ram but it is not essential. Adjust the spring-tension bolt and stroke bolt together to get the best period for the particular ram. Support the drive and delivery pipes so they do not bounce and vibrate.

This is a small ram but larger ones can be built—two have been built with 3 in. drive-pipes and correspondingly larger ram parts. One lifts water about 150 ft. and drives it through 3,600 ft. of pipe.

The drive-pipe should be fitted with a strainer. This keeps out rubbish, animals, and leaves, any of which will stop the ram if they get inside. The drive pipe should be 1½ in. or larger and, if possible, new, solidly put together, straight, and well-supported throughout its length. A gate valve on the drive-pipe about 4 ft. from the ram is often recommended. It is a great convenience but not absolutely necessary. Another gate valve on the delivery-pipe is necessary to avoid draining the entire delivery-pipe whenever the ram is cleaned. The ram should be connected to the delivery- and drive-pipes by unions so it can be removed for cleaning. If it is desirable to use two rams, they must have separate drive-pipes but the delivery-pipes can be joined, provided the pipe is large enough to carry the water.

The delivery-pipe should start from the ram with about two lengths of 1 in. galvanized-iron pipe. From there, ¾ in. pipe can be used to deliver all the water from the ram directly into a storage tank for use from there. Use the overflow for irrigation purposes.

The small bolt at the end of the clack spring controls the length of the stroke of the ram. The bolt at the back (rounded) end of the spring controls the tension of the clack spring. Experiment for the best length of stroke and tension for local conditions. Adjust the length of stroke first, then the spring tension. The greater the tension and length of stroke, the slower the ram will work and the more water it will pump, but it will take more water to keep it working.

In case of problems . . .

○ See that the clack valve closes squarely, evenly, and completely. If it does not, the clack spring may have been bent somehow, and will have to be straightened.
○ See that the clack valve does not rub on the front, side, or back of the valve body.
○ Check for rubbish in the ram or delivery valve or air-valve.
○ Check to see that the air dome is not filled with water. If it is the ram will knock loudly and may break something. The air-valve allows in air between each of the strokes and this keeps the dome full of compressed air.
○ Check rubber clack and delivery-valve for wear or looseness.
○ If drive water is in small supply, speed up the stroke by loosening spring tension and shorten the stroke by lowering the stroke-adjusting bolt. More water is delivered by a faster stroke and continuous running than a slower stroke that stops every day.
○ Check for leaks in drive-pipe. If air bubbles come out of the drive-pipe after it has been stopped for a while, air is leaking into the drive-pipe and the ram action is spoiled.
○ Clean the ram occasionally. It deserves it after working constantly day and night for weeks and months on end. Protect it from outside injury and inquisitive children.
○ When the ram runs out of water it will usually stop, remaining open and losing all the water available until it is closed again. Listen at the storage

tank to hear if it is still running, and, if not, go to the ram and close the
drive-pipe until water has accumulated in the cistern.
○ Long delivery distances require larger pipes to reduce friction.
○ It is a good idea to have a cistern at the top of the drive-pipe to let dirt
settle out of the water. The outlet from the cistern to the ram should be a
foot or so above the bottom to allow room for dirt to settle out.
○ To start up a hydraulic ram it is necessary to hold down the impetus valve
for a few seconds and allow the water to run to waste. Then allow the
valve to rise and shut off the flow of water. It may be necessary to repeat
this on several occasions before the ram will start automatically.

(*Appropriate Technology* Vol. 1 No. 4, Winter 1974–5)

Windpumps bring water to the Turkana Desert
VIVIEN ABBOTT

Kenya is a country we have come to think of as one of the most stable in
Africa; a developing country, yes, but fairly wealthy with a good coffee
industry and a sound tourist trade. But many parts of Kenya are extremely
poor with basic problems like famine and lack of water for drinking,
washing, irrigation and livestock. These conditions exist in parallel with an
engineering industry based around the capital, Nairobi, so Kenya is the ideal
country to find an engineering solution to these problems.

In 1975, ITDG began work on the design of a windpump using modern
engineering knowledge, materials and fabrication methods which also had
to be suitable for building and using in a developing country, and had a
planned life of 20 years with minimum maintenance requirements. In the
early stages of the project ITDG identified collaborators in Kenya, Botswana, Egypt, Oman, India and Pakistan who were willing to try to build the
windpump locally.

Prototype

The Kenyan collaborator, Bobs Harries Engineering Ltd (BHEL), is the
most advanced of these manufacturers. BHEL completed its prototype
early in 1979 and small-scale production of the 'Kijito' pump (Swahili for
'stream of water') started in June 1979. (In 1988 there were more than 120 in
operation in Kenya and surrounding countries.)

Two of these windpumps have been installed at a village called Kaikor in
Kenya's Turkana desert. The Turkana is an arid area in the north of the
country supporting about 190,000 mainly nomadic Turkana people.

There are normally two major rainfalls each year, although some areas sometimes do not get any rain at all. During the dry season the hills provide only just sufficient grazing for the livestock (mostly goats, cows and camels). After the rains, the people bring their animals down on to the plains to graze, and draw their water from hand-dug wells in the sandy river-beds which soon dry up. The water is dirty and contaminated, so both humans and animals are susceptible to water-borne diseases.

In about 1977, the numbers of people and animals in the Turkana increased sharply and the area became over-populated. During the following two years rainfall was lower than normal, so that the ground water was depleted and grazing became very poor. The next two rains failed, and the effect of the resulting drought on both human and animal population was very severe. Very little accurate information is available on human losses, but early figures indicate that more than half the livestock perished.

Initial aid programmes were in the form of famine relief and some wells were dug and supplied with handpumps. Excellent work was done in this field, although it resulted in many people settling near the relief points because they had lost their cattle and hence their need to be nomadic.

Rehabilitation

The Turkana Rehabilitation Project was set up to teach these people to support themselves again and be independent of famine relief. The teaching programme included lessons on basic livestock husbandry and cultivation techniques.

One of the major problems was the lack of water for drinking, livestock and irrigation. As an experiment, the Project installed Kijito pumps at Kaikor, 15 miles from the Sudan border, which had a small existing borehole with a poor yield. It is unusual to find a windpump producing water for human consumption.

The well was rebored to a depth of 150 ft. and a similar new one dug nearby. Two Kijito windpumps were bought from BHEL, one with a 16 ft. diameter rotor and one with a 20 ft. diameter rotor. They were installed in November 1981 when the population of Kaikor was 400. There was also a school nearby which 400 to 500 children attended irregularly.

As the handpump was removed and the first windpump installed people started to drift in from the surrounding areas to watch the proceedings. By the time the windpump was pumping water, more than 3,000 people were trying to collect water from its single 2 in. outlet pipe. This resulted in what can be described as a good-natured riot, which naturally required a certain amount of good-natured riot control. The water pumped was, and still is, clean and good to drink.

One of the most rewarding sights at Kaikor is that of the children using the water for washing. The teachers at the local school want to teach hygiene and one of the new rules is that all the children are to wash all over twice a day, before meals. This is a rather special experience if you have been brought up to regard water as a rare and valuable asset. The windpumps at Kaikor are 1 to 2 km from the main settlement and are used as a social centre, particularly by the women.

With clean water available, the population of Kaikor has begun to increase. The two Kijito machines now supply 4,000 people and their livestock. Excess water pumped is used in a small-scale self-sufficient furrow irrigation scheme and the people are growing sorghum to supplement their diet. Two more Kijito machines have now been installed within an 80 km radius of the first two, but the drastic increase in population around them seems to indicate the need for more projects of this kind in the Turkana desert. If there were more windpumps of smaller capacity it is quite possible that they would not attract so many people from the surrounding areas, artificially boosting the population.

(Waterlines Vol. 1 No. 2, October 1982)

Solar pumps—a ray of hope in Somalia

Compiled from reports by GARY COCKETT and ROBERT FRASER

A combination of the hostilities over the disputed Ogaden (western Somalia) region of Ethiopia and severe drought forced about a million refugees to flee over the border to Somalia in the early 1980s. Five hundred thousand of these were thought to be living in camps in three of Somalia's border regions assisted by the Somalia National Refugee Commission in conjunction with the United Nations High Commissioner for Refugees. Non-governmental organizations such as Oxfam ran programmes such as the water project described here.

Gary Cockett[49] was seconded to the project through the Register of Engineers in Disaster Relief (REDR) from the UK Anglian Water Authority in 1981. Two days after his arrival he was put in charge of water supply for two of the six camps in the Hargeisa area: Las Dhure and Agabar. They are sited on the banks of 'tugs', (sand-filled river-beds between 50 and 100 m wide) which are dry on the surface for most of the year but which flood with water for a few hours after a bout of heavy rain to a depth of 1 to 2 m. The impervious bedrock of the tugs is typically covered by between ½ metre and 2.5 m of partially saturated sand, and from these shallow aquifers the Oxfam water project draws its supplies.

Estimates of the combined population of the Las Dhure and Agabar refugee camps varied between 50,000 and 70,000 while Gary Cockett was there. Accurate figures were not available as refugees were not registered

Rock masonry gutters channel water into Ngamione rock catchment
(Jeremy Hartley)

A rubberized pan, viewed from the rock catchment area, showing rock masonry guttering (Jeremy Hartley)

Construction of a catchment tank at Mutomo, Kenya. A pillar of earth is left at the centre of the excavation, and the labourer measures the arc from it
(Jeremy Hartley)

An arc dam in Kenya showing rock masonry gutters (Jeremy Hartley)

and a daily bus service between the camps and Hargeisa, about 45 km away, gave the population mobility. In the face of such a high population density, Oxfam devised a system of standpipes near each well to give a bare minimum emergency supply of 5 to 10 litres a person a day.

Between 10 and 20 permanent wells, from 4 m and 6 m deep, were hand-dug by the refugees with the assistance of a Pionjar petrol-driven rock-breaker in the hard rock areas.

These wells were mainly sited in the bank aquifer just outside the tug-bed where they were safer from flooding, though from time to time a small number of temporary supplementary dry season wells or sumps were built for convenience directly in the tug-beds. They were lined with Armco corrugated galvanized steel sections 0.9 m high and available in either 1.8 m or 3.5 m diameters. Below the water-table the liners were perforated, either with a hammer and chisel or by burning holes in them with welding rods.

Wells were constructed in open cut above the water-table and lined with 3.5 m diameter corrugated sections up to 2 m below ground and 1.8 m diameter at depths greater than 2 m below ground. Below the water-table, 1.8 m diameter sections were used throughout. Excavations were back-filled with graded rocks and stones to above the level of the water-table, and then with the sand and gravel previously excavated. Because the well-liners were made of corrugated steel they would not readily descend through gravel and sand-beds by gravity, even with the assistance of heavy cantledge and the undermining of the toe.

Pumping methods

Thirty pumps driven by solar energy were used in the Oxfam water project[50] plus a number of diesel and petrol-driven models used for back-up at times of peak water demand. Twenty-five of the solar pumps were donated by Oxfam America and five by the German 'Freedom from Hunger' organization.

In a solar pump, solar radiation is converted directly into electricity by a photovoltaic (solar cell) array. The electricity produced drives a high-efficiency electric pump set.

The main advantages of photovoltaics as a source of electrical energy are that there are no diesel or petrol fuel costs, they are simple to maintain and their working life is long. Their lack of reliance on hydrocarbon fuels is especially useful in areas such as Somalia where supplies are unreliable or fuel is dirty. Solar pumps could be maintained in the field with a screwdriver and a couple of spanners instead of needing complex tools and a greater supply of spare parts. The intrinsic complexity of diesel and petrol-driven pumps, and their many moving parts, caused special problems of maintenance which resulted in considerable downtime as they generally had to be sent back to the water project's Hargeisa workshop. Lifespan of a solar array is estimated at 20 years and for an electric submersible pump at 15,000 hours, compared to 2,000 hours for a small petrol pump. Nevertheless, if the electrical circuitry went wrong, solar pumps had to be sent back to the manufacturer.

Thus it seems that photovoltaics have the edge on other types in a purely technical comparison. The high capital cost of solar cells is 'the only economic stumbling block to the whole solar pump concept', says Robert Fraser, a master plumber working with Oxfam. In the three years, 1980 to 1983, he says the cost per peak Watt of mass-produced photovoltaic power has dropped from about US$60 to US$10. The price is likely to continue to drop, although US Government predictions of US$2 per Watt by 1985 is now considered to be very optimistic but could conceivably be achieved in the medium to long term.

From his experiences in the Oxfam water project Robert Fraser feels that solar pumps are a better investment than their conventional, although cheaper, equivalents. For example, the Somali Water Development Agency relies heavily on donors for capital investment in the form of pumping equipment. Every few years it receives equipment which lasts for a relatively short time. It seems better to spend more for equipment with a longer working life and use money to add to the stock of equipment available than to renew equipment completely every two or three years.

The particular solar pumps used in north-west Somalia were manufactured by Solar Electric International. They consisted of two aluminium frames and used photovoltaic arrays from ARCO Solar, which had a total area of 8 ft. × 4 ft. (just under 3 cu.m square). The frames could be set at three angles to optimize their exposure to the sun and were mounted on wheels.

Each array had a box of printed circuits called a 'maximum power controller' (MPC) attached to it which was designed to sense the load required by the pump and control the output of the array. The MPC was claimed to increase the efficiency of the equipment by 5 per cent. The manufacturer later decided to discard the MPC and compensate for the loss of efficiency by incorporating extra modules in the solar array because 10 per cent of MPCs created surges of power to the pump every two seconds after a few days or weeks of use. This reduced the efficiency of the pump considerably.

The solar pumps used are of an electric submersible type manufactured by the German company KSB. The model is all plastic with a brushless d.c. motor directly coupled to an impeller. The bearing of the impeller is water-lubricated and the pump can be floated at the surface of the water or submerged to any depth. It needs relatively solids-free water as it is easily blocked by particulate matter. Nevertheless, flushing out the blockage is a relatively simple matter. The inlet grille was enlarged to make blockage less likely. On the basis of experience the standard delivery outlet was also altered to allow the pump to hang vertically in the water where it previously tended to lean over. Pumping capacity was 2.5 litres/second, the outlet was 2 in. BSP, and it was useful only during the bright daylight hours.

Other types

Three other models of pump are used on the Oxfam water project. Gary Cockett notes the only petrol-driven pump, a Villiers Texmo four-stroke single cylinder centrifugal pump with an output of 3 litres/second, for the many breakdowns it suffered. The most used type of pump was a Petter/ Atlanta single cylinder diesel-driven centrifugal pump with an 8 litres/ second output, which he describes as 'robust and easy to work with'. Also available was another diesel-driven pump: a Lister-Pegson centrifugal type with an output of 12 litres/second of water. This type was less suitable for the conditions met at most camps and was limited to the few where relatively high flows had to be pumped at low heads of pressure.

Gary Cockett estimates that the output of the solar pumps used in north-western Somalia is 3 litres/second at the lowest heads and between 1 and 2 litres/second at the more typical 5 m heads met in the camps. With the favourable light conditions met in the region, these magnitudes of flow can potentially be maintained for 8 to 10 hours per day most days of the year.

Gary Cockett feels that overall, the relief agencies in Somalia were doing a very good job under poor conditions. But he makes suggestions that would make engineers' tasks in the Third World easier and ensure that equipment, including solar pumps, arrived in the field in better working order.

Choosing the best method of transportation is a matter of balancing cost against the time taken and possible damage to equipment in transit. For the project he worked on, he felt that air freight would have been a better solution than sending equipment overland. Containers should be checked before despatch to ensure that no parts are missing. A detailed manifest should arrive at the destination point before the equipment is delivered so that losses can easily be identified and rectified. Failure to do these things wastes the time of workers in the field.

(*Waterlines* Vol. 1 No. 3, January 1983)

CHAPTER 7
Handpump Testing and Development

Handpumps installed in wells where ground water is easily available provide one of the simplest and least expensive methods of supplying rural communities with water. Indeed, because of lack of capital or local conditions, handpumps are often the only method that can be considered. However, selecting the right handpump is no easy matter; many have been developed but there has been little guidance for purchasers.

To provide more information and to help manufacturers produce better pumps, the Consumers' Association testing and research laboratories have carried out detailed assessments of hand- and foot-operated pumps, initially for the UK's Overseas Development Administration, and subsequently for the World Bank with UNDP funding to coincide with the start of the Water Decade activities. Their programme, culminating in the 1982 Interim Progress Report is outlined in the first article.

Saul Arlosoroff is the UNDP's project manager for handpumps' testing and development within the World Bank. He points out that supplying rural areas with pumped water requires an enormous capital investment for the five to seven million handpumps needed to meet the goals of the Decade: the effectiveness of this massive investment ultimately depends upon the proper performance of the handpumps installed. The UNDP/World Bank programme for laboratory and field-testing is directed at improving dependability and reducing costs.

Pump development is undertaken in several countries to meet local requirements, as illustrated by the last two articles. The first describes some of the laboratory research and the simple technology developed at the Blair Research Laboratory, including the Blair 'walking stick' and 'bucket' pumps. Mention is also made of the Blair hand-operated drilling rig. The second outlines the development by the University of Malaysia of a PVC handpump which could provide an interim solution to the problem of village water supply in Malaysia and other countries. Field-testing is in hand with funding from Canada's International Development and Research Centre.

The articles in this chapter, as elsewhere in the book, were written at the initial stages of original development work. They are important because they introduce imaginative ideas and programmes so essential for improving community water supplies. Following the publication of several progress reports and two applied research and technology notes on the Handpumps

150

Project, the World Bank have now published *Community Water: the hand-pump option*[51] which presents the conclusions of five years of work.

The Consumers' Association's handpump testing programme

KEN MILLS

The problems of how to select a handpump for a particular site are legion and the difficulties are compounded because little objective information is available to the purchaser. Many early pump breakdowns in the field can be shown to be caused by inadequate design in all its aspects, low manufacturing quality, wrong installation or simply the wrong pump selected for the job it has to do.

The CA Testing and Research Laboratories has devised and carried out a handpump assessment programme to provide more detailed knowledge for the purchaser and to help the pump manufacturer produce better and more reliable products.

Since 1977 the CA has been carrying out detailed assessments of a wide range of hand- and foot-operated pumps to provide drinking water in developing countries. The CA was originally asked by ODA to help find pumps which would give reliable performance in the field and provide better 'value for money' for the available overseas aid. It examined a range of pumps from manufacturers in the UK, Europe, America, Canada, India and east and west Africa, covering not only the traditional types of pump, but also more recently-designed types which use less conventional methods of pumping water.

In 1979, with the help of the International Reference Centre in The Hague, the CA held a conference on the testing and evaluation of handpumps.[52] Following on from this, in 1980 the World Bank commissioned the CA to continue work on handpump assessment, with UNDP funding. This work coincides with the start of the IDWSSD in 1981.

The first of a series of reports[53] on the work, which covers pumps from Thailand, Indonesia, Bangladesh, the Philippines, Kenya, Japan, the USA, Finland, Ethiopia and France, has been circulated world-wide by the World Bank.

If pumps are first tested in the laboratory, components failures can be detected more cheaply and quickly. By carrying out detailed engineering assessments, areas of weakness in design and manufacturing can be detected. 'Endurance tests' can telescope three years' field use of a handpump into a six-month period.

Field trials in developing countries are expensive and the majority have not been well-controlled for a variety of good reasons, so the usefulness of the information is limited. The CA ran pilot field trials in Lesotho at the same time as laboratory testing, and this gave some insight into the problems of data collection and management of field trials. The World Bank will use this and other field trial data to produce an improved protocol and data collection system to run a planned series of field trials in 20 developing countries.

Before the CA decided on a test programme it tried to put itself in the position of a purchaser of handpumps: it was obvious that there was a great shortage of available information. The CA talked with the big institutional buyers like UNICEF and ODA at one end of the purchasing scale and, at the other end, consultant engineers working for small charitable organizations who could only afford to buy a few pumps at a time. From these discussions the CA identified information needed to decide which pump to purchase.

Detailed information is available from the ODA and from the World Bank based on CA's work.

Choosing a pump

When selecting a pump, consideration must be given as to who makes the decision to purchase and whether the pump is to be manufactured locally.

A large organization like UNICEF has the resources to make a much more efficient decision about where to manufacture handpumps. In the case of the India Mark II pump, it chose four or five Indian manufacturers and gave them detailed information about the pump. UNICEF then employed the UK Crown Agents as quality control supervisors to ensure that the manufacturers kept to the specifications. This strategy was used after the failure of some UNICEF field trials as the result of faulty pumps; since making manufacturing firms compete, the success rate in UNICEF field programmes has been much higher. The small purchaser, however, cannot run such a scheme, and so needs information from laboratory testing.

Testing a pump builds up a picture of the technical ability of the manufacturer and the pump design. Bad pumps need to be identified and taken off the market. There is no such thing as 'the best pump': all have both advantages and disadvantages.

To choose a suitable pump, information is needed on the number of people who are likely to use it, plus the estimated hours of use per day. Some pumps were originally made for one family to use in a country like Canada or the USA where there is some knowledge of maintenance. It is unfair to expect such a pump to survive continuous use in a village where there is no hope of any maintenance.

The amount of effort required to operate the pump is important as is its efficiency. The purchaser should remember that it is usually women and children who draw water, so the pump must be physically comfortable for them to use.

It is essential for the pump manufacturer to provide adequate, preferably pictorial, information on installation and maintenance. This should show the correct height for the pump to be installed and the best way of making a good sanitary seal at the base of the stand to prevent contamination from surface water. It should also mention whether any special tools are needed to repair the machine.

Some pumps are packed in containers for delivery to a central depot, but others are available in individual packages. The CA investigates whether the manufacturer has really thought of transport problems, both for export and overload carriage. A crate that is easily moved by a fork-lift truck in the factory may not be manageable by people alone when it reaches the bush. It is ridiculous to believe that experienced engineers will always be on hand to install a pump.

Weights and measures

The CA has built a unique 'pump testing tower' (Figure 7.1) to gather most of this information. Weighing the principal components of the pump is part of the CA's testing scheme. The main dimensions are measured, including the cylinder bores to check that the piston fits snugly. Handle and spout heights are recorded, the angle through which the handle travels in the course of a stroke and the mechanical advantage of the handle. The water pattern as it comes out of the spout is measured to ensure that the pump is suitable for filling narrow-necked vessels.

The CA then examines every part of the pump and determines what it is made of and how it is manufactured. It estimates the degree of technical competence the manufacturer needs to make the pump, to assess its suitability for manufacture in developing countries and whether it could be repaired with local materials.

Resistance to contamination and vandalism are also important. The CA looks at the sanitary sealing of the pump-stand and well-stand. It also checks how easy it would be to dismantle the pump and pilfer parts. Safety hazards investigated include potential finger-traps, insecure fastenings and sharp projections.

To test pump performance, strain gauges are put on the pump handle to measure the applied force, and a rotary potentiometer is fixed to the body of the pump. This measures the angular movement of the handle. The pump is operated at uniform speed over a fixed number of strokes and the volume of water delivered is measured. This information is fed into a micro-computer which records it and calculates the work done on the pump by the operator. The computer then compares this with the amount of work done by the pump in lifting water, to calculate the efficiency. Where possible, the CA

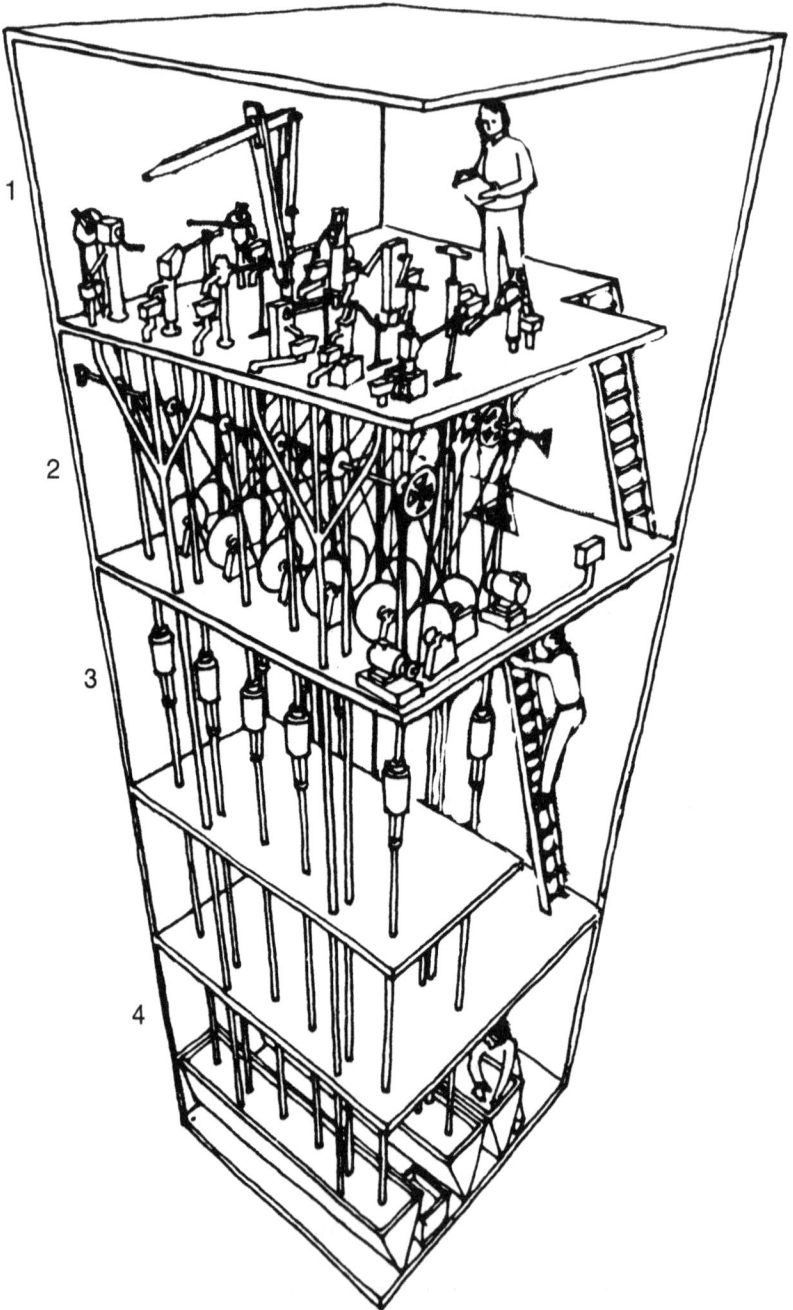

Figure 7.1 *The Consumers' Association handpump testing tower. (1) Pumps on test, (2) endurance drive mechanism, (3) head simulation valves, (4) water tanks*

pumps from simulated depths of 7, 25 and 45 metres, each at 30, 40 and 50 strokes or revolutions a minute. Shallow-well pumps are only tested at 7 metres, the greatest depth from which water can be raised using this type of pump.

A test for leakage through the valve is made by checking whether water drops back down the bore of the well overnight.

The CA carries out user tests to iron out difficulties in people's interaction with pumps. A test group of 60 people, mainly women and children of various heights and ages are selected from the CA's 'user panels'. They are allowed to familiarize themselves with the workings of the pump and are then asked to fill a 10-litre bucket with water, watched by a trained observer. The time and number of strokes required to fill the bucket are recorded and users are asked to complete a questionnaire on comfort, height and ease of operation. A statistician analyses the results and they are compared with notes made by the observers. The CA records some of the users on video to assess any difficulties they have experienced in adjusting to operate the pump. This identifies pumps which are awkward or difficult to operate.

Impact and endurance

The pump is put through an endurance test in four stages of approximately 1,000 hours each incorporating a total of 10 million strokes or revolutions of the pump. The first stage is carried out with clean, hard water and the second stage with clean acidified soft water. In the third stage 'Kieselguhr', a fine abrasive, is added to accelerate wear in the moving parts. In the last 1,000 hour period, fine sharp quartz sand is added to the water. During the last two stages the water is agitated to ensure that the particles are still dispersed in the water. The pump is then dismantled to inspect for corrosion and wear.

Pump durability in the field is vital for the success of any rural water programme, and the CA's endurance tests have revealed problems in almost every pump tested. Knowing this, the potential purchaser can check whether the manufacturer has modified his product to overcome the failures.

The final test is an impact test using what has been christened the 'careless cow'. This is a leather bag filled with lead shot and sawdust, which is hung as a pendulum and swung at the handle of the pump-stand at impacts of increasing severity.

After all these tests, the CA has a very much better idea of how much skill is required to maintain the pump, having dismantled it several times. Many breakdowns are expected during the endurance period and this also gives a good idea of the problems likely to occur in the field.

The CA would nevertheless appreciate information from people with experience of using pumps in developing countries.

The CA is an independent association which hopes through unbiased, comparative testing, to be able to provide manufacturers with information on ways of improving their pumps, to encourage better design and to upgrade the packaging and handling. It hopes the work will lead to real improvement in rural water supplies and health in developing countries.

(*Waterlines* Vol. 1 No. 1, July 1982)

World Bank handpumps testing programme
SAUL ARLOSOROFF

In 1983 the United Nations estimated that more than 1,500 million people in developing countries had inadequate supplies of safe drinking water. Based on studies dealing with the problem and its possible solutions, experts from the UN, the World Bank and other related organizations believe that handpumps provide the most reliable and adequate means for combating this growing problem.

UNDP established global and interregional projects for laboratory testing, field trials and technological development of handpumps as part of the IDWSSD; these projects are being carried out by the World Bank through the Office of the Senior Adviser for Water and Wastes.

The ambitious goal established by the UN is to provide drinking water to about 1,200 million rural people who presently do not have access to adequate safe water. As handpumps installed in wells where ground water is easily available provide one of the simplest and least costly methods of supplying the rural population with water, meeting the goals of the Decade would require the manufacture and installation of between 5 and 7 million handpumps.

Supplying pumped water to rural areas requires an enormous capital investment in engineering, hydrology, borehole drilling, well digging, and pump installation. The effectiveness of this massive investment depends ultimately upon the proper performance of the handpumps installed.

Despite the research and development of handpumps already undertaken by manufacturers, governments, bilateral and international agencies, a number of serious technological problems remain. These problems are manifested in poor design, unsatisfactory performance, shortened working life, and often in pump failure. There is also a lack of reliable data on handpump performance and on the comparative performance of different handpump designs. These data are required to facilitate selection from among the range of available handpumps.

Improvements

The UNDP/World Bank programme for laboratory trials, field testing and technological development of handpumps addresses these problems. The main objective is to improve the dependability and reduce the costs of rural water supply systems that employ handpumps, so that the majority of people in developing countries can have access to safe drinking water. I it hoped that the programme will provide the necessary technological basis for the development of new low-maintenance and cost-effective handpumps for installation in developing countries.

The first project consists of laboratory testing to select and evaluate a limited number of handpumps. Pumps being tested include both established and new designs produced in developing as well as developed countries. Hand- and foot-operated pumps with different pumping mechanisms are being tested. Laboratory testing began in 1980 at CA Testing and Research UK, and was concluded in 1982. A summary of the testing programme precedes this article.

The second project, started in 1981 includes field trials for a variety of handpumps, including the pumps and components found most promising in the first project.

Extensive field trials of 2,000 pumps will be conducted in approximately fifteen countries in various regions of the developing world. Each test site will be of a defined area and will include 25 to 50 pumps each of three to four different types, giving a total of about 100 to 200 pumps per site. Handpumps will be monitored by the project staff and the local project participants. Detailed data will be collected, analysed and disseminated.

One of the main objectives of the project research will be the development of 'village-level operation and maintenance' (VLOM) pumps, which can be manufactured in the developing countries and repaired by trained village operators. Unlike the conventional pumps, these light, simple pumps can be repaired without incurring the delay and expense of employing heavily equipped, highly skilled mobile maintenance units.

International co-operation

The pumps to be field-tested will be bought with funds from international, bilateral and national agencies, since the UNDP funds are intended mainly to cover technical assistance and management costs of the project.

To provide maximum impact and to encourage continuing support for the project's objectives, the World Bank, as executing agency, will co-operate with other international organizations such as UNDP, UNICEF, WHO, UNEP, UNIDO, the major bilateral agencies, and others. In particular, the project will co-ordinate with the WHO/UNDP Water Supply and Sanitation

Programmes, the UNDP/World Bank Project on Low-Cost Sanitation and the UNICEF Rural Water Supply Programmes.

'The handpumps' projects are expected to make significant contributions to programmes for low-cost water supply in developing countries. They will develop a standard methodology for handpump testing leading to the identification of effective pumps. The World Bank projects will provide local training and technical assistance to district-level handpump operation, maintenance and monitoring teams. Manuals will be prepared to assist in the selection, installation and maintenance of pumps. The projects will promote and assist in the development and local manufacture of appropriately designed handpumps.

Governments will be able to obtain greater benefits from funds available for rural water supply. Moreover, by improving the effectiveness of hand-pumps, the World Bank projects are also expected to encourage increased investment in rural water supply during and after the Decade.

The rest of this article consists of excerpts of the interim laboratory report on handpumps,[54] to give an idea of the type of information that will be made available by the project.

Testing and trials

Eighteen handpumps, each produced by a different manufacturer, are being examined by the CA laboratory, with testing in accord with the following criteria:

○ Time required for ordering and delivery.
○ Cost of pumps.
○ Suitability of packaging for export and overland transportation.
○ Engineering assessment on safety; resistance to contamination; resist-ance to abuse; ease of maintenance and repair; degree of skills required for manufacture; and suggested design improvements.
○ User preference by gender, age and size.
○ Endurance.

As an example of the laboratory tests, Table 7.1 below shows the labora-tory's assessment of a first batch of six pumps with respect to the degree of skill required for each activity in the pump manufacturing process, based on a scale of 1 ('very low level of skill required') to 5 ('very high level of skill required'). In the table the pump names are coded by the letters A to F.

With results of other laboratory tests, this table will help decision-makers to choose a pump type suitable for local manufacture, operation and maintenance. It must be emphasized that this table shows only one of a number of evaluations, and therefore cannot be used independently to assess handpump suitability.

Table 7.1 Degree of skill required to operate pumps (1 = simplest)

	Pump					
Manufacturing process	*A*	*B*	*C*	*D*	*E*	*F*
Iron foundry	3	4	–	2	4	3
Brass/gunmetal foundry	3	–	3	–	2	–
Steel forging and welding	–	3	4	2	4	3
Hot brass pressing	–	–	–	–	3	–
Sheet-metal forming	–	–	3	–	–	3
Simple machining*	2	–	3	2	3	3
Complex machinery**	–	5	3	–	–	–
Leather cutting and forming	2	–	–	2	–	–
Rubber/plastics mouldings	–	5	1	2	2	3
Woodwork	1	–	–	–	–	–
Soft soldering	–	–	–	–	2	–
Hard chrome plating	–	5	–	–	–	–
Specialized processes	–	5	–	–	–	–
Total score	11	27	17	10	20	15

* Turning, drilling, tapping, etc.
** Gear, cutting, etc.

The World Bank has prepared a series of forms for the field trials which request information on pump installation, maintenance and repair; pump operation; pump deterioration, damage and breakdown; some well and water characteristics and sociological and cultural conditions related to pump use.[54]

(*Waterlines* Vol. 1 No. 3, January 1983)

The Blair Research Laboratory's contributions to the Water Decade

PETER R. MORGAN and HARRY J. McPHERSON

For many decades, the Blair Research Laboratory, the research wing of the Ministry of Health in Zimbabwe, has undertaken practical research work related to the fields of malaria and schistosomiasis in Africa. Much of this work, especially that concerned with malaria control, has played an important part in reducing the illness caused by malaria in the region.

In the early 1970s a small unit within the laboratory began working on rural health technology, placing particular emphasis on water supply and sanitation. The unit has remained small, but its work has influenced the provision of low-cost water and sanitation technologies in Zimbabwe and elsewhere for some years. The Ventilated Improved Pit latrine, known locally as the 'Blair latrine' was pioneered in Zimbabwe more than 12 years ago. By 1976 large numbers were being built in Zimbabwe; over 100,000 have been built since that time. All rural sanitation programmes in Zimbabwe are based on the Blair latrine design.

Many low-cost water supply schemes also use Blair Research technology and these include the 'Blair pump', designed in 1976 and mass-produced in 1980, and the 'bucket pump' designed in 1982 and put into mass-production in 1984. A water-wheel pump designed in 1979 shows promise for use in irrigation schemes and a swing pump has been designed to use 'child energy' to pump water.

In addition, a considerable amount of practical research has been undertaken on small- and medium-sized sand filters for use in rural areas, as a means of purifying heavily contaminated surface water. Bacteriological studies have been undertaken for many years on these filters and also from water extracted from wells and tube-wells of different types. These studies have made it possible to upgrade very traditional methods of raising water so that its quality is very much improved. Recently, more use has been made of a locally designed and manufactured hand-operated drilling rig, which permits villagers to drill their own tube-wells. The laboratory has encouraged any efforts which allow more community participation. The drilling rig, designed by a local manufacturer, facilitates full participation by the villagers. A sense of ownership results, which has beneficial effects on the long-term care and maintenance of the installations.

Using schools

The laboratory has been able to introduce many of these technologies into the primary and secondary school curricula in Zimbabwe, so that techniques related to water supply and sanitation become familiar to future generations. Several films on the technologies have been made by the Ministry of Information, these are shown by the mobile cinemas which tour the country. For many years laboratory staff have taken on large numbers of training programmes where local builders and craftsmen are trained in the various techniques which offer the most practical answer to water and sanitation problems in their areas.

Training schemes allow the practical fruits of research to be channelled directly into the rural areas. The Ministry of Health has always played a vital part in this process—and is actively participating in Decade plans at present. Some provinces in Zimbabwe are constructing up to 6,000 new latrines every year for rural folk under the direct supervision of the Ministry of Health, with the villagers themselves playing a major role in the development plan. A great deal of emphasis is now being placed on the maintenance of water-supply schemes, and training techniques have been developed by laboratory staff. One such scheme includes deliberately dismantling the

A Zimbabwean woman uses a Bucket Pump, a modernized version of the traditional bucket and windlass, developed by Blair Research in Harare (Blair Research Laboratory)

Handpumps designed especially for heavy use in villages can also be operated by children. Sri Lanka (UNICEF/Vivianne Holbrooke)

The Blair Pump — a simple light-duty pump designed for the family or small community. Down-the-hole components are made of PVC (Blair Research Laboratory)

simple Blair handpumps. Trainees under instruction follow a route through the rural areas where the pumps, pre-broken, are waiting for repair, under the close scrutiny of their fellow trainees and members of the Ministry of Health. This very practical 'nuts and bolts' approach takes precedence over teaching techniques involving written materials, although these, too, are available. Builders learn about latrines by building them; they learn about pumps by breaking and repairing them. The Blair Laboratory has built a training centre at the Henderson Research Station near Mazowe.

Emphasis on simplicity

Blair Research staff have always emphasized the importance of simplicity and relate this to elegance of design. When they develop a design, every attempt is made to reduce the number of parts to the bare minimum. It was once said, 'The designer knows he has reached perfection, *not* when there is no longer anything to add, but when there is no longer anything to take away.' This principle is nowhere better illustrated than in the Blair latrine, which is little more than a common pit latrine fitted with a ventilation pipe.[59]

The Blair pump also uses very simple principles; it is little more than two pipes, one fitted inside the other, with a non-return valve at the lower end of each pipe. The earliest pumps were made for heavy-duty use and were all handbuilt from standard fittings. Later, mass-produced models were designed for lighter use by an extended family of up to 50 people.

The Blair pump has no levers and no water-seals. The outer pipe works like a cylinder, the inner pipe like a long piston. The inner pipe also acts as a push-rod and water spout; water comes out of the handle on the downstroke. Pipes of PVC are used underground while steel is used for parts above ground. When the push-rod/spout is pushed down, the valve at the base of the cylinder pipe closes and the water is under pressure, forced past the descending valve at the base of the inner pipe. Water is thus forced up the inner pipe to the surface. Pumps of this type can deliver water from a 12 m-deep well and yield between 15 to 25 litres of water per minute depending on depth and the strength of the operator. Like the latrine, local designers have interpreted and built Blair pumps in their own way: the principle is sound, so the precise method of construction is less important.

The simplicity of the Blair pump design was deliberate. If the design is simple, so is maintenance. A complete pump can be taken out of the ground and all the parts replaced within a few minutes. The rising main unscrews from the concrete head-block and the pump can be fully dismantled for inspection. There are no nuts and bolts, and upper and lower valves are identical and are thus interchangeable.   The Blair pump has had its teething problems. The first 1,500 pumps mass-produced by a commercial company, were subject to breakdown due to a defective thread assembly joining a plastic part to a metal one in the head. The head assembly has now been substantially improved by making it entirely of metal and the valve design made more efficient and robust. A full tool-kit is available from the manufacturer, which includes a simple spanner, a saw and spare parts. When placed in the right setting, this simple pump provides good service at a very low cost. A 6 m pump commercially produced currently costs about US $90. This is much less than the cost of other pumps.

In an attempt to simplify water-lifting even further, Blair Research staff designed a 'bucket pump' and successfully coupled it to their hand-operated drilling rig.

The bucket pump consists of a cylindrical 'bucket' about 400 mm long which fits inside the 150 mm casing of a drilled well. The bucket is raised and lowered using a windlass and has a valve at the bottom. When the bucket enters the water, the valve opens and the bucket fills. When the bucket is raised the valve closes and the water is lifted to the surface. The bucket must be raised three times to fill the standard container used by women in Zimbabwe.

The bucket and windlass is the most common technique for raising water from wells in many parts of the developing world. It is perhaps the most successful water-lifting device, but it often allows water to be contaminated when transferred from one container to another. The design of the bucket pump ensures that the bucket and chain rarely touch the ground, and the head of the well or tube-well is well-protected against surface contamination. The bacteriological quality of water raised by these simple devices is very similar to that extracted from handpumps, and thus makes it suitable for improved water-supply installations. Maintenance and repair can be carried out locally.

The bucket pump can be made by local craftsmen, but is also mass-produced like all Blair designs. Currently, bucket pumps are being prepared for a water project in the Masvingo Province of Zimbabwe funded by the German agency GTZ. Because the system is very similar to those in traditional use, it is hoped that it will be understood by local people. It will then be easier to maintain than many of the complex handpumps currently being imposed on the developing world.

Each development made by the laboratory has been described in a Blair Research Bulletin. However, the research staff are very clear that what might apply to Zimbabwe does not necessarily apply elsewhere. There is an ever-increasing need for researchers within each developing country to tackle the technical and developmental problems of that country, and to rely less on the outside world. Self-reliance is all important to development and national pride.

The Blair Research Laboratory's work within the Ministry of Health in Zimbabwe aims to improve public health country-wide. The provision of the hardware alone is not sufficient to have a substantial impact on health, and other aspects of an integrated primary health care programme also play an important part. No programme of health improvement can possibly have any impact if the community, and especially the young, are malnourished. Neither can any family attain good health without the help of immunization programmes against such killers as measles and tuberculosis.

Health education is of prime importance at the grass-roots level, as simply providing a tap cannot improve people's standards of hygiene. The Blair Research Laboratory has encouraged health education campaigns based around its water and sanitation technology. These are carried out through the schools. Often, very simple factors act as stimuli for development. In Zimbabwe, for instance, the Blair latrine is popular *because* it doubles as a washroom. Family wells are popular because they make it possible to plant a vegetable garden nearby. Themes of this type are actively being introduced into the school curricula.

(*Waterlines* Vol. 4 No. 1, July 1985)

Malaysian villagers comment on simple plastic handpumps

GOH SING YAU and LOW KWAI SIM

Handpumps made from PVC could provide an interim solution to the problem of village water supply in Malaysia and other countries. Not only is the use of plastic parts technically feasible, but a preliminary study of village users indicates a high degree of satisfaction with plastic pumps supplied by the University of Malaya (UM).

The Government of Malaysia hopes eventually to supply piped water to the country's 13 million people. But right now less than half of rural Malaysian households have piped water and it will probably take a few decades to achieve this. In the meantime, handpumps remain one of the cheapest and simplest ways to supply potable water to the more than 833,000 households that still have to rely on traditional sources such as streams and rain-water.

Since the 1960s, the Ministry of Health has been installing imported, cast-iron handpumps as part of its rural water-supply programme. But their reliability has been dismal. Although some pumps are relatively inexpensive, Ministry staff have found that they rarely work properly for more than a year. Moreover, spare metal parts are hard to come by and this means some pumps are cannibalized, then abandoned to keep others in working order.

In 1979, the Ministry of Health joined forces with the Department of Mechanical Engineering at UM to try to overcome these difficulties. With funding from the IDRC, a Canadian public corporation that supports scientific research for the benefit of Third World countries, development work began on an appropriate pump for rural use. As a potential substitute for the imported models, it had to be easy to operate and maintain, and capable of being manufactured locally at low cost.

Academic institutions such as universities are rarely seen as the best places to look for practical solutions to practical problems. Academics, it is sometimes argued, tend to concentrate on the theoretical aspects of technology and ignore its less glamorous side—implementation. But UM's approach to handpump development has been a multi-disciplinary one involving three university departments, government personnel and a production expert from local industry.

Canadian prototype

A lightweight PVC handpump was developed in the late 1970s by IDRC's Health Sciences Division in collaboration with mechanical and chemical engineers at the University of Waterloo, in Canada (Figure 7.2). This prototype was the raw material from which the Malaysian model was developed. UM's design retains a number of essential elements of the Waterloo model. First, the pump uses a piston equipped with two polyethylene ring seals to draw water. Secondly, most of the below-ground components are made of PVC. But the design details of the below-ground components such as the piston, rings and valves have been optimized for maximum mechanical efficiency. The above-ground components such as the handle, leverage system, spout and casting have been developed according to local needs and the availability of materials; thus the design is still evolving. After the first year of the project, in which the UM pump design was adapted, a two-year production and testing phase began. Seventeen prototype pumps were fabricated and tested in two rural areas. Kuala Pilan (in Negri Sembilan) and Malim Nawar (in Perak). Installation and subsequent maintenance were carried out by personnel from the University and the Ministry of Health.

The project ended in 1982. By that time, the pumps had withstood two years of everyday use and had required only minor maintenance and repair. Only the PVC cylinders had worn substantially, but subsequent design modifications reduced this problem.[55]

It should be noted that while theft and vandalism of above-ground parts have not been a problem in Malaysia where social discipline is good, engineers in other countries around the world may have to design the visible components of their handpumps with these human foibles in mind.

The UM design has three major advantages over the traditional cast-iron designs. First, the handpump is easy to fabricate because PVC parts can be solvent-welded together and worked on with light hand-tools. This, of course, opens up the important possibility of large-scale local manufacture, thus avoiding the need to import. Secondly, it is feasible for villagers to

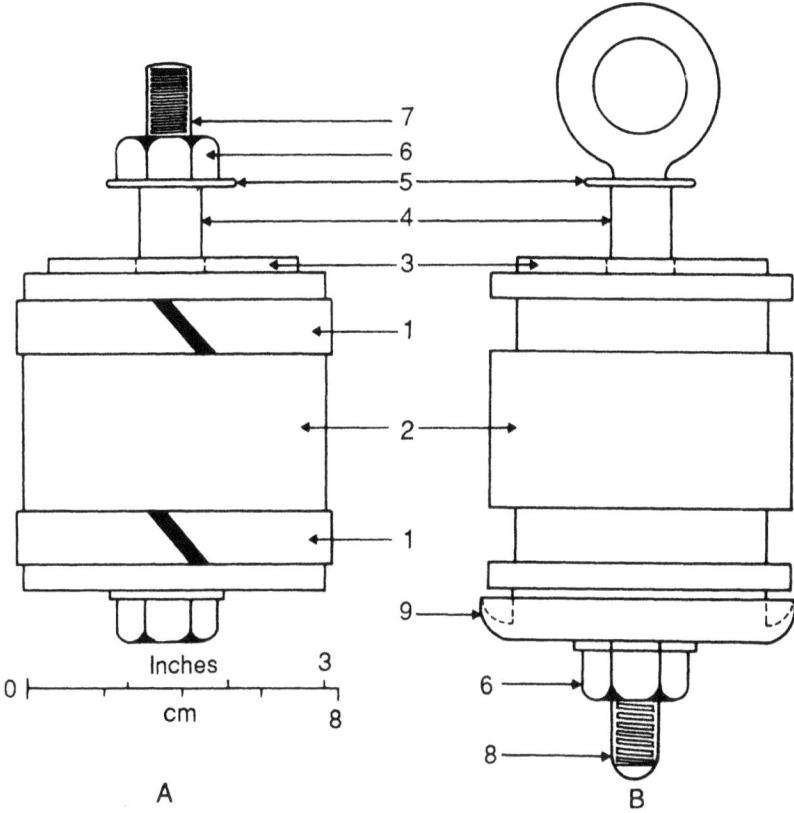

Figure 7.2   *The Waterloo handpump: (A) Piston and (B) foot-valve assembly (1) polyethylene ring; (2) piston; (3) PVC plate valve; (4) brass valve guide; (5) flat washer; (6) nut; (7) bolt; (8) bolt with eye; and (9) polyethylene foot-valve adapter*

maintain the pump themselves because PVC is light and the main components—the foot-valve, piston and piston rod—can be removed, inspected and repaired with relative ease. Thirdly, plastic parts do not corrode or rust.

The field tests of the 17 pumps verified the technical feasibility of the design, but UM needed to know whether or not the villagers would accept the pump. Technology, no matter how attractive in the laboratory must pass the test of user-acceptance, the first step in the development of a successful implementation strategy.

In August 1983, with IDRC support, studies were carried out to determine the acceptability of the UM pump to villagers in the Kuala Pilah district. The study area consisted of a number of traditional agricultural villages, populated mainly by paddy farmers. The total population was 869, living in 169 houses (237 households) scattered over 1,000 hectares.

The houses can be divided into the following categories: those serviced with piped drinking water (35 per cent); those with handpumps including the UM design (41 per cent); those with shared wells (12 per cent) and those relying on traditional water sources such as the river and rain (12 per cent).

A total of 160 survey participants, each from a different family, were selected and categorized according to a number of factors including age, educational level, and number of children. They were broken up into eight groups of 20, each consisting of 10 men and 10 women, and each group was interviewed together, as a group. The respondents were further categorized as follows: users of the UM handpumps; users of non-UM handpumps; users of UM and other types of handpump and those with no handpumps at all.

The questionnaire was designed to encourage spontaneous response from both users and non-users. Each question was based on the answer to the previous one and did not have to be answered by the same respondent. Thus, questions were designed to be a reflection of the respondents' concerns and opinions.

Consistent supply

UM pump users said their supply of water had been consistent since the pumps were installed, except during a prolonged dry spell. Because the pumps were located close to their homes, they saved much time and effort compared to fetching water from the river which was some distance away. All UM handpump users expressed satisfaction with the pumps, noting that they had never needed repairs except for the replacement of worn or broken pins on the leverage systems.

The UM pumps were considered light and easy to operate, especially by children. The water was said to be of higher quality than from metal handpumps because it was free of rust; the colour was often described as 'pure' rather than 'yellow'.

Negative views of the UM pump were few, but there were complaints regarding the low volume of water from tube-wells. There was insufficient water for festive occasions and for bathing, laundering and cleaning. Most of the users believed that the tube-wells were simply not deep enough to tap the ground water and some suggested alternative well locations. Other users blamed the shortage on the large number of households sharing each pump and asked for more to be installed.

The survey indicated a number of factors that explain the acceptance and desirability of the handpumps.

First, in areas serviced with government-installed pipes, the water supply was cut off during the rainy season. In addition to containing a level of chlorine to which the villagers could not accustom themselves, piped water was reported to be turbid and to exude a bad smell. Pumps were considered to supply good-quality water and to be more reliable and less sensitive to the vagaries of weather and government water policies.

Second, traditional sources of water, including rivers and streams, were often highly polluted and could be used only for washing and bathing. The water obtained from the pumps, on the other hand, was clean, clear, tasted good, was always cool and had no unpleasant smell. The villagers said they suffered no ill-effects from drinking pump-water.

Third, the handpumps supplied three or four houses daily with adequate water for drinking and cooking.

Fourth, the use of handpumps afforded users, especially women, the opportunity to meet and talk with their friends while performing an important daily chore. The pumps therefore encouraged social gatherings and acted as focal points for the dissemination of local news.

Finally, it should be remembered that the UM handpumps were installed free of charge. The villagers generally agreed, however, that even if they had to pay for a UM pump themselves, it would still cost less than piped water supplied by the government in both the short and the long term. For piped water, the installation charge alone would be about double the price of a UM PVC handpump.

All users said they were willing to work out a maintenance scheme both at the household and community levels so they would not have to rely on the Ministry of Health or UM personnel to carry out repairs. Furthermore, the male users demonstrated a keen interest to learn more about the installation and maintenance of the pumps. A few even asked to take a course on the subject.

Those respondents with access to non-UM handpumps complained that the devices consistently malfunctioned and were difficult for women and children to operate. It is noteworthy that in a separate survey in Kuala Selangor, 100 km north of Kuala Lumpur, all such metal handpumps proved to be out of service for several years because of malfunctions. Villagers were relying on rain and drainage canals for their water.

For comparative purposes, group interviews were also conducted in a village with no handpumps at all, Parit Empat in Kuala Selangor. Villagers there were in the habit of collecting drinking water from polluted drainage canals and supplemented their supply with rain-water. Occasionally, a van carrying potable water would come by and fill up the containers left by villagers near the roadside.

The Parit Empat respondents were shown photos of UM handpumps and asked if they would like to have one installed. As might be expected, all said yes, induced perhaps by their desperation for good-quality water they also expressed an interest in learning more about the workings of the handpump and asked for an experimental pump to be installed.

Some respondents said that if the pumps were as reliable as they thought, they would try to obtain the money from co-operatives to buy one com-munally. All showed a willingness to share the cost and maintenance of a pump among a few households even though the total price could be as much as M$300 (about US $130).

This contrasts sharply with the attitude of the respondents in Kuala Pilah. There, despite obvious satisfaction with the performance of their free handpumps, the villagers seemed reluctant to purchase the devices. For some, the claim that the handpumps are expensive may be genuine; but for others, the reluctance to pay may be for other reasons. Free installation during the pilot-testing phase may have given people the impression that handpumps are a social benefit requiring nothing in return from the bene-ficiaries.

In any event, because the UM pump components are mainly plastic, injection moulding holds great promise for the mass production of hand-pumps which can be afforded even by poor villagers. The University of Malaya, with support from IDRC, has already embarked on another important phase of the handpump's development in this vein. A commercial plastics manufacturer is to use injection moulding to produce 550 pumps for field-testing in 10 rural areas.

(*Waterlines* Vol. 3 No. 2, October 1984)

CHAPTER 8
Handpump Maintenance

In 1977, Simon Watt wrote an article for Appropriate Technology[56] which highlighted the problems and causes of the mechanical failure of village water-well pumps and outlined the redesign and development of new pumps, with particular reference to the hydraulically operated 'Vergnet' handpump. The article dates from the publication of an Oxfam document compiled by Arnold Pacey.[47]

An early conclusion of the UNDP/World Bank Handpumps' Project was that strong involvement of the user community in maintenance was essential. Hence the development of the VLOM (Village Level Operation and Maintenance) concept. Handpump maintenance systems can be differentiated by the number of levels or tiers in their organizational structure. In a one-tier system, all maintenance is undertaken by a single entity, usually a central organization or the community itself. In the two-tier system, the work is shared by the community and another agency. In the three-tier system, a local authority also assumes responsibility for specific maintenance operations.

The first three articles of this chapter deal specifically with the India Mark II handpump, developed in close collaboration with UNICEF, with alternative approaches to maintenance. Jim Baldwin reports on the Indian experience with the government three-tier maintenance system comprising a village caretaker, a 'block' inspector-mechanic for every 60 to 100 villages and a four-man mobile unit at district level covering five to ten blocks. Sanjit Roy advocates the one-tier system developed by the Tilonia Social Work Research Centre involving repair and maintenance by a village youth, trained and employed by the community. In the third article, Ken Gray responds to Sanjit Roy and refers to a further alternative, the two-tier system which eliminates the block mechanics by having mobile maintenance teams at the block level.

In the final article, Will Lynch describes his work as a rural water supply technician with the US Peace Corps in Morocco, where he worked on a handpump rehabilitation programme.

Continuing development of handpumps to satisfy VLOM standards will inevitably reduce dependence on central government support by facilitating maintenance at village level.

The Indian Mark II handpump and its three-tier maintenance system

GEORGE BALDWIN

India has now about 12 years' experience developing and testing an in-novative maintenance programme for deep-well handpumps, a technology notorious for its failures. The new programme appears to have overcome years of failure and discouragement with earlier types of handpumps and maintenance systems. The lessons from India should have much relevance for any country using large numbers of handpumps in boreholes of 15 to 100 m depth.

There are five factors underlying the Indian experience:

○ The design of a new type of handpump with far lower maintenance requirements.
○ Rigid control of pump manufacturing standards to assure very high quality control.
○ A high standard of initial pump installation.
○ The careful design of a three-tier maintenance organization that depends on district-level four-man mobile units.
○ Top-level government recognition of the maintenance problem and a commitment to finance the programme's recurring costs. These costs are estimated at about US $30 per well per year, roughly one-sixth the usual cost of maintaining deep-well handpumps.

The Indian system has been developed in close co-operation with UNICEF, which has played a major role in development and financing. By the end of 1982, UNICEF had signed standard maintenance 'Plan of Operations' agreements with a quarter of India's 22 states. A standard technology and maintenance system is therefore being encouraged in the regions of India where the deep-well handpump is the chosen technology today.

Since about 70 per cent of India has similar hydrogeological conditions (a thick soil overburden on a hard-rock base), the following description has wide application in the country. Indian conditions, technology, capital and recurring costs, and maintenance requirements differ markedly from neigh-bouring Bangladesh, with which some comparison is instructive.

Developing the technology

For many years over much of India, state governments have been drilling boreholes and fitting them with cast-iron handpumps of traditional design. And, for many years, the performance record of these handpumps has been shockingly bad, with half or more normally out of service. Survey data are not available but the word of knowledgeable observers gives overwhelming

INDIA MARK II PUMP-HEAD

Inspection cover

Self locking bolt

Machine chain

Coupling x lock

Guide only no gland required

Riser Pipe to this point

Vandal proof spout

Solid sq. bar handle
8:1 advantage

Heavy duty stops

Sealed ball bearings

All bolts std. $^1/_2$" Whit
c/w lock nuts

Pedestal 6" Shrouds
Standard casing pipe

Installation mark

Level of platform

Angle iron Spragg legs

Base grouted
to this depth

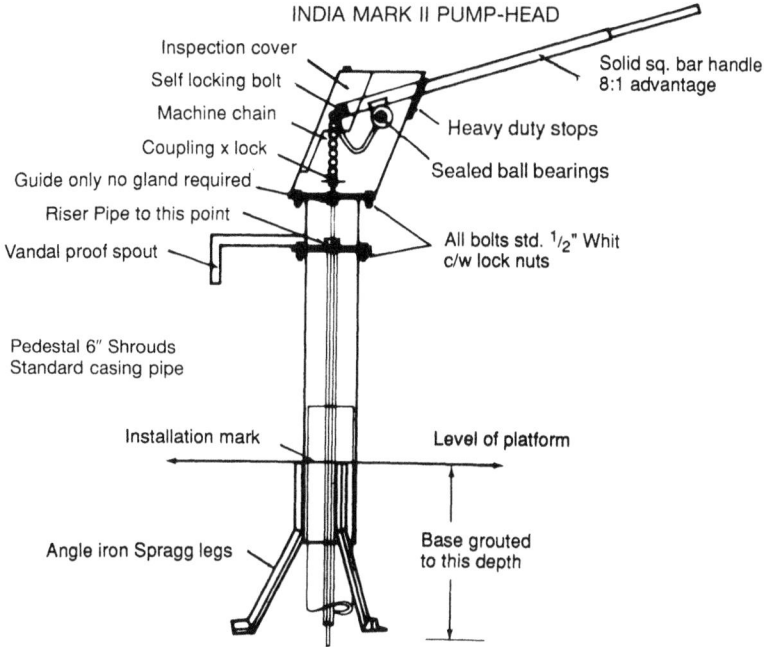

Figure 8.1   *The India Mark II pump-head*

evidence. These observers have always been field personnel rather than the higher-level officials who control resources and make investment decisions. On the rare occasions when such officials visited handpump installations, they were shown the minority of pumps that worked.

It required persistent educational activity by UNICEF to drive home the truth. Tamil Nadu in the south and Madhya Pradesh and Marashtra in the central plateau were the first states to take steps to improve handpump services, and it is here that most of the progress has been made.

When the new maintenance scheme was first announced and established in Tamil Nadu in August 1976, it was an order issued by the Governor himself; this gave the programme the highest political backing.

UNICEF has written an account of the pump redesign effort of the 1970s which has led to the present Mark II pump, which describes the weak points of traditional handpumps and how these have been eliminated in the Mark II. The result is a pump-head (the part above ground), which is expected to need no servicing for a span of 12 months (Figure 8.1).

Considerable progress has been made in the pump's down-the-hole cylinder, now based on an adaptation of the American Dempster pump's cast-iron shell with a polished brass lining. The difficulty of getting leather 'buckets' that have been properly tanned and impregnated has made this the weakest element in the whole system. Many cylinders do not stand up to the planned 12 months' operation planned for by the preventive-maintenance schedule, forcing mobile teams off their schedules to give corrective maintenance.

Although some attention has been paid to redesigning the cylinder, it has not received nearly as much attention as the pump-head. The aim is to design a cylinder that will either require infrequent maintenance or can be drawn up without pulling the rising main (this would allow village- or block-level personnel to make most of the repairs). While block mechanics, with village help, can sometimes pull up the rods and rising main to reach the cylinder, the task usually has to await the mobile team.

In addition to the design improvements which have eliminated the major friction points, the Mark II is manufactured to rigid standards and must be carefully installed: but not more carefully than a well-supervised public health engineering crew can easily learn.

Despite considerable pressure to award contracts to several suppliers, UNICEF originally refused to approve more than two firms as suppliers (Richardson and Cruddas in Madras and Inalsa, a subsidiary of the Delhi Cloth Mills in Delhi). Attempts were made to use other, small-scale firms but these proved unable to meet the rigid standards laid down. UNICEF does not itself inspect supplies delivered by the manufacturers; it has delegated this task to the UK Crown Agents, which has officers competent not only to spot defects but also to go back to the manufacturing process to identify the source of defects and help put them right.

Since 1979, some 11 or 12 additional Indian firms have been accepted as producers—one in most of the states in which the Mark II has become standard technology. This expansion of the manufacturing base, after an initial failure, has been made possible by technical assistance from the Crown Agents. The Crown Agents are paid 2 to 7 per cent of the ex-factory price for their services. A few producers have won small export orders, but the Mark II has not yet become an important export item. Nor is it yet manufactured anywhere outside India, despite the fact that it is not protected by patent and that designs are available to anyone wishing to manufacture it.

Features of the Mark II

It is worth calling attention to some of the features of the Mark II (Figure 8.3). It is made from welded steel plates, not cast iron. This gives more strength per kg of material and greater uniformity in fabrication; it also rusts, unlike cast iron. The original anti-rust treatment was to use an epoxy paint on sand-blasted metal. This was not good enough: when Britain's Consumers' Association testing laboratory found that the pump was susceptible to rust, UNICEF and the Crown Agents moved to hot-dip galvaniz-

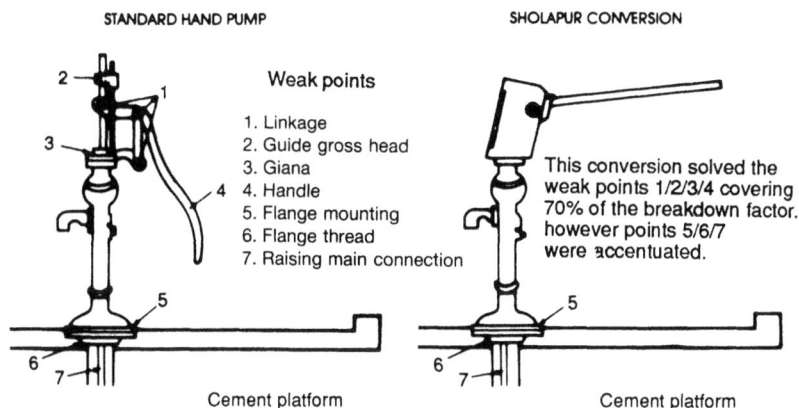

Figure 8.2   *The original standard handpump design and the Sholapur head, showing improvements*

ing. This increased the pump unit-cost by nearly 10 per cent.

The number of fulcrum points has been reduced to one, which rotates in a sealed ball-bearing with a life of several years. Thus, there are no points which need oiling or greasing. It was a Swedish engineer, working for a voluntary agency in Maharashtra in the early seventies, who deserves the credit for this critical innovation which led to the 'Sholapur' head (Figure 8.2).

The handle is a mild-steel bar with an 8:1 mechanical advantage. A normal pump handle has an advantage of around 4:1. This improvement allows one person to lift a column of water 20 to 25 m in height with ease. When the water-table is at these depths, conventional pumps often require two or more adults to pull the handle which, in addition to being harder work than some can perform, exerts great strain on several pump parts.

The pump is not attached to the well casing; it is embedded independently in concrete. This means there are no base-plate nuts and bolts to come loose, and no possibility of contaminated water finding its way into the well.

Except where the handle enters the head, the latter is completely enclosed. Children cannot drop pebbles into the mechanism, which is sometimes a source of trouble.

With the change from a hollow pipe handle to a solid bar handle, most of the shock-loading was eliminated from the connecting rods, resulting in a substantial reduction in failures in this area.

The pump's attachment to the concrete platform is strengthened by iron legs (sprags) set at an angle to the pedestal. The casing pipe is no longer under stress as it is not attached to the pedestal. This 'sprag' mounting has

CWD—M

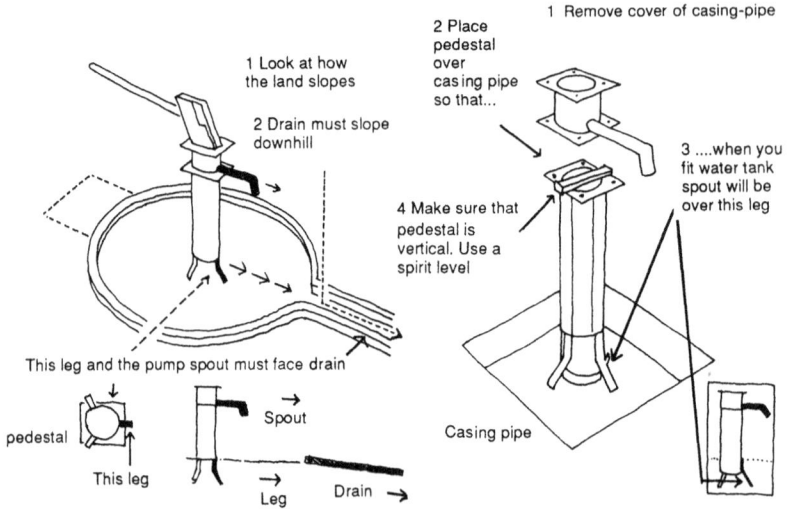

Figure 8.3   *Key aspects of installing the Mark II (UNICEF, Delhi)*

also reduced failures in the top connection of the rising main, if installation is properly carried out.

In early 1979 a complete Mark II, including cylinder, rising main, and connecting rods, cost US $182 of which the pumphead itself accounted for about one-third. The Mark II costs less than an imported pump and only modestly more than a conventional Indian-made cast-iron pump with much lower reliability. The estimated annual recurrent cost per well fitted with a Mark II is about US $30. This includes full cash costs of the mobile units and their district workshops but excludes any allowance for vehicle or building depreciation.

This compares with an estimated US $5 a year for the shallow wells of Bangladesh: however, the latter cover only about one-quarter or one-fifth the number of households served by a typical Mark II, so the recurrent cost per family is almost the same. The Indian maintenance structure requires much more costly inputs (motor vehicles and mobile teams compared with single individuals on a bicycle) but because the Indian pumps now require less maintenance, the mobile teams can look after five times as many units, spread over much larger areas, as their bicycle-mounted counterparts in Bangladesh. Thus the costs per beneficiary (that is, per family or per capita, not per well) of these quite different handpump technologies look surprisingly similar, for both capital and recurrent costs. This means that the per capita burden on public budgets in the two countries would be roughly similar.

Maintenance system

At the end of 1982 there were some 150,000 Mark II pumps in operation in 14 Indian states. These were being maintained, in large part, by 230 mobile teams: the key element is a three-tier maintenance system. The latter consists of a village caretaker, a block inspector-mechanic with tools and a bicycle for every 60 to 100 villages, and a four-man mobile unit at district level (comprising 5 to 10 blocks) where there is a small district workshop for the overhaul of pumps, cylinders and rods.

With the three-tier system, primary responsibility for mechanical maintenance lies outside the village with the mobile units. This is a radical change from the earlier system with the old, 'unimproved' handpumps: the state government had built the wells but then turned over complete responsibility for their maintenance to the villages. That system simply had not worked.

The new system does indeed preserve roles for two layers of maintenance staff below the mobile units—a village-level caretaker and a block-level mechanic (sometimes referred to as an inspector).

The caretaker (normally an unpaid literate youth who does something else for a living and who has been given two days training for this job) is primarily responsible for 'housekeeping' around the well, especially for seeing that the drainage system works properly to prevent the build-up of muddy areas and of stagnant water-pools that support mosquito-breeding. The caretaker's training also includes some simple health education. His second main responsibility is to notify the block mechanic and the mobile team when anything goes wrong. He does this by sending off pre-printed, pre-stamped, and pre-addressed postcards on which he has to write nothing, only make a tick mark against the appropriate space (Figure 8.4).

There are some situations, however, in which caretakers may be expected and competent to perform minor mechanical operations, such as regularly tightening nuts and bolts at those pumps which have been 'converted' by the attachment of a new Mark II head to the old cast-iron pedestal. This is an interim measure designed to improve the performance (and lower the maintenance requirements) of old but still useable pumps until production of the Mark II's increases to the point where old pumps can be replaced. The caretaker can easily carry out this sort of inspection with one or two tools.

Caretakers are initially appointed by block development officers on the basis of nominations made by the 'gram sevaks' (community development workers responsible to the block development officers); thus they are not responsible to any village-level authority. Indeed, the literature on the promotion of the new handpump programme and its maintenance scheme gives much more emphasis to spreading understanding of the programme among lower-level government officers than it does to the formal lines of responsibility for tube-wells within the village.

Formally, the wells and pumps belong to the state government (through

Three-tier maintenance vs VLOM

The Indian three-tier system is one approach to keeping as many handpumps as possible in operation at once. Another is the village level operation and maintenance (VLOM) concept formulated by an international panel of experts brought together under the UNDP/ World Bank Handpumps Project.

The idea of VLOM is that it should be possible for a village caretaker to carry out routine maintenance with the minimum of tools and equipment. This would reduce the high costs incurred under the three-tier system by heavily-equipped mobile teams which have to travel great distances from their base. It has been estimated that the average annual maintenance cost of a single handpump in India is $200. This figure implies a bill of $300 m a year for maintenance alone if the 1.5 m new pumps needed to meet India's Water Decade target are installed.

The main barrier to the Indian Mark II pump being compatible with VLOM is that the rising main is of galvanized iron and requires special lifting equipment to withdraw it from the well for down-the-hole repairs. For a 30 m-deep well, the main may weigh 130 kg. Much work is in progress to modify the Mark II or develop other pumps to overcome this.

For instance, Inalsa, one of the two original manufacturers of the Mark II in India, has brought out a modification in which the piston can be drawn up through the riser pipe by one person in a short time, assisted by using a rising main with an internal diameter greater than the plunger diameter. Water can thus drain past the suction valve and the operator does not have to lift the weight of the water as well as the hardware. This makes it a lot easier to replace the fastest-wearing parts—the leather cup washers that seal the piston. Inalsa also gives the option of replacing the standard galvanized iron pipe with rigid PVC or *abs* plastic. The reciprocating steel connecting rods are kept central in the raiser main by specially-designed spacers. Without spacers the rods might damage the internal surface of the plastic pipe when they flex over the 25 to 80 m total depth.

In Malawi, the locally-manufactured Maldev pump allows all down-the-hole components to be withdrawn through the pump-head. It is spreading into the other African countries, where it is known as the Afridev.

its designated water-supply agency); responsibility for their maintenance is put squarely on the shoulders of the state, not the village. Largely because the technology is different, this evolving Indian system is a much more

Date ....

Sir | ஐயா,   Panchayat ....

The following repairs are noticed in the hand pump No. ... ...

...... எண் உள்ள கைப்பம்பில் கீழ்கண்ட குறைபாடுகள உள்ளன

1 G. I. Rod cut (கம்பி துண்டாதல்)

2 Pipe loosening (குழாய் கழலுதல்)

3 Cylinder fall (சிலிண்டர் விழுதல்)

4 Cylinder repair (சிலிண்டரில் பழுது)

5 Repairs in top end mechanism
   (மேல் பகுதி இயந்திர பழுதுகள்)

Signature

Figure 8.4 *Caretaker's postcard for notifying faults in handpumps (Tamil Nadu)*

'top-down' system than found, for example, in Bangladesh where nature permits use of shallow-well technology.

Above the village caretaker is an inspector-mechanic, a paid full-time tradesman who works from the block headquarters. His territory will normally include 50 wells, which he is supposed to visit on a fixed schedule, roughly every two weeks. The inspector-mechanic can fix most problems that arise in the pump-head but he cannot deal with problems down the well or perform any masonry repairs that require cement. He also provides a surer source of notification to the district engineer than the caretakers' postcards.

The block mechanics existed before the mobile units were created and formerly represented the only outside help available to village authorities. A key problem with the old system was the sheer physical difficulty—often impossibility—of transporting the heavy tools, and some parts, needed to attend to any problems that arose down the well.

Mobile Unit

'Pulling' a rising main, the connecting rods, and the cylinder requires more tools and equipment than it was realistic to expect a mechanic to transport around on a bicycle, often over very bad roads and in rainy weather. The inevitable result was that the work almost never got done and the majority of pumps fell into disuse.

The district-level 'mobile unit' is the new, and key, element in the modernized and tube-well maintenance programme. Theoretically the teams consist of four men, a diesel pick-up truck, and a small workshop at their district office. Each team is issued three sets of tools, two for carrying on the jeep or pick-up truck, one for the workshop.

One of the vehicle sets consists of specially designed tools for installing the Mark II pump and for pulling up cylinders and rods. The team members consist of a mechanic, a helper, a mason, and a driver (in India, drivers function only as drivers, preventing use of a three-man team). The team is responsible to a junior engineer in the state water-agency. In some states this is a specialized agency; in others it is part of a multi-purpose public health engineering department. Each team is expected to look after 500 to 600 tube-wells, doing both preventive and corrective maintenance. Until the number of 'converted' pumps is reduced to almost zero by the installation of Mark IIs, corrective maintenance dominates preventive maintenance. Eventually it is hoped that the mobile units will have to visit each well no more than once a year, mainly for preventive-maintenance work: pulling up and replacing the cylinder, inspecting the pump-head and making any necessary cement repairs.

This planned system calls for a strategy of exchanging broken pumps and *all* cylinders for new or reconditioned units, rather than trying to do repairs in the field. This service-exchange strategy saves time in the field, and moves repairs closer to stocks of spare parts. Besides, better repair work can be done in a workshop than in the field. This policy requires that the mobile team carries somewhat larger stocks of components. It also means that the actual task of repairing and reconditioning broken units becomes seasonal, since the personnel who do this work at the district workshop are also the members of the mobile team. The latter can do the workshop tasks only on days when they do not go into the field—the rainy season creates many such days.

Although the service-exchange system is recommended practice, so far the majority of the units have been unable to follow it because they have too many pumps to look after. With a high ratio of pumps per unit, the latter is under pressure to be in the field for more of the year than planned, reducing the time available to carry out reconditioning work at the workshop. The system cannot afford the cost of carrying a large stock of extra cylinders, or the labour cost of adding permanent workshop staff to keep up with the reconditioning in order to hold down those stock costs. Indeed, many of the mobile teams do not yet have a workshop to allow the service-exchange system to operate. So the service-exchange scheme is more an ideal than a well-established practice today, except for the minority of districts where the wells-per-team ratio is low. In practice, a majority of teams are forced to do all repairs on-site.

(*Waterlines* Vol. 1 No. 4, April 1983)

A one-tier system: the Tilonia approach to handpump maintenance

SANJIT ROY

The precise number of villages in India lacking safe drinking water is still a matter of speculation. A 'problem' village is defined as one:

○ Which does not have an assured source of drinking water within a distance of 1.6 km.
○ Where the source of drinking water is susceptible to water-borne diseases like cholera and Guinea worm.
○ Where the water has excessive salinity, iron or fluorides.

In 1972 to 73, 152,000 villages were identified as problem villages. By 1978 when the Planning Commission of India was optimistic that 96,000 villages had been covered, a revised list was submitted which stated that 190,000 villages still lacked safe drinking water in 1979 to 80. By the winter session of Parliament in 1982 the number had in fact *increased* to 213,000 villages. Six months later in the next session of Parliament, the number of villages suffering remained the same.

The reasons why this deplorable state of affairs continues to plague rural communities are explained in the Planning Commission's sixth Five Year Plan for 1980 to 85, which states:

'Lack of involvement of the local communities in the maintenance arrangements, shortage of staff and inadequate funds are the main reasons why the existing water-supply schemes have failed to yield the expected results. It is clear that the operation of the small rural water supply system can only be ensured with the participation of the village community. It has been noticed that wherever maintenance arrange-ments have been adequate the beneficiaries are not unwilling to pay a nominal charge for the water supplied to them. The effort should be in all cases to recover at least the operating expenses.'

The Government, with UNICEF, has opted for a three-tier maintenance system to tackle this and one hears that it has worked in many parts of the country (see previous article). But it is too vast a problem to be left to the engineers and experts alone. By far the most serious flaw in this main-tenance system is the marginal and cosmetic involvement of the community which will actually be using the handpump. The 'experts' have come up with the idea of a caretaker who is normally an unpaid youth doing something else for a living and who, after being given two days' training, is responsible for keeping the handpump clean, the bolts tightened and also doing some health education. For any major repair he corresponds with the block mechanic by a system of postcards.

It is immediately evident that the three-tier system has been designed by engineers and economists who have never lived and worked in a village. They have never experienced what it is like to live without safe water for months because the handpump is out of order, when neither the block mechanic nor district maintenance units have shown the slightest interest in responding to repeated calls from the community.

Community contribution

The three-tier system is yet another example of one designed by people who do not have confidence in the community. It has not made allowances or used the knowledge and skills available in the village itself and, quite clearly, it has ignored the fact that villagers do not appreciate what is given free and feel that things which are set up by the government are not really theirs. The stability, continuity and credibility of any community-based programme depends on two critical issues: the extent to which the continuity contributes towards the programme in both cash and kind and how much village knowledge, skills and experiences are used for the people's own development.

Since 1981, when the Social Work Research Centre (SWRC) at Tilonia started installing handpumps to provide safe drinking water in Rajasthan, financial contributions from communities have reached over Rs 100,000. More than 300 handpumps have been installed in 'scheduled caste' and backward communities, schools and dispensaries. Communities have contributed cement, material and labour for construction of the pumps' foundations totalling more than Rs 50,000.

A handpump costs Rs 10,000 and it is not too much to ask for a poor community to contribute Rs 300. Indeed, it is an exercise in building-up pride and self-respect as this response has been observed in many areas: 'This is our pump. We paid for it. No one had better touch it without our permission.' In many villages the village mason has rejected the UNICEF design of the foundation and improvised his own with a kerb on which village women can stand their earthen pots.

The question that has been constantly asked by the community is *who owns the pump?* Using the Tilonia system the answer is clear: 'the community, because it has paid for it.'

But with Government handpumps installed free of charge it is far from clear. The community has no stake in the handpump and the Government has made it clear that the pump is Government property. This is again reflected in the three-tier system where neither the block mechanic nor the district maintenance unit will allow the community to act on their own initiative and get the pump repaired by someone in the village. Why? Because the person is not trained.

One-tier system

These are some of the issues that were responsible for the birth of the one-tier system. It came gradually and grew out of the SWRC's handpump programme. The ideas came from the community using the pumps: the SWRC only laid it out in an organized manner and, with government support, provided the institutional framework to make it work.

The idea grew out of a discussion in a village tea-shop. Among those having tea with us was the owner of a cycle repair shop. He saw the UNICEF district maintenance team zooming past and said, 'All for a washer in a handpump! Isn't it too silly for words? We have wayside machine shops in large villages repairing tractors, diesel and electrical pumps, bullock carts and agricultural machiney. And the Government thinks we are incapable of changing a leather washer on a handpump! How stupid can you get? It is just another way for engineers to make money and for them to use their jeeps to go to the cinema or drop their children at school in the morning. The last thing they use it for is maintaining handpumps.'

Tilonia started experimenting to find out if it was possible for semi-literate boys to repair the 300 handpumps the SWRC had installed. We trained them initially for a month. Where the service they provided was good and efficient, covering major and minor repairs, the community was willing to pay between Rs 40 to 100 for repairing the pump. We found it just required some manual labour and common sense. We demystified the technology that goes into the repair and maintenance of handpumps:

○ A trained mechanic or degree-holder in mechanical engineering was not needed to repair handpumps. A semi-literate village youth with some training could do the same job.
○ This semi-literate village youth could carry out all major and minor repairs on the pumps. In other words he could perform the function of the caretaker, the block mechanic and the district level maintenance unit required by the three-tier system without leaving the village, given the proper training and the right set of special tools.
○ He did not need jeeps and trucks. He could do the same job on a bicycle.
○ He was in a position to persuade the community to pay for repair and maintenance.

Rajasthan's approach

With the results of this experiment we approached the Government of Rajasthan and proposed that the strategy be given serious consideration. UNICEF, for all its talk of community participation, was opposed to it from the start. The engineers from the Public Health Engineering Department (PHED) opposed it virulently on the grounds that Tilonia was over-simplifying a very complicated technical issue. They seemed to be saying

Table 8.1 Comparison of one-tier and three-tier handpump maintenance systems

Item	Three-tier system	One-tier system
Cost/pump/year to maintain	Rs 400 to 500	Rs 100 per pump Rs 50 for spares
Tools and equipment	Trucks, jeeps, heavy repair tools, special tools	Cycle, special tools
Educational qualifications	Mechanical degree holder: Diploma from Industrial Training institute	Fourth standard pass: primary school level
Personnel	Superintending engineer, executive engineer, assistant engineer, block mechanics, caretakers	Handpump *Mistri* (HPM) at the village level
Training	No long-term training programme at any level. Only orientation time for engineers and two days for caretakers	Three months' field-training under TRYSEM, two months' practical training on-site. Regular in-service training
Community participation	Marginal—at caretaker level	HPM identified and selected by the village community: priority given to scheduled castes
Community accountability	None Answerable to the Government	The village has the right to recall the HPM. If he is not working satisfactorily he can be replaced
Institutional finance	No provision Tools are free to caretakers	HPMs take a loan from the nearest bank for Rs 2,500. There is a 50 per cent subsidy if the HPM is a member of a scheduled caste

that a technical solution and a well-designed system is the answer to community participation at the village level. In fact, the response to problems is infinitely more human.

In the State of Rajasthan the three-tier system had not worked: more than 50 per cent of the 20,000 handpumps were out of order. Already, disturbing reports were coming in that handpumps installed by private contractors through the PHED were poorly installed. Poor cement and adulterated materials had been used for foundations and washers and threads on the pumps' rods were beyond repair. The Indian Government had recently declared that the community would be given more responsibility in planning and decision-making through village-elected bodies. Both these factors contributed to the decision to implement radical plans taken by the Rajasthan State Government. No other state government has so far put similar plans into practice. They are:

○ The repair and maintenance of handpumps is the responsibility of the community and not the Government.

○ A rural youth with some mechanical background (for instance cycle repair, blacksmithing, diesel-pump repair) is selected by the community and is sent for three months' training to Tilonia. He is then officially called a 'handpump *mistri*' (HPM).

○ Training is provided under a Government of India scheme called TRYSEM (Training of Rural Youth for Self Employment) and includes how to conduct major and minor repairs both above and below ground. The training is practical and on-the-spot. For two months out of the three he is under training, the HPM works on faulty pumps in the villages.

○ The HPM is not to be a Government employee, but is answerable to the community. The employment is part-time.

○ After training the HPM looks after between 36 and 40 handpumps within a radius of 5 to 10 km of the village where he is based.

○ The State Government pays the HPM Rs 100/handpump/year under his charge and Rs 50/handpump/year for replacement of spare parts. After training the HPMs get a grant of Rs 250 from the Government, under the terms of the TRYSEM scheme, to buy tools. A set of special tools costs Rs 2,500. The Government or training institution arranges for a loan from the bank so that the tools become the property of the HPM within a year.

○ Tilonia instructs trainers from Industrial Training Institutes from six other districts of Rajasthan so that the HPM system can be used all over Rajasthan for handpump maintenance.

○ HPMs are selected mainly from the socially vulnerable groups, the 'scheduled' castes. Since March 1981, 133 HPMs have been trained at Tilonia to cover the districts of Ajmer and Bhilwara in Rajasthan. Trainers from the six Industrial Training Institutes are holding their own HPM training programmes. These are not as successful as we had hoped but at least the process has begun.

The people

Aziz Mohammed is the main wage-earner of a family of nine and lives in Patan village. He is 25 years old and passed eighth standard at school. Apart from repairing cycles occasionally, he is fully trained as an HPM and knows how to use the special pump tools. Village-level health workers have discussed the importance of health education with him during his training programme. He has also put on some puppet shows in the village to help educate people to use the handpump for safe drinking water and thus help prevent water-related diseases. The State Government has allotted him 36 handpumps in two village *panchayats* (local governments). If they are kept in working order the village headman, Jawan Singh, Rajput of Badgaon village, gives a yearly certificate which Aziz takes to the *panchayat samiti* headquarters in Silora. There he collects his money from the block development officer. The village headman has been given a Sarpanch guidebook (Figure 8.5) which explains his responsibilities and functions in the monitoring of the handpump maintenance programme.

Nathu Lal, HPM from Kotri village (aged 35, educated to fourth standard, a small farmer) is convinced that a top-heavy infrastructure of chief engineers, superintending engineers and executive engineers is not really necessary if HPMs like himself are placed all over the state to repair the 30,000 handpumps.

Narpat Singh, HMP from Beeti village (aged 22, fifth standard pass, his family has nine members) was critical of his role as caretaker in the three-tier system. He was grossly underemployed and had to work free of charge

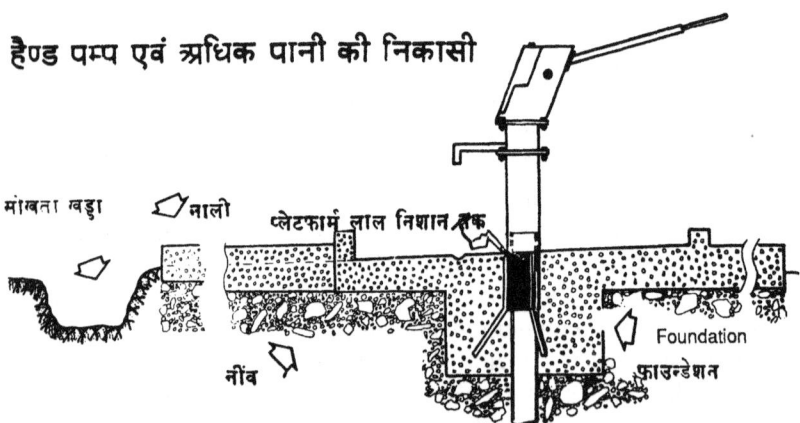

Figure 8.5 *Illustration from the Sarpanch guidebook, issued to every village leader, showing detail of handpumps installation*

(which is supposed to be an indication of community participation) when everyone above him, doing less work and with more comforts, was getting paid. Why were they not working for free as well?

Girijesh Kumar, HPM from Harmara village (aged 22, education to ninth standard, family of seven, part-time repairer of diesel pumps and electric fitter) was trained in March 1981. He rattles off the names of villages where handpumps have been out of order for months and the community is tired of sending postcards. Where is the accountability? Who else can they write to and what is the point? There should be someone closer than block level, someone they can actually go to.

HPMs, it was decided, should receive Rs 100 for each handpump they look after per year and Rs 50/handpump/year for spare parts installed. But even this small payment was criticized on grounds that the money could be misused. The critics were again showing their appalling ignorance of rural realities. Only the poorest people work without payment because they have no choice.

People who attack the one-tier system conveniently forget that what an HPM earns in one year looking after a handpump an international expert claims as his allowance for half a day's work.

(*Waterlines* Vol. 2 No. 3, January 1984)

Working towards village-based handpump maintenance—UNICEF's approach in India

KENNETH D. GRAY

If there is one thing that UNICEF has learnt from over 30 years of experience in development, it is the necessity of involving the community for the long-term success of any programme. One aspect of community involvement in the development process revolves around the operation and/or maintenance of programmes meant to improve living conditions. In India, UNICEF has been involved since 1967 in assisting the various state governments in providing drinking water to the rural areas through drilled bore-wells fitted with handpumps.

This system of water supply was identified as the most cost effective (current capital expenditure of US $7 per beneficiary) and the most capable of eventually being operated and maintained by the users themselves.

Even before the India Mark II design was finalized, UNICEF recognized the need to encourage the development of handpump maintenance systems which involved the users. In 1976, a pilot project was initiated to field-test a three-tier system (described on p. 170) in one district of Tamil Nadu. The innovative feature of this system was the participation of a volunteer village handpump caretaker (one for each pump) chosen by the villagers. The main role of the caretaker has been to help spread the message of the importance of clean drinking water and to report when the handpump needs repair; the caretaker is also expected to do some preventive maintenance.

The results from the pilot project were encouraging enough to convince the Government of India (GOI) and UNICEF to begin to advocate and promote the adoption of three-tier systems in the various states implementing this programme (each state government decides its own policies with regard to water supply). Although no state has come near to implementing fully a three-tier system, each now recognizes the need to establish an appropriate system. The skeleton maintenance infrastructures which have been established alongside the proven sturdiness of the India Mark II have resulted in villagers and government authorities regaining confidence in handpumps as a viable solution to the drinking-water problem. This in turn has helped create a foundation so that the people who benefit from the pumps can begin to take a more active role in the maintenance of their own handpumps.

By 1980, UNICEF had already begun looking at alternative methods to the three-tier maintenance system which would involve the community more. One approach was to help encourage the introduction of mechanics from the private sector to supplement the Government's efforts and thereby give villagers an alternative choice for repairing their handpumps. The idea was to use training funds under a centrally funded GOI programme for Training of Rural Youth for Self Employment (TRYSEM). In this scheme, unemployed youth receive training in various trades (such as carpentry, plumbing and mechanics) and assistance in obtaining a bank loan and necessary tools in order to take up their chosen trade.

UNICEF agreed to field-test this scheme with the Social Work and

---

India Mark II

Unfortunately, the first ten years of experience (1967 to 77) with handpump systems brought only limited success due, in large part, to the poor quality of the many unsuitable types of handpumps being installed by the state governments. In 1974, the Government of India requested UNICEF's assistance in the development of a sturdy, community handpump. Three years later, the India Mark II design was finalized (after one year of field testing), and in late 1977, a Government of India company began mass production. Since that time, UNICEF has been co-operating in the standardization, quality control, design improvements, and development of manufacturing units throughout the country.

Research Centre (SWRC) at Tilonia, Rajasthan. This is one of several non-governmental organizations UNICEF co-operates with in the training of handpump installation and maintenance personnel. In March 1981, the first group of 18 handpump *mistries* (mechanics) was trained at Tilonia. UNICEF assisted SWRC with technical personnel and training equipment and materials. Four of the first trainees are mentioned in Sanjit Roy's article.

Training

In the following year, several training programmes were conducted, and the curriculum was developed. The plan was to try first to introduce this system in Ajmer district (where SWRC is located) and thereby have an opportunity to work out the various problems with obtaining bank loans, purchasing appropriate tools, the distribution and provision of spare parts, and the method of payment for the *mistries*.

Before this could be done, however, the Government of Rajasthan decided in mid-1982 to abandon its maintenance system under the Public Health Engineering Department (PHED); this was not, however, a three-tier system, as caretakers had never been introduced. The maintenance responsibility was handed over to the *panchayats* who were expected in turn to hire the handpump *mistries*. UNICEF argued against abandoning the current system until a proven alternative system was ready to take its place.

A programme was worked out to begin training the 1,000 handpump *mistries* who would be needed to cover the more than 36,000 India Mark II handpumps in Rajasthan. Six Industrial Training Institutes (ITIs) in Rajasthan were selected for this purpose. An orientation programme to train the ITI instructors at SWRC was supported by UNICEF, and UNICEF has also assisted the six ITIs with training materials and special tools developed by UNICEF for easier installation and maintenance of the handpumps. Most of the *panchayats* have so far not assumed responsibility for the maintenance of their handpumps. The provision of bank loans, tools, spare parts and payment of salary is still being worked out.

By the summer of 1983, a large number of handpumps were out of order due to the lack of any maintenance and the PHED was requested to undertake a massive one-month campaign to repair all handpumps.

Evolution

Although the maintenance of all handpumps is now theoretically with the *panchayats*, a new form of the three-tier maintenance system has evolved in Rajasthan: PHED mobile maintenance teams for 'major' repairs (there are no UNICEF maintenance teams); 120 former PHED block mechanics who are being posted to block development offices under the Rural Development Department; and self-employed handpump *mistries*.

In other states, UNICEF continues to assist efforts to establish viable maintenance systems based on local conditions. For example, in Andhra Pradesh State which has a high density of India Mark II handpumps (80,000), a two-tier system—which eliminates block mechanics in favour of increased numbers of mobile maintenance teams posted at the block level—is being promoted. Furthermore, field-testing is currently underway on the use of rigid PVC rising mains-cum-cylinders for the India Mark II, so that heavy lifting gear will not be required to lift the down-the-hole parts of the pump. This should make village-based maintenance by the community itself more feasible and widespread before the end of the decade.

(Waterlines Vol. 3 No. 1, July 1984)

Handpumps in rural Morocco

WILLIAM LYNCH

To many people's surprise, handpumps are both wanted and needed in Morocco. Until 1983, this was not a widely-held belief. Instead the Government was putting emphasis on diesel-powered systems, wanting to jump from water drawn from a well in a bucket straight to piped supplies with taps. Not only did this approach miss much of the country's rural population, it was plagued by parts' shortages, a lack of maintenance and no clear-cut ownership or responsibility.

The minds of some people in the Ministries are being changed due partly to surveys conducted by Peace Corps volunteers working in concert with UNICEF and Catholic Relief Services. These surveys have not only indicated that there is a need, they have also shown there is a desire for handpumps. Subsquent work has indicated that the people are willing to contribute their own resources to mount the pumps.

History

During the early 1970s a UNICEF representative struck on the idea that handpumps could be used as the first step to development in rural parts of Morocco. Eventually, some 761 Briau Dauphines, Briau Africas and Bodin Solo 2 pumps were shipped from France to Casablanca. These pumps arrived between 1974 and 1977 and were transferred to the Provinces of Beni Mellal, Tetouan and Ouarzazate.

The Provinces were responsible for the delivery and installation of the pumps once they cleared customs. Although each pump and length of pipe was marked with its eventual destination, some pumps went as far astray as Safi, hundreds of kilometres from the nearest programme site. Because pumps were delivered incomplete and there was no programme for installation, many were left sitting in private houses, stables and municipal stock-rooms.

During the spring of 1983, Lewis Brittain (a fellow Peace Corps volunteer) and the author toured the Province of Ouarzazate to appraise UNICEF of the current situation and develop a parts list. We visited 215 sites, 11 store-rooms and accounted for 339 of the 432 pumps originally designated for the Province. It was found that 89 pumps had been installed and subsequently removed; 42 pumps were working (including 13 that we repaired); 47 pumps were still mounted, but not working; and 161 pumps had never been installed.

We did not visit all the sites listed on the manifest of even the Province's own tally sheet because the provincial technician accompanying us deemed it impractical to make 100 km trips to see one pump, on roads that even our Land Rover could not handle safely. Later, I discovered that some villagers were afraid we would remove the pump if they showed it to us and so denied that they had ever taken delivery.

Through this survey and subsequent interviews, it emerged that there had been no concerted installations programme. It appears that the entire process was put into the hands of the local government, and often the local administration did not see the handpumps as important, since there was a major interest in the purchase and installation of motorized pumps. As a result, village-level personnel were responsible for getting the pumps to their wells. In some cases where the village or *cercle* (county) did not have the money to install the pumps, they were given to a private citizen who had the means. In other cases the pumps were left in storage.

Lack of maintenance

With one short-lived exception, there had been no maintenance team or programme. After three years there had been a change in administration in that *cercle* and the new *caia* (the King's lowest uniformed executive, in charge of a *cercle*) advised the villagers to remove the pumps as they broke down, and use a bucket instead to get their water.

In other cases the local administration had used the drop-pipes as flag-poles to celebrate feasts and visits by dignitaries. Since both pipes and rods found other functions, often only the pump-heads were delivered to the well sites. In most cases, the recipients of the pumps lacked the resources to buy the pipe and rod.

Another problem with transport and delivery was the fact that crates had often been dropped or rolled without regard for labels saying 'this end up' or 'fragile'. This resulted in many dented cylinders and shattered cast-iron

CWD—N

parts. No Briau Africa pump made it from port to well intact, although all Dauphine and Solo 2 models inspected appear to have arrived in serviceable condition.

Further complicating the matter, installation directions were written in French, the language of the former colonial rulers and the manufacturers. Unfortunately, in many rural areas Berber is the first language, Arabic the second and French is as incomprehensible as Japanese.

Despite the problems, in a fair percentage of cases, pumps were actually installed. This was often done without the benefit of instructions and resulted in pumps being lashed to timbers or covered with cement to halfway up the pumphead. In other cases shallow-well pumps were mounted on deep wells. The pumps were never worked, but were left in place if they did not interfere with drawing water from the well with a bucket.

A major problem for pumps that were installed and functional was children. Youngsters would often swing from the handle, or jerk the handle rapidly while pumping water. Sometimes the children pushed small stones into the spout and delighted in the sounds the pebbles made as they rattled down the drop-pipe.

Other pumps were made unserviceable by acts of vandalism. One man recounted how, when he was a boy, he and some friends smashed several pumps to bits with rocks.

In other cases the pumps had been mounted on wells that had insufficient supplies of water. The villagers did not understand the need either to wait for the water to rise to a workable level or to prime the pump. Since most installations did not include an access door, the pumps had often been removed so the users could get at the water. During the course of removal, pipe and rod were bent and often the pump-head itself was smashed.

At the village-level alternative uses were found for drop-pipes. During our inspection we found pipes supporting television antennae, serving as roof drains or as rafters in livestock barns, or even being used for irrigation.

Another problem cited by many local people was the fact that they had to wait to use the pump, so pumps had been removed to improve access to the well.

The Province of Ouarzazate has now committed itself to a programme of repair, rehabilitation and installation of the handpumps scattered across the countryside. This is being made possible by further donations from UNICEF, and the involvement of Catholic Relief Services and the US Peace Corps.

Rehabilitation programme

Bernard Gilbert, UNICEF's potable water engineer and water projects director in Morocco, has committed himself to the project's success. In August 1983 he was able to secure 93 3 m lengths of pipe, 135 3 m lengths of rod, and numerous leathers and other parts that had been in storage in Morocco for many years. These were shipped to the Province and are already in use.

In November of that year he pledged a further donation, from newly arrived shipments, of 1,200 m of 1¼ in pipe and 1,200 m of 12 mm sucker rod, 20 complete pumps and 35 cylinders and accessories. The equipment is available in-country or at Casablanca Port, where it is awaiting customs clearance. We expect delivery during the first half of 1984.

The Province has given the Department of Rural Affairs *carte blanche* with regard to use, installation and removal of pumps and parts now in the province. They have also provided a plumber, mechanic, 6-ton truck, re-rod, lumber to use as forms for casting cement, and cement.

Catholic Relief Services has provided a petty cash of 28,500 Dirhams for the purchase of pipe connectors, pipe cutting and threading tools, pipe vices and other essential materials.

Peace Corps sent me to help implement the programme on the local level from site selection to installation and maintenance, armed with a well-stocked tool chest.

Using pumps, parts and equipment left over from when the pumps originally arrived, we were able to make 31 new installations and repair eight existing pumps between late August and November 1983. All installations and repairs were made at hand-dug wells ranging in depth from 4.9 m to 26 m with an average depth of 1.25 m.

The Governor and the Secretariat General of Ouarzazate Province have stated that they want the maximum number of pumps possible installed. They have also agreed that the maintenance of these pumps is essential to the success of the programme.

We plan to use additional UNICEF pumps to replace Briau Dauphines and Bodin Solo 2s that we removed from local store-rooms. This is necessary because many of the pumps are incomplete due to scavenging. We have found that we can generally mount two pumps using the parts from three.

There is, however, no sanitation component in the plan. Apart from the lack of a feeling that sanitation is necessary to ensure health benefits from an improved water supply, the programme has insufficient money to include it.

The usual procedure in the countryside is to 'go for a walk' after dinner. People usually squat next to a wall, wipe with their left hands, and then clean their hands with water from a pot they bring with them for the purpose. Pour flush toilets are common in the towns, but since they are often clogged or poorly vented, people often resort to the ways of the countryside even in urban areas.

Installation

There is a great resistance to giving up a pump even if it can never be mounted. Villagers see the pump as theirs, and experience a certain loss of prestige when a pump is removed. The new UNICEF pumps will enable us to cannibalize old unmounted pumps without depriving the trustees of the right to a working pump.

We are also attempting to avoid the problems that have beset the programme in the past. Since Berber is the only language that many of the people understand, we use technicians who are from the Berber tribes of the south. They are readily accepted and are able to explain the programme and my role clearly. The technicians have been impressed with the importance of letting the people get hands-on experience with the pumps. They have turned out to be excellent teachers.

We arrive at the site of a kerbed well that has a ready supply of water and serves the general public. These wells are generally located in mosques, schools or squares. We explain to the people that we are there to mount the pump we inspected in the spring or else to mount a new pump; and that we will supply everything else if the villagers give us sand, stones and water for cement, and help in making the installation.

We then construct a two-piece mounting. One slab of cement has the pump base mounting bolts cast into it, the other will serve as an access door. We explain the importance of using the trap door and not removing the pump when there is a breakdown. This visit usually lasts two or three hours, during which time the benefits, maintenance and repair procedures are discussed.

Repair requests are put through the local *caid*, who in turn notifies the Province. We have had good results with this oral system so far, but are now working on a check-list/postcard and a simplified manual in Arabic. In all breakdowns so far, the villagers were making use of the door, which means our discussions during the first visit are not in vain, as I initially feared they might be.

During the second visit we mount the pump. There is a great deal of excitement, with everyone participating. To keep things from getting out of control, we generally work with the local work leader and three or four skilled or semi-skilled workers, such as masons, blacksmiths and farmers. Usually there is also a large audience, whose questions must be answered, which further heightens local understanding of the programme and the pump.

With the villagers' help, the entire pump is taken apart and reassembled. We inspect and clean the parts and explain their functions, maintenance and possible problems. We then work together to mount the pump.

After the head is mounted and the handle is attached, we show how to use the handle gently, often simulating misuse by rapidly and roughly jerking somebody's hand up and down. We then have a race to compare the performance of the pump with a bucket on a rope. In any well deeper than 10 m, a 70 to 80 mm cylinder usually fills a bucket faster than a rope and pully. We then explain that the pump is worth in excess of 100,000 Ryals (5,000 Dirhams), without the cement, re-rod, transport and labour. It is not hard to explain the people's looks of awe.

As in most countries, collecting water is more often women's work than men's in Morocco, and usually takes place in the early morning. But if the water point is far from home, men may collect water in a large container carried on a cart, or with a mule loaded with large jugs.

Decisions about the siting of handpumps do not involve women directly, as men from outside must communicate with the village men of authority, even though women are most often the ultimate users. In rural Morocco, women often have their own area of the house where they work, socialize and eat.

If wells are sited in mosques, where they are likely to be taken care of by a group of concerned men, women do not have access to them. Mosque wells are used for ritual washing before prayers, and are fitted with pumps when there is known to be insufficient water at other sites in the village. The aim is also to ease acceptance of the technology by at least some of the population.

Afterwards, we are usually given a meal and are then shown several other wells that the locals feel could make good handpump sites in the future. We record the diameter and depth and promise to do what we can. For each pump we mount, we find several more places where people want pumps. Unfortunately, we do not have the funds and equipment to satisfy everyone.

We hope that UNICEF's input will set Ouarzazate's handpumps programme on its feet, but how long the pumps continue to function in the future will depend on the capacity of the Provincial administration to set up a viable maintenance system.

(*Waterlines* Vol. 3 No. 1, July 1984)

CHAPTER 9
Water Transport and Storage

There is a great disparity in the availability of potable water over the earth's surface, both in space and time, hence the vital importance of transport and storage. In the first article, a summary of a study[57] for ITDG and IT Transport Ltd, Val Curtis assesses some possible aids for Kenyan women carrying water and identifies the use of donkeys for the transport of water to remote rural communities. In the next article, Barbara Rogers stresses that women would favour water projects which ensured more abundant and accessible supplies, such as a well-digging programme, not only to reduce the physical burden of carrying water but also to combat health problems.

T. N. Lipangile, project manager of the Wood/Bamboo project in Tanzania, reports on a cheap and labour-intensive technology at Mwanza by the shores of Lake Victoria, which achieved remarkable success in the implementation of bamboo pipelines and wooden tanks. The article on ferrocement storage tanks is by Steve Layton, project manager at the Village Industry Research and Training Unit (VIRTU) based at Kieta in the North Solomon's Province of Papua New Guinea. (Further information on the technology can be obtained from an IT publication by Simon Watt.[58]) Francis Hillman describes work of prefabricated fibre-reinforced cement channels, undertaken by the Khabura Development Project funded by Petroleum Development, Oman and managed by the Centre for Overseas Research and Development at the University of Durham.

Water distribution, comprising transport and storage, is a wide subject as indicated by the variety of these articles. It encompasses both domestic and farming supplies. Gravity flow supplies are the first choice and reference should be made to the handbook written for rural communities in Nepal which is generally applicable elsewhere.[59]

Doing the donkey work
VAL CURTIS

Every country has a distribution network for getting water to the home; in developing countries the equivalent of modern pumps and pipes is the daily labour of the women carrying vessels from rivers or wells to their households. This work is arduous, can lead to injury and deformity and consumes time that might be better spent. The IDWSSD is aimed at solving these problems by encouraging the provision of clean supplies to all by the year 2000.

Yet it is increasingly obvious that this will remain a pipe-dream; that the task is far more difficult than was first imagined. It seems that the number of women who are having to carry water will go on increasing and that the distances they have to cover are getting greater.

So might there be another way to help women to improve matters? All over the world there are different methods in use for carrying water which could reduce the effort and time needed to provide a daily supply. This article summarizes some of the findings of a study undertaken for ITDG and IT Transport Ltd to try and find out about problems related to water carrying and to look at labour-saving technologies that might help Kenyan women to lessen their burden.

In those cultures where women are allowed out of their homes, the drawing of water is a large part of their daily domestic duties. Even if a woman lives near a stand-pipe, the size of her household may mean that she has to make about 15 trips to it a day to keep her family clean and provided with drinking and cooking water. In rural Africa, a woman will commonly walk 6 or 8 km to a water-source and back with a 25 litre vessel on her head or her back. If water retreats further than 25 km it becomes impossible to sustain a household and the disruptive migrations that mark the beginnings of a serious famine are precipitated.

Carrying water in Kenya

In Kenya, the work involved in fetching water is as different for individual women as is the variety of climate and terrain. As one might expect, the pattern tends to be that those in the wetter, more prosperous areas have to spend much less time on water-carrying than those in the dry, marginal and more remote areas. An hour spent per day is an average from a survey in the less remote areas[61] whilst a study in dry Kitui District showed average distances to water of 1.5 km in the wet season, and 6.1 km in the dry seasons.[62]

These long distances limit the amount of water that can be carried back to the household, even if there are daughters who can share the work. A quantity of water, rather than its quality, is, generally, more important for the health of a family; at least 40 litres per capita per day is needed to keep clean enough to be able to avoid infection. For an average household of 10 people this would require about 20 trips to water. Clearly, in dry periods, fetching enough water to keep the family healthy is impossible.

In the poorer, drier areas, periods of water shortage coincide with periods of food shortage. Hence a woman has to walk farthest when she has the least energy to spare and this will exacerbate malnutrition. If a woman is also pregnant, then the hard work and little food can cause her baby to be born underweight, and the quality of her breast milk will be reduced.

The burden of water-carrying has other effects which are detrimental to a woman's health. For example, a study of broken neck cases in a rural clinic in Bangladesh revealed that half had been caused by falls whilst carrying heavy loads.[63] In Kenya, doctors tell of broken backs and strangulation caused by accidents with heavy loads. They feel that the work of water-carrying is at least partly responsible for the distorted pelvises that cause the death of mothers and babies in childbirth. Kikuyu, Kamba and Masai women carry water with the aid of a head-strap. This leaves a dent in their skulls and is probably the cause of the frequent headaches that many report. Many Kenyan women who have had to labour with loads of water since childhood are crippled with backache while they are still in their thirties and almost all complain of back pain when asked about their general health.

A woman's heavy workload also leaves her at an economic disadvantage; she may well have had less education than a man because, as a child, she was kept at home to work.

The amount of food or cash crop she can grow is, in many places, limited by the time she has free to cultivate the land, and lack of time also reduces her potential to earn from other activities such as handicraft production. An ODA study in Swaziland found that when women were saved the trouble of water-carrying, their output of handicrafts doubled. Development projects often serve to reinforce women's economic disadvantage by only training men. I visited a weaving project in Northern Uganda where Karamajong warriors were able to make a useful income from the blankets they had been trained to weave. The French development worker explained that he did not offer training to the women because they had far too many domestic tasks to perform. The women lost out further because the extra income was spent, not on their local home-brewed beer, but on city-bottled beer, so their income is not increased.

One way to reduce the workload of rural women would be to have a tap, in or near every household. But in Kenya this is not going to happen in the near future, if ever. So far, between 10 and 20 per cent of the rural population has an adequate, safe supply of water (the exact figure depends on your definition of 'adequate'). The Kenyan Government has to spend the majority of its water development funds in urban areas because the potential for social and political disaster is much higher in cities. This leaves only 35 per cent to be spent on the 86 per cent of the population that lives in rural areas.

But the fact that the majority of the budget has to be spent in urban areas is not the worst problem that development planners face; along with problems of access and communication, they have also found it very difficult to develop programmes that respond to what the community really wants.

Partly as a result of their failure to involve local communities, and especially women, installations are misused and rapidly fall into disrepair, necessitating the spending of scarce funds on rehabilitation and maintenance of equipment. Small projects have a better track record because they can be flexible but they can only reach very limited numbers of people.

The population of Kenya will have doubled by the year 2000, so unless there is a massive increase in investment in water supply, then the number of women who have to carry water will steadily increase. The growth in population is also forcing people to live in drier areas, so it seems that the distance they will have to carry water will also increase.

Other countries

If an increasing number of women will be without improved water supplies nearby, could their workload be reduced by other means? The technology of water-carrying has been evolving since humans first learned to make vessels from skin. Many different ways have evolved in different parts of the world. In Tanzania and Burma, for example, men use a shoulder pole to carry about 40 litres of water to sell, and in Thailand women swing bamboo vessels over their backs. In Korea farmers carry their produce in a type of wood and rush frame rucksack called a *chee-geh* which it might be possible to adapt to water-carrying.

In China, handcarts are used extensively, while in Burkina Faso and Uganda wheelbarrows or homemade trolleys are often used to carry jerry cans of water. Wheeled devices allow greater loads to be transported because the ground takes some of the load.

In most cases where animals or a transport aid are employed to carry water, a man or boy will do the work, either for the family or to sell. This is one case where men's tendency to appropriate the technologies brought by development can have dramatic benefits for women.

Domesticated animals such as donkeys, horses, buffaloes, elephants, camels, llamas, and yaks are used in different continents to carry loads and, where the terrain is suitable, to draw simple sleds or carts. This can much increase the amount of water which can be carried.

To assess whether any of these transport aids have potential for use in rural Kenya, I had to do some 'market research'.

I selected photographs and drawings of our examples which were simple, cheap and suitable for the terrain and took them with me on visits to women's groups in various parts of rural Kenya. Informal discussions with individuals and groups and observation of the terrain soon showed that different socio-economic and physical circumstances were going to suggest very different approaches.

In richer, peri-urban areas, hard roads and relative wealth meant that animal carts were both affordable and efficient. In some cases they were already being used, though they suffered from many faults in design. In poorer, drier areas where the study largely concentrated, dry conditions meant that paths were loose and sandy and less suitable for wheels. Also people could not contemplate the relative expense of carts.

Also in these areas, water supply was often at the top of the list of problems that women wanted to discuss and, though they felt that the government should provide them with clean water, they did not believe that this would ever happen. Some women felt their best option was to get together to build some sort of structure for storing water but they felt they did not have the expertise. The pictures of improved transport ideas were much pored over. Some women felt that a shoulder yoke could help to carry more water but would be difficult to learn to use and awkward on the narrow bush-paths. Others had tried to manage wheelbarrows but found them difficult to manoeuvre in sandy soils and on stony, steep paths. The idea of using a donkey for carrying water met with almost unanimous approval. Donkeys can carry 50 to 100 kg, can cope with almost any terrain, are long-lived and hardy in drought. They are also relatively cheap (half the price of a cow) and produce more offpspring (an average of 3 to the cow's 2). All the women said that they would like to own donkeys to help carry water, produce and firewood, but that they were hard to get and men did not see the point in buying them whilst they had the women to do the donkey work.

Women's groups are accepted as part of Kenyan society. They offer women the opportunity to pool funds, to try to make money and to make their own decisions as to how the money will be spent. Groups could (and, it seems, would) incorporate the raising of donkeys into their activities. They felt that as well as helping with their chores, donkeys could be hired out or used to irrigate cash crops to generate income. Cash is probably the women's greatest need and desire.

In some parts of the world, donkeys are an essential part of the economy as load carriers, water-raisers and taxis. In parts of Kenya, donkeys are already used to carry goods and water for many miles but their use is becoming less and less common despite their obvious advantages. Part of the reason for this decline seems to be that donkeys have come to be regarded as backward and not part of a modern way of life by men with money.

Development agencies also regard donkeys as low in status, and confine their research to western breeds of cattle and fighting the diseases to which they are prone. If they wish, as they say they do, to reach the poorest of the poor, who are always the women, then to advocate and develop the use of donkeys in remote rural communities is a path that could have important benefits for women.[57]

(*Waterlines* Vol. 4 No. 2, October 1985)

Water—women's work

BARBARA ROGERS

'Are you digging wells here? Back home your agency is advertising that it's digging wells in the desert.'

'Well no, we've been very disappointed with this well-digging business, as a matter of fact we've given up. Everybody thinks wells are so important for village water supplies, but we've done everything we can think of and we still can't get the villagers to take any responsibility for them. I've been to villages, collected all the men together, talked with them for hours. Then we come along with the equipment, dig downwards until about midday, and there's some water at the bottom. I can't persuade them that we've got to go a lot deeper still, otherwise the well will dry up as soon as the dry season starts and they really need the water. Those people just refuse to go on digging, and of course their wells dry up and then they come and ask for more help. I'm fed up with wells.'

'But why were you only talking to the men? It's not the men who go out to the well every day, have to carry all that heavy water year in and year out, who actually see the water-levels going up and down according to the time of year . . .'

Pause.

'I wasn't actually thinking of that at the time. That was before I became enlightened about getting women involved in things.'

Talking with the women

Water experts need no reminder that they are dealing with a basic necessity of life, in fact the most important of them all. But they manage to ignore the fact that women are responsible for fetching water, for rationing it out, and for basic decisions about where it should be obtained.

Contaminated water supplies for drinking, which are such an immense health problem, may be the only choice open to women whose own health and strength is severely over-taxed; a great deal of energy and time must be spent on fetching water and they may well not have either to spare for seeking out cleaner sources. Large amounts of water have to be brought in for drinking, especially in hot climates, with extra amounts for cooking and, with luck, a little left over for washing.

Questions of village water supplies may be a little more complicated than they seem at first sight, because women have reasons of their own for a particular preference. For example, in some places they may prefer to walk some distance for their water, since this provides the only time when they can get together and talk. So a well which is away from the centre of the village will give them time away from the scrutiny of others.

A little time for relaxation and meeting others is perhaps just as much of a basic human need as the more obvious physical necessities of life, and for women the well or river provides both. The only way to find out the best way of meeting these two needs is to ask the women involved. If it is not too radical an idea, the planners might even bring themselves to meet the women separately, away from the men, who sometimes silence them in meetings and impose their own interests and demands.

It seems to be very hard for men working in development to deal with village women on equal terms with men—a problem for westerners in particular. Nor is this inhibition peculiar to experts in high technology. Many field-workers for voluntary organizations see themselves as one-man problem solvers, with the depressed areas of the Third World as the last frontier for their pioneering spirits. There is a certain *machismo* involved in work on appropriate technologies, which can be blind to the importance of women and the need to involve them in decision-making. Attitudes to Third World men have changed a great deal—they are no longer dumb, 'backward' peasants but, at least in theory, are suppliers of ingenious technologies of their own, and partners in the development process. This more realistic attitude needs to be extended to Third World women as well.

Women's needs

Poor women, in both rural and urban areas, have to use great ingenuity in their everyday lives, in the struggle to feed increasing numbers of dependents. Conditions have changed very fast for them. The rapid growth of the cash economy largely excludes them, yet imposes demands for cash for vital services, and the younger men feel free to travel in search of paid jobs and leave the women of the subsistence household with a double shift—their own *and* the men's work.

Many western men, with their double standards of work—that is 'real work' being paid and 'not work' being unpaid—fail to recognize the crippling work burden borne by Third World women. Yet if there is one bold generalization that it is safe to make, it is that women will respond positively to any innovation which reduces their work-load and/or increases their cash income. It has been observed that women are in fact more sensitive to these kinds of direct incentives to innovation than are men. Water projects which provide more accessible and more abundant supplies of water, in places that women find convenient and socially desirable, offer perhaps the most direct help in this regard. Not only is the extremely heavy work of water-carrying reduced, but during a dry season extra supplies of water can produce a good crop of marketable vegetables.

There is also, of course, the health benefit where contaminated water is replaced by clean water. This is another area where women are particularly sensitive. Health problems arising from water contamination particularly affect the children of which women have charge and they contribute substantially to infant and child mortality. A project in Burkina Faso, part of a programme to help women and girls, managed to make the women aware of the connection between dirty water and disease, and they became highly motivated to use simple water filters, using their own pottery jars with sand and charcoal.

They would even carry the heavy jars to the fields during the rainy season, to filter supplies to drink while they worked. Unfortunately, hopelessly inadequate water supplies in the dry season—which meant they had to walk several miles daily—made it physically impossible to bring in enough water, and the children could not be stopped from drinking the extremely dirty water before it had gone through the long filtering process. Better dry-season supplies of water have become an urgent demand of the women involved in this particular project.

It is ironical that the well-digging programme which could have helped them had already been stopped because consultation with the villagers, through the men only, had proved hopelessly impractical.

(*Waterlines* Vol. 1 No. 1, July 1982)

Bamboo water pipes and wooden tanks

T. N. Lipangile

Ten years ago, when the Tanzanian political party CCM and the Government introduced a village settlement policy, a project was started at Mwanza, by the shores of Lake Victoria to investigate using wood and bamboo for village water supplies. Since then, work has continued on researching, planning, constructing, maintaining and managing bamboo pipelines and wooden tanks and fittings. Today, about 200 km of bamboo pipeline have been laid in 28 villages and around 100,000 people are being supplied with water.

The bamboo pipes are made from bamboo stems which are cut from the forests. There are two types of bamboo in Tanzania, 'yellow' and 'green' (the species *Bambusa vulgaris* and *Arundinaria allpina*), growing between altitudes of 0–1,500 m and 1,500 m to over 2,000 m respectively. One hectare can contain about 5,000 bamboos and these are fully mature after four years. The greatest length with a uniform section (width) is about 4 m. The space inside the tube varies in diameter for each stem of bamboo, ranging from 38 to 100 mm, although recently some 250 mm- and 300 mm-wide bamboos have been reported in China and Burma.

All these sizes are suitable for village water schemes. A single 100 mm bamboo pipe can easily provide water sufficient for a village population of at least 4,000 people while a double system (two pipes) can provide water for not less than 10,000 people under the same conditions.

The bamboo pipe is made by hollowing out the internodes which grow naturally across the bamboo stem at intervals of about 1 m. This drilling operation is done manually with a special drilling tool such as an auger attached to a steel bar 2.5 m long. This can drill half-way down the bamboo and then the bamboo is turned to drill the other end. The bamboo pipes are reinforced by galvanized wire (about 3 mm thick), knotted at intervals of about 50 mm. The knots are made by twisting the wire with pliers or a small bar of iron or wood. Since bamboo structures are naturally longitudinal, the steel knot provides the cross-sectional support necessary to sustain the water pressure.

Bamboo pipes can withstand a pressure of three atmospheres, but one atmosphere is sufficient for one village. They have a flow efficiency which is better than steel pipes if the internodes are removed with proper care.

The best joint for bamboo pipes is class B and C polythene, which forms a watertight joint. A piece of polythene tube about 20 cm long and the same diameter as the bamboo is warmed to expand it. The ends of the pipes are sharpened using a tool like a pencil sharpener, then pressed into the polythene tube. As the polythene cools, it contracts and hardens to fit the bamboo exactly. A treated cow-hide (leather) joint has been successfully tested as an alternative to the use of polythene. The joint is formed by wrapping the leather round the two bamboo ends like a bandage. A pipe-laying crew of six men can lay half a kilometre of bamboo pipes in one day.

Bamboo pipe technology

The most critical question about the bamboo pipes' technology has been their durability when buried in the ground. A lot of research has been done on this for the past seven years and some solutions have been obtained and are now in practice, while others are still under research.

The main problem is the presence of micro-organisms. They originate outside the soil surface and are brought in by rain-water and by direct contact with the soil. The micro-organisms include fungi (vegetable kingdom) and also subterranean termites. Fungi cause rotting and are very sensitive to changes in the weather, temperature and water quality. They are very aggressive to bamboo in hot climates in dirty water derived from lowland areas (altitude 0 to 4,000 m), but less aggressive in cold temperatures with clear waters derived from upland areas (altitude 1,500 m or more). Similarly, termites are active in the hot areas and less active in colder areas at the same altitude. There are 2,000 species of termites.

The best method of protecting bamboo in the ground from fungi is to design the system so that it is constantly full of clean water. The maximum time without water should not exceed 60 days, and should be followed by a strong dose of chlorine sterilization (maximum concentration 10 mg/litre) after any interruption. A storage tank which acts as a balancing tank during peak flow hours is the best solution. The tank should be installed above the village so that gravity flow ensures that it can provide full pressure and flow even during the hours of maximum use.

By incorporating chlorine solution constantly or intermittently, the interior surface of the bamboo pipe is perfectly preserved against all forms of decay. The external bamboo surface is coated with hot, dipped tar or an epoxy lining incorporated with copper naphate preservative to prevent the soil coming into contact with the bamboo surface. Alternatively, the pipes can be dipped in cold epoxy or hot bituminous paint. With this coating, chlorine sterilization is not necessary.

To protect against termites, the trenches are treated with pesticides or water-borne preservatives impregnated into sawdust, which is glued to the bamboo surface.

At the moment the project is researching the impregnation and fixation of water-borne preservative in a bamboo culm to protect joints against fungi and termite attack. Some operating schemes have pipes which are seven, six and five years old respectively and still operating well. The pipes in other schemes were repaired after five to six years of operation because they were not treated with effective preservatives during construction.

A well-preserved bamboo pipe can last for 10 to 20 years in the ground. The lifetime of unpreserved bamboo constantly exposed to dirty water in hot climates is one year. In cold climates it is up to seven years. In both cases termites are eliminated by pesticides. The largest economical distance from the bamboo forest to a village site is 1,000 km provided that the system lasts for not less than 10 years.

The wooden tanks are made from pine timber planks (100 mm × 50 mm × 2.5 m). The planks are milled accurately with tongues and grooves by a planing machine at the sawmill. The timber pieces are held together by steel hoops. The tank consists of a wooden bottom, walls and a top. The timber is treated with water-borne preservative to give a lifespan of more than 20 years. The planks can be stored on the ground or put on a wooden platform.

The cost of a small wooden tank mounted on a wooden platform is 50 per cent cheaper than a concrete masonry tank. The costs of bigger tanks are becoming progressively cheaper. A crew of six men can construct a wooden tank at ground level in three weeks.

The wooden fittings are made from hardwood blocks which are naturally durable, for instance *Pterocarpus angolensis*, *Chlorophora excelsa*. The fittings include bends, elbows, tees, flanges, all made at the Wood/Bamboo Project's workshop. They are competitive in price with steel fittings and have a lifespan of more than 15 years when buried in the ground.

Maintenance and economics

Daily maintenance work is done by two villagers selected during the construction period. One 7 ton truck (carrying 300 bamboos) is enough for short-pipe extension and maintenance in the village for five years, assuming that only one pipe bursts and requires repairing each month. Spare bamboos are stored in a river or a pond of sterilized water so that they do not dry and crack. Domestic water taps are of the lock type with a turn of 90 degrees to close and open the orifice. They do not need maintenance and are wear-free. The village maintenance system is logged by a performance return sheet indicating monthly bursts, leaks, insect attacks and stock of spares and chlorine. The report is submitted to headquarters monthly for monitoring.

The bamboo and wood used are not toxic materials. Fungi are prevented by contact with clean water, chlorine or the bituminous paint lining. Care is required when preservative is incorporated in the system. If pesticide is used to treat the pipeline trenches, all preservatives are fixed to the ground where there is no chemical movement. The pipes are kept away from direct contact with preservatives and the water quality is excellent. Water analysis conducted in Tanzania and abroad (at Delft University in The Netherlands) has shown the water quality from pipes in trenches treated with Aldrin and Dieldrin pesticides meets WHO standards. Water analysis was also done to determine the water quality of pipes treated with copper chrome arsenate sawdust outside. Again, the water quality at the distribution point was within the WHO limits. Protective clothing (for instance, masks, gloves, gumboots and overalls) is provided for the workers dealing with preservatives. All preservatives are buried in the ground at a depth of 1 m.

The bamboo pipes are between four and six times cheaper than conventional pipes made of steel and plastic. The main materials which have to be imported are galvanized wire and tar. The whole technology can be handled by local people with very little training.

Recently, an independent evaluation mission from SIDA studied the engineering and economic aspects of the project and concluded that a well-preserved wood/bamboo water technology is viable. The cost per capita of bamboo/wood water technology is between US $4 and US $16. The use of wooden tanks and fittings treated with preservative is responsible for a substantial amount of the savings. A small wooden tank is 50 per cent cheaper than a conventional one made from concrete or masonry, and for larger tanks the savings are greater. The wooden fittings made from hardwood blocks are competitive in price with steel fittings.

When we have developed the impregnation and fixation of preservative to bamboo culms so that the bamboo does not rot if the water pump stops, the Wood/Bamboo Project aims to use pumps driven by wind, gas, water and alcohol. Enough material has been gathered to start work on a pilot level.

Ferrocement tanks in Papua New Guinea
STEVE LAYTON

VIRTU (Village Industry Research and Training Unit) is a technical (appropriate technology) section of the Division of Commerce in the North Solomons Province of Papua New Guinea. VIRTU was initially funded from a national government grant, but now is completely funded from within the province. The aim of the Unit is to promote rural-based income generating activities primarily in the less developed areas of the province.

VIRTU's ferrocement tank project was started as a 'community project' rather than one designed to generate income, VIRTU's normal method of working. However, it has become a profit-making venture.

During the second half of 1982 and the beginning of 1983, large areas of the North Solomons Province of Papua New Guinea (PNG) were experiencing a prolonged period of drought. In the worst affected areas on the outer atolls the provincial government was forced to ship water in 44-gallon drums. Although the province had been promoting rural water supplies for some time, the drought illustrated the extent of the problem. Because rain-water harvesting was looked upon as one solution to providing water in these areas, and as commercially available tanks were not appropriate to the needs or resources of the people, the community works section of the provincial government requested VIRTU to look into the possibilities of transferring ferrocement tank technology to the rural areas of the province.

We have no recent data on the water consumption rate of the rural population or rainfall in the North Solomons Province. However, a survey carried out on Nissan Island in 1983 which gathered information from 10 villages indicated that the average storage capacity per person was 178 litres. The minimum requirement is 12 litres per person per day (supplied by a community stand-pipe) according to the World Health Organization, so this capacity is only enough for a 15-day supply. The survey results also showed that 66 per cent of the total amount of water was stored in old 44-gallon oil drums.

Based on the Nissan survey it is estimated that the present storage capacity on the 11 islands and atolls is about 874,000 litres. Allowing for a 60-day period, the storage capacity required is in the region of 3,547,000 litres, a shortfall of some 2,673,000 litres. And to meet this demand by supplying fibreglass tanks, the provincial government or the people themselves would have to purchase tanks to the approximate value of K 326,700.

At present the PNG National Weather Service, which is based on Port Moresby, only has active recording stations on Bougainville and Buka. The most recent station to operate on the islands and atolls was located on Nuguria and was closed in mid-1979. However, it is possible to estimate a mean rainfall figure based on figures recorded between 1949 and 1979. We estimate that the average mean annual rainfall on the islands and atolls is 3,520 mm.

After three months of design and trials VIRTU's first promising tank began to take shape, and soon after this field-trials were carried out on Nissan, the largest of the outer atolls. Nissan was used not only because of its regular air services, but also because it has the Province's largest population and hence the largest demand for water. Experience has shown that in general, the meagre ground-water resources of the outher islands and atolls of the North Solomons cannot be successfully exploited.

Therefore, it is felt that the collection of rain-water is the only viable option open to the people living on these islands and atolls.

VIRTU's approach

Although initially the project was requested as a community development project, it was very soon realized that this approach had not succeeded in many parts of the country. And after reviewing a number of projects undertaken by various groups throughout PNG, it was found that their approach to the transfer of ferrocement tank technology had been very similar. In most cases the technology was 'given' to the people in the form of demonstrating the construction of one or two tanks at 'appropriate technology workshops' or 'village technology courses' with most of the effort being channelled towards encouraging the participants to construct one or two tanks on their return to their villages.

The approach taken by VIRTU is very different. We very quickly realized that if a tank could be designed to meet the criteria below, it would be not only possible to produce large numbers of tanks in rural areas but also to give a financial incentive to the rural people to construct the tanks.

○ The production process should use local rural labour resources and encourage the establishment of small-scale rural industries.
○ Materials, equipment and production techniques should be not only understood, but sustained by the people who are going to use them.
○ Where possible, raw materials should be obtained locally; if they must be purchased they should be commonly stocked by local sales outlets.
○ VIRTU tanks should be able to compete with commercially available tanks.
○ They should be structurally sound enough to withstand the earth tremors which are common in the region.
○ The size of a tank should meet the water needs of an average rural family and be within their financial reach.

The first trials were carried out on Nissan Island, but first members of VIRTU staff made a number of visits to the island to discuss with government officers, community government officials and village leaders the most

Installing an India Mark II pump in Angola (UNICEF/Murray-Lee)

Piped supplies can bring water nearer home. In Sri Lanka this stand-pipe supplies between 10 and 20 families (Jeremy Hartley)

The communities' skills should be tapped and the villagers trained to help install and maintain their supply, fostering a sense of ownership and pride (WaterAid/Jeremy Hartley)

Involving the community in the maintenance of water supplies is essential. Central African Republic (UNICEF/Murray-Lee)

appropriate way for the project to be established. During discussions it was identified that the majority of the skills and resources were already present on the island and that if VIRTU could transfer the technology needed to construct the tanks the other aspects involved in the project would follow. The main non-technical aspects of the project were:

○ Identification of a group of potential entrepreneurs who would be able to give the time needed to establish and maintain the project.
○ Assisting these would-be entrepreneurs to develop the non-technical skills required.
○ Identifying ways in which the community government and village leaders could assist the project.

Given the interest shown in the project by the people of Nissan, it did not take long for the project to develop. Nissan has a large number of young, educated people who had insufficient land to grow coconuts to produce copra (49 per cent of the Nissan population is under 17 years of age). There were few other opportunities to earn money, so it was decided that the tank construction project should use the resources these young people represented.

After a number of meetings the 10 main youth groups on Nissan decided to send one member from each group to work and train with VIRTU staff, and after training to form Nissan Construction (NISCO) to generate income from the sale of ferrocement tanks.

Also working with the VIRTU staff on Nissan was a Business Development Assistant (BDA). BDAs are employed by the Division of Commerce in the North Solomons to assist village businesses and to act as a liaison between the District Business Development Officers and village businessmen. Because the role of the Nissan BDA was important, he was sent to Kieta to work at VIRTU during the construction of the first few successful test tanks. This gave him an insight to the types of problems which could be faced in Nissan and the extra training needed to advise on possible solutions to these problems.

The training of the would-be entrepreneurs on Nissan took just under a month and was designed to be as intensive as possible. It consisted of NISCO's first contract to supply four tanks at two schools, a health centre and a village. The tank construction technique used a glass-fibre mould designed to:

○ Support the reinforcement wire during plastering and thus avoid the need for excessive wiring purely to support the reinforcement during construction.
○ Support the cement mortar during construction, thus reducing the level of skill needed to construct a tank and speed up the plastering operation which in turn allows for the mortar to dry uniformly.

Table 9.1   Comparative costs of different types of tank

Material	Cost per instalment	Cost per litre after 10 years
Glass-fibre	K835 (US$ 950)	1.5t (US$ 1.7 cents)
Corrugated iron*	K260 (US$ 295)	3.8t (US$ 4.32 cents)
VIRTU tank	K200 (US$ 227)	0.5t (US$ 0.5 cents)

* A corrugated iron tank has to be replaced on average every 18 months on the North Solomon's atolls

○ Assist the entrepreneurs to monitor the standard of their workmanship and the amounts of materials used.
○ Be lightweight and robust and withstand repeated re-use.
○ Ensure that all the tanks produced would have a uniformly attractive appearance.

The fibre-glass mould is made by adapting a commercially available fibre-glass tank. The tank moulds are made up of a top and bottom mould both of which are in two parts. The construction of a tank has been broken down into easy steps totalling 13 hours' work over three days.

Besides the tank production technique, other factors have made the project a success, not least the price of the finished tank compared to the cost of other commercially available tanks. Table 9.1 illustrates the marketability of the VIRTU-designed tanks.

In the first year, NISCO generated a gross income of K 7,200 (US $8,193). There is a potential market for 30 to 40 tanks per year.

Following the project's success on Nissan, a number of other groups on the two main islands of Bouganville and Buka have been established and either supported by or wholly owned by community governments. Also the Provincial Division of Health has established a small team of workers to construct tanks at rural aid posts around the province.

This means that in the first year of production small-scale rural businesses in the province gained approximately 6 per cent of the annual market for water tanks which represents a total gross income of K 13,000 (US $14,794).

(*Waterlines* Vol. 3 No. 2, October 1984)

Prefabricated fibre-reinforced cement irrigation channels

FRANCIS HILLMAN

After several years without significant rainfall along the Oman Batina coast, an expanding irrigated area owing to the advent of diesel and electric pumps, groundwater resources and their careful and efficient use are an issue of ever-increasing importance. Agriculture can demand up to 50 cu.m. of water (50,000 litres) per day per hectare during the summer months. If this water is not carried from the wellhead to the crop in an efficient manner this figure may be doubled by unnecessary losses. There are two main causes: firstly, the lowering of the water-table as ground water diminishes, and secondly, the intrusion of sea-water as the interface between salt and fresh-water moves inland.

The options open to the richer farmers are numerous since companies offering commercial irrigation equipment have been set up over the past decade to cater for a landscaping programme in the area of Muscat, Oman's capital. The majority of the Sultanate's small farmers, however, have neither the know-how nor the funds to invest in such systems. The farmers of the Batina coastal strip rely mainly on traditional channel and basin irrigation methods. The water is usually lifted from a shallow well (5 m to 20 m deep) or from deeper boreholes. The lifting power now comes almost entirely from diesel and electric centrifugal or multi-stage pumps.

The distribution of water on a farm is typically by cement block and plaster channels or unlined earthen channels. The Khabura Development Project (KDP) began to look into alternatives because earth channels lose large quantities of water due to seepage. They require constant maintenance due to weed growth, rely on the lie of the land to give them a slope and it is difficult to control the flow of water in them. Good block and plaster channels have many advantages but are expensive to construct and install correctly. Cheap block and plaster channels are made with weak cement and plaster. They become infested with grass and are often installed badly, resulting in excessive leakage and water not reaching its intended destination.

What was required was a channel liner which would overcome these problems but still be competitive in price and be produced locally. In addition, competent installation giving uniform slopes and an efficient layout was required as a service by the project to farmers in the area.

Over the past few years several different materials, shapes and sizes of channel liner have been tried and in the process a system for making prefabricated fibre-reinforced cement channels of semi-circular cross-section has evolved (Figure 9.1).

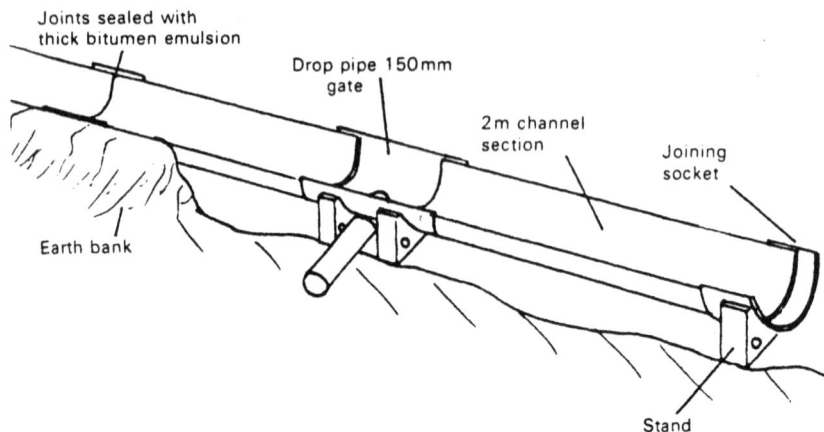

Figure 9.1 *Sketch of a Khabura Development Project fibre-reinforced cement irrigation channel showing the two types of joint*

Development phases

Initially, earthen irrigation channels were lined with polythene, but this had numerous disadvantages. As a result, there was no local interest in this modification and it was discontinued.

At the end of 1978, ITDG was approached to investigate other alternatives, and came up with the idea of using date-palm fibre to reinforce an ordinary cement mix. This fibre-reinforced cement (frc) would be used to line earth channels. The initial cross-sectional shape used was that of a natural catenary curve—this results when anything flexible is suspended between two points and allowed to hang by its own weight. Thus, a thin (15 mm) sheet of frc laid and tamped flat on strong polythene and subsequently suspended along its two long edges would be a catenary-shaped channel when dry. After curing, these channels could be laid end-to-end on the soil surface or on stands, the joints sealed with tar emulsion and the channels surrounded with earth along their length. The deep cross-section of these channels would allow the use of syphons to remove water and obviate the need for gates, which are always a potential source of leakage.

Several hundred of these channels were made and installed both on the project farm and on other local farms. The main problems which emerged over time included vertical cracking of the channel sections and lack of acceptance by farmers. They did not like the deep shape and the syphoning system.

During 1983 the basic material and manufacturing principle was slowly adapted to come up with a product which was not only functional but also socially acceptable. The commercial viability of the product could then be assessed under Omani conditions.

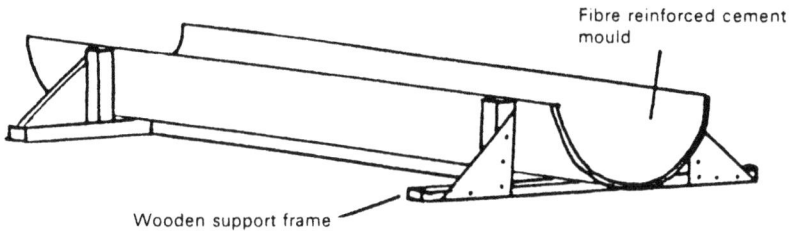

Figure 9.2 *Fibre-reinforced cement mould for making fibre-reinforced cement irrigation channels*

Present system

The main changes were made in shape and thickness. Sockets with stands to join sections and prefabricated gates were also introduced, positive moulds were used, initially made from 300 mm and 400 mm PVC pipes cut in half lengthways and mounted in a wooden frame. The two drawbacks of these moulds were size, and the tendency to warp when exposed to sunlight. Neither size was suitable for the water flows commonly encountered, so an intermediate size was required. Both these problems were overcome by using 350 mm-diameter steel pipe cut in half lengthways to act as a template for casting moulds from frc. In this way any number of virtually identical moulds can be made cheaply (Figure 9.2).

The basic principle of casting any of the components is the same. Fibre-reinforced cement is prepared. The fibre for this is the sort found behind the date palm leaves after they have been pruned, which is done twice a year. This is a waste product, so can be obtained free. It is moistened and fed in rolls into a hand-powered Simplex chaff-cutter. This produces fibres between 25 and 35 cm in length. A suitable powered machine for this activity has not yet been found: suggestions are welcome!

The frc is mixed in a Benford half-bag capacity petrol-driven mixer, which can hold enough to make one channel and joining socket at a time. The mixture is made up of 40 kg sand, 28 kg cement and 3 kg fibre. The quality of the sand is poor: dusty and not sharp. There is not doubt that washing improves the quality of the mix, but better sand can usually be found to avoid this necessity.

Water content is determined by experience, but totals approximately 10 litres per channel. A compromise must be made between the maximum ultimate strength of the channel when dry and how workable the mixture is when wet.

Laying up

To make a channel, the wet frc is taken by wheelbarrow and shovelled on to the laying-up board. This consists of two pieces of plywood upon which a

9.3

57cm gate section

50cm PVC pipe push fit

150mm PVC elbow

50mm cut off from elbow, filled with frc to make stopper

9.4

57cm gate section

50cm 150mm PVC pipe cut at an angle and cemented in place on installation

9.5

150mm hole for elbow insertion

frc 75cm mould section

9.6

50mm PVC pipe pulled out before concrete sets

End board

Base board

Side board held on with wing nuts

$1/2$ PVC pipe fixed to base board

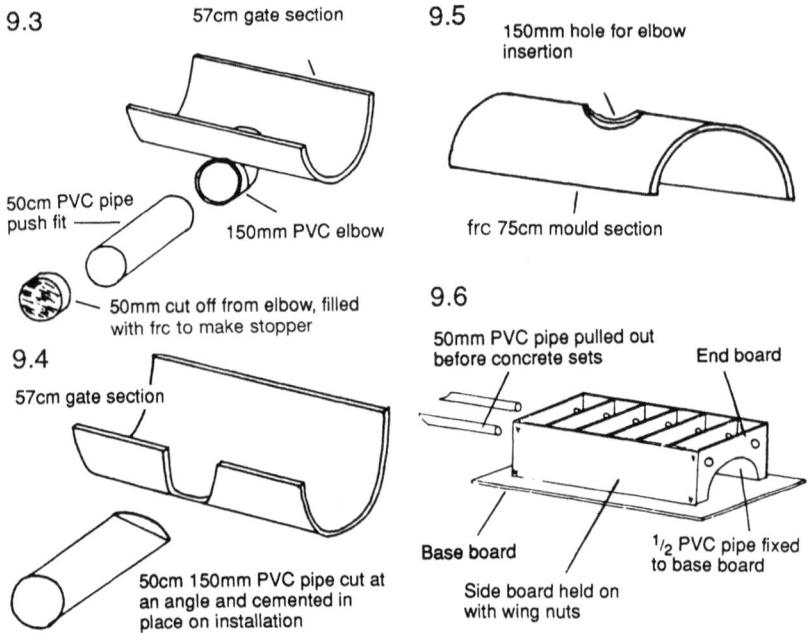

Figure 9.3   *Drop-pipe gate for releasing water from the irrigation channel, showing construction of stopper. 9.4 Straight-pipe gate. The outlet pipe is cemented in when the channel is installed. 9.5 Mould for drop-pipe gate. 9.6 Box mould to make six pipe stands*

plastic sheet is laid. The sheet is made of reinforced plastic tarpaulin with wooden laths screwed to the two long edges. A 20 mm angle-iron frame of the same dimensions as the channel (2 m × 57 cm) is laid on top of the plastic. This frame keeps the frc mixture uniform in thickness and the right size for moulding. The mixture is spread evenly in the frame and thoroughly tamped down with a wooden bar. Pneumatic vibrators mounted on a cement float have been used to remove air but this is not essential. The surface is smoothed with a trowel, then the iron frame can be carefully lifted up.

With a person at either end, each grasping the ends of the wooden laths, the wet sheet of frc is carefully lifted and placed into a mould. The laths are left resting on the wooden frame of the mould. They must not be pulled in any way in case the straight edge of the wet channel becomes distorted. The inside of the channel is then smoothed as much as possible using a bottle.

The moulds are made in the same way but using a slightly longer angle-iron frame (2.1 m × 57 cm) with the same size plastic sheet and laying-up board. The wet frc sheet is lifted on to the inverted steel template, then smoothed over with a trowel. It is better to use a slightly wetter mixture for the moulds than for the channels.

Only a small piece of plastic sheet is needed to make the sockets for joining lengths of channel, on a frame measuring 25 cm × 68 cm. They are moulded over the outside surface of a completed channel.

Pipe gates are of two types. There is a drop-pipe style, where a 150 mm PVC elbow is set into the base of a short channel (Figure 9.3). There is also a straight-pipe type, where a short section of channel is moulded with a space in the side, and a pipe is cemented in when the channel is installed (Figure 9.4).

The mould for the drop-pipe gate consists of a short length of channel (75 cm long) with a 150 mm diameter hole in the base (Figure 9.5). Wet frc is laid in a 57 cm frame which has a 150 mm hole left in the centre. When the wet frc sheet is laid over the mould, a 150 mm PVC elbow is inserted through the hole and cement is packed around it to seal it in place. Stoppers for these outlets are made from a 50 mm length of PVC pipe cut from the elbow before moulding. The centre of this is filled with frc to make a stopper (Figure 9.3). Stands are made of conventional concrete poured into a box mould, as illustrated in Figure 9.6. This makes six stands at a time.

All the items which make up the prefabricated channel system are left overnight to set and carefully demoulded the next day. They are placed in a tank of water for three days to wet cure, then in a shaded area to damp cure for at least a week. They are hosed down each day.

Installation

As with the production process, installation methods have evolved over time. With these particular channels and water-flows of anything between 6 and 15 litres per second it has been found that slopes of 0.25 per cent to 0.5 per cent are most satisfactory. This is roughly similar to the lie of the land in the area, which slopes gently towards the sea.

The course which a channel is going to follow is first set out with a piece of strong builder's twine stretched very tightly. The slope of the land is then surveyed and markers placed every 20 m or so. A surveyor's level and staff is used for this purpose, but a clear pipe with water in it can be used, although it tends to be less accurate and more time-consuming. A stand with joining socket placed on it makes a good level-marker, or just the socket placed on the earth, depending upon the height above ground at which the channel is to be installed. The string running along the top of all the level-markers then represents both the line and slope along which the channel will run.

To install a channel, two stands and joining sockets are positioned so that when a channel is placed between them the strings run exactly along the lowest point of the inside of the channel. Before placing a channel, a bead of bitumen emulsion is spread in each socket. This squeezes out to seal the

Table 9.2 Daily costs	£
Cement (6 bags)	17.14
Sand (400 kg)	1.90
Repayment of loan for setting-up costs (£3,570 over 3 years, interest free)	4.05
Depreciation of equipment	1.19
Fuel	0.48
Labour (3 expatriates @ £6.43)	19.29
Total	44.05

Assuming: production is 10 channels, sockets and stands per day, there are 290 working days per year, three expatriate workers are employed.

Therefore, production cost per channel (2m) is £4.41. Adding a 20 per cent profit for the factory owner, the sale price per channel, with socket and stand, will be £5.29. By these calculations, the owner has an income of £8.80 per day from the channel production unit.

If installation costs are £2.38 per length of channel, the total installed cost would be £7.62 per 2m length, or £3.84 per metre. For comparison, concrete block and plaster channels range in price from £2.78 to £2.95 per metre, depending on their size and the amount of plaster used.

In these calculations, the rate of exchange has been taken as £2.38 to the Omani Riyal.

joint, and any spaces remaining are filled when the channel is placed in position. A piece of angle-iron the exact length of a channel (2 m) and a long spirit level are invaluable in ensuring that the slope and distance between the two sockets is correct before going to the effort of lifting a channel—weighing 60 kg. Gates are installed in the same manner between two stands, and they act as elongated joints between two sections of channel. Once a length of channel has been installed satisfactorily, earth is trodden well down all around to provide support.

Having arrived at an apparently acceptable system for manufacturing prefabricated irrigation channels with several thousand metres installed on local farms and constant orders for more, it was decided to look at their commercial viability.

A local farmer with an existing concrete block factory expressed interest in starting up a small unit for producing channels. An application was made to the Oman Bank for Agriculture and Fisheries for a small loan with which to build a 10-channel production unit. This has now been constructed and has been in production for six months. The KDP purchases channels from the factory at a price which enables the owner to make a small profit and pay three expatriate workers. Channels are sold to local farmers at a subsidized price. The installation side of the work is still supervised and subsidized by the KDP using Omani workers.

It is ironic that a technology designed to improve small-scale irrigation in an area by using mainly local materials and labour can only achieve this end if cheap imported labour is used and a degree of subsidy is forthcoming from some suitable body. Such are the contradictions of the socio-economic system in present-day Oman.

Are the social and economic benefits of agriculture justified? If so, water is the essential basic ingredient and realistic ways of using it more efficiently are of vital importance to the long-term sustainable exploitation of this precious resource.[64]

(*Waterlines* Vol. 4 No. 4, April 1986)

CHAPTER 10
Education and Training

The first article is drawn from a wide-ranging study of the Singida Region in Tanzania by the Institute of Resource Assessment at the University of Dar es Salaam. The theme is that water is women's business and ways of involving women are discussed. Kevin Taylor of WEDC argues that water development in Southern Sudan has been unsuccessful because of lack of finance and trained staff. He outlines the steps being taken to train through work experience in local institutions. From my own experience, high turnover of trained staff is a major obstacle. This is often due to lack of recognition of the crucial work done during unsocial hours.

WASH have undertaken intensive technical training courses. Fred Rosenweig, writing as their Associate Director for human resources, discusses programme planning procedures and suggests a timetable for this planning. The results of the WASH projects has shown that these steps lead to training workshops that have a significant impact on participants.

The final article is a condensed version of a paper by Gus Liebenow, Professor of Political Science at Indiana University. He outlines the demonstration effect of a successful pilot scheme in promoting self-help to achieve a large programme of gravity-fed water supply systems. Other essential ingredients were political will and support which encouraged external funding. Demonstration schemes are undoubtedly very necessary to achieve enthusiastic support at all levels for the completion of major development in a short time. Such schemes also require a blending of technically trained staff with a spirit of community self-help, both in construction and maintenance. The Malawi initiative has provided the basis for a practical model for a World Bank Paper on self-help programmes.[65]

The International Training Network for Water and Waste Management has been established by the World Bank and UNDP with several bilateral and multilateral development agencies to promote lower cost water technology in the urban areas of developing countries. Network Centres are being established in existing institutions in developing countries to familiarize staff with lower cost technologies. These Centres will also act as national or regional focal points for the Network, providing other institutions with training assistance at all levels. The information and training materials developed by the World Bank include films and 45 structured lessons. The Network will eventually have up to 15 Centres throughout the developing world.

Ways of involving women in water projects
CAROLYN HANNAN-ANDERSSON

It is becoming increasingly clear that water for domestic use is 'women's business'. Women, of course, have always known this. The men in the village will confirm it, laughing at the mere suggestion that men should be involved with such work. The surprising fact is that it took so long for those at the planning level to recognize the importance of women as a target group in improving rural water supplies. In the mid-seventies, women were 'rediscovered' and 'reintroduced' into the water supply sector. Much has been said and written about the need to involve women, but as yet little has been put into practice. The challenge is now to work out practical methods for ensuring women's participation.

The key to success in involving women is an acknowledgement of the importance of their contribution to development and the provision of adequate information and motivation for them. Because of their subordinate position in rural societies, special efforts will have to be made to ensure their participation. After studying three villages in Tanzania where water and sanitation programmes had brought no improvements in health, we were able to make some practical suggestions for involving women.

Traditional roles

Water collection in rural areas is traditionally women's work, even if they are assisted to a great extent by children, especially girls. In spite of this, women have been consistently excluded from all dialogue about the priority of improved supply, the possible improvements, the implementation and arrangements for operation and maintenance. Unfailingly they have been involved in any 'self-help' construction activities, but they have not always been reached with the necessary promotion or instructions on the proper use of the improved supply, nor with adequate water-related health education.

The almost total exclusion of women from the whole process of improving water supplies may well be the most significant factor in the disastrous failure rate for improved supplies. If women are not included in the planning and implementation of the improved water source, as they have been in the past for traditional water sources, their motivation to use and maintain the new source will be small. In short, they are overworked but underused.

The need to learn more about the situation of rural women and their priorities is increasingly evident. This is an essential prerequisite if women are to be involved and if the planned change is to improve their living conditions and social status.

Nyaturu women have a relatively weak position in Nyaturu society. They are subordinate to their husbands and have limited access to resources such as information, credit or technological innovations. They play a very passive role in community affairs and traditional social norms require that they are outwardly deferential to men and do not express themselves at public meetings in the presence of men. These are obvious hindrances to involving them in social change.

Attempts have been made to improve water supplies, health standards and sanitation among the Nyaturu since the early 1900s. Little effect has been achieved. While the Nyaturu cannot be said to be opposed to change as such, they are unwilling to accept innovations which upset the traditional system too much, or which cost too much in terms of money, time and effort. If changes are to be made, the advantages must be clear and the means of attaining the changes comprehensible. Communication at the level of individual households is crucial. So is an adequate knowledge of the traditional conditions under which the communities live.

Village study

In all three villages studied—Unyianga, Unyangwe and Nkhoiree—the majority of households rely on hand-dug unlined wells for their supply of water for domestic uses. This is in spite of the fact that two of the villages have already received improved supplies, according to the programme for improving water supplies in Singida. The water from the traditional wells is of questionable quality. While the supply is plentiful in the wet season, the wells sometimes dry out completely in the dry period, or the water seeps in very slowly, resulting in long queues at the wells. Separate wells are dug for cattle. Most domestic wells visited had no hedge or barrier to keep animals out, so that contamination from cattle, dogs and hyenas was possible.

Unyangwe village had an improved supply which was actually functioning at the time of the field-work. This village had received two foot pumps, one of which had been out of order since shortly after installation. The second pump has continued to function without problems.

Unyianga village has a windmill which has a long history of breakdowns and slow maintenance. The second supply system planned for this village has never been finished and is unlikely to be, completely due to an inadequate supply of water. Nkhoiree village has not yet received any improved supply but a survey has been carried out.

The improvements which had been made in the two villages, Unyianga and Unyangwe, were totally inadequate. Two foot pumps in a village for a population of 1,671 and one windmill supplying one domestic point and cattle trough for a village with a population of 2,158, cannot possibly meet the needs. Even when the improved supplies are working, only a small percentage of the population benefits. Given the problems experienced with breakdowns, this percentage is lowered even further.

It could be said that the impact of the improvements made was non-existent. Households using the improved supply and those using the traditional sources had similar water-use patterns and standards of health, hygiene and sanitation. The involvement of the communities had been minimal and almost no information at all had been given to them on planned improvements, the use of improved supplies or health aspects. There was no integration at all with health education or sanitation inputs.

The percentage of households actually using the improved supplies (when they were working) expressed satisfaction with the quality of the water. They claimed that stomach problems had decreased while the supplies were working. The main complaints about the improved systems were that they were inadequate for the needs of the community. There were also many complaints about the slow maintenance when the pumps or windmills broke down. The suggested improvements were to build more wells with hand-pumps so that they are closer to all households. Only a small percentage of households in Nkhoiree expected the government to deliver a piped supply.

Only very small amounts of water were carried home for domestic use in all three villages. The average consumption was as low as 8.7 litres per person per day (with a range of 2.6 to 20 litres). However, most washing of clothes was done at the wells and the amount of water used for this activity is thus not included in the calculations. Some bathing was also done at the sources. However, even allowing for those additional litres, the per capita consumption is still a far cry from the recommended 20 litres.

In addition to very low consumption, which did not appear to change noticeably when households were using improved supplies, the handling of water in homes left a great deal to be desired. Standards of personal hygiene were very poor. Sanitation aspects are still unclear, as it is difficult to accurately estimate the actual usage of latrines in a short survey such as this one. However, it was presumed that household members use the bush as much as they use the latrines, especially since many latrines were neither private nor safe enough for regular use. The standard of construction of the latrines was very poor, in keeping with the general standard of housing. Health education on the relationship between health and water, personal hygiene and sanitation are urgently required, in conjunction with the improvement of the water supplies.

The health situation revealed through interviews with the 75 households is not good. There were many stomach problems experienced in the area, as well as bilharzia, malaria and some skin and eye diseases. Diarrhoea is also a problem though not all households considered it an important one.

Practical suggestions

By asking women what they considered to be their greatest burdens, it was possible to obtain an impression of their perception of the problem of water supplies. Not one of the women mentioned water collection as the greatest

CWD—P

burden they carried. The main burdens were rather agriculture, firewood collection and grinding flour. Of interest and relevance is the fact that when asked about the activities which they enjoyed, 20 per cent of the women mentioned water collection. Since firewood collection and gathering wild vegetables were also mentioned as enjoyable activities, we presume that they offered an opportunity to get away from the house and meet other women.

In spite of the fact that the problem of water supply was not the first priority for women, only 17 per cent did not consider there was any need for improvement, or could not suggest any improvement. The response of most women indicated that they saw the need for improving water supplies, in order to reduce health problems. However, there was still the attitude that the government should deliver the services promised. Shallow wells with hand or foot pumps were quite acceptable to the majority of the women.

If the effective involvement of women in improving water supplies is to be achieved, changes will be necessary at the practical level of organizing and managing projects. On the assumption that water projects will be integrated ones, directed at men and women, special efforts need to be made to include women more fully.

This can be done by employing female project staff, involving village women in village planning meetings, all-women meetings, village water committees, women's promotion groups, dance and drama groups and pump and well-caretaker programmes. To mobilize village women, every existing group can be used: traditional women's groups, Umoja wa Wana- wake wa Tanzania (UWT, a political organization), adult education and Maendeleo (development) groups, religious bodies, primary schools and health-care facilities.

The hope is that women staff members will identify more easily with village women than their male counterparts, but there is the possibility that better-educated 'town' women may hold some of the negative attitudes that have prevailed towards peasants in general and women in particular. Training in community development methods will be needed for both male and female staff members. Men should be able to accept women staff because water is traditionally a woman's sphere.

Even women of a higher educational standard may have difficulty in asserting themselves in a mixed group, so it might be necessary to appoint more than one so that they can support each other. The most suitable type of woman for the work is a matter for discussion. For instance, unmarried girls may be better qualified educationally than older women. However, they would be less likely to be respected.

When trying to involve village women in village planning meetings, it must be remembered that women will often not speak in large groups containing men, such as village planning meetings. So one strategy is to ensure that they at least attend the meetings, which must therefore be at a time they can manage, and then allow them to express themselves at all-women meetings. The convening of meetings for women alone should not cause objections from the men, since water is women's work. It would be a boost for the women's self-esteem to know that the project team values their opinions and suggestions.

Older married women are likely to remain in the area, but have family responsibilities. Young married women with small children are more likely to be under the control of their families, but older women often have only a poor knowledge of Swahili, the official language. The project must be careful to avoid recruiting women from only the higher levels of the village hierarchy: there is inequality and conflict even among women.

UWT groups, where they exist, may be quite elitist, so efforts would still need to be made to reach the poorer sections of the female community.

In the case of village water committees, it seems that women's role will continue to be low-key for the foreseeable future, though it is important that they are represented, as it does signal an increase in status for women.

Material on water, sanitation and health can be included in literacy programmes, perhaps as simple readers, and the effort should be made to use as many visual aids as possible, and to develop discussion techniques. Teachers of adult education groups, who sometimes know little more than the groups they teach, will need to have their information supplemented and supported.

Talents in the field of drama and dance often have no relation to status or educational standard, and are therefore an area where women from all social categories in the village could participate, as can children.

'Women's promotion groups' of five to ten women (one from each 'area' within the village) can be democratically chosen by the women at the start of the project, to observe at all meetings and report back to their areas.

Giving women responsibility

Appointing women pump attendants sometimes becomes a goal in itself, and then it is assumed that the business of women's involvement has been attended to. This sort of token attention is not enough. There are practical problems to appointing a woman, especially since training usually occurs at a regional centre and is often for several weeks. Family responsibilities will make it more difficult for women to attend, and they would find it impossible during the peak agricultural period, as they are responsible for producing food crops.

However, it is very important that women should have proper training, as it should improve their chances of being accepted in their villages. If women fail as the result of lack of training, it will be taken as a general indication of their unsuitability for the job. A practical compromise might be to have most of the training in the village, with a short period at the regional headquarters. The duties of a pump attendant include preventive maintenance, minor repairs and reporting breakdowns to headquarters. There must be adequate resources available: equipment, spare parts and back-up support.

Women well-caretakers might be elected, or a large number of women involved by rotating the post monthly. Responsibilities could include ensuring that all women receive information on the use of the well, that a fence or hedge is constructed around it and properly maintained. Well-caretakers would also have to prevent children misusing the well and playing inside the enclosure, keep the well-site clean and properly drained, and report problems to the pump attendant.

It would make the well-caretaker's job much easier if provision for washing clothes, in the form of a cemented area, was provided close to the well without the risk of polluting the water supply. The well has always been the traditional site for washing clothes, and prohibiting the practice would be unworkable, as women would be unwilling to carry home all the water needed to do washing at home.

Aspects of personal hygiene and sanitation should be appealing to the followers of Islam, and Christian groups could also be motivated for changes in patterns of living which lead to improved health and well-being.

Special programmes for primary school could be used to encourage children to accept changes, especially in terms of water-use patterns, and influence their mothers. Methodology is especially crucial here, however, as 'forced labour' with little or no explanation has been used to construct school fields and assist with reafforestation programmes in the past. Project staff and other qualified people should supplement the efforts of local teachers. Programmes in schools must above all be realistic. Marguerite Jellicoe who conducted an earlier study, noted the discouragement that schoolgirls in Singida experienced in the 1960s when they had learnt standards of cleanliness, home-care and dress that were often impossible to realize in their mothers' homes or in houses of the men that were willing to marry them.

For changes to be accepted and internalized, it is necessary to build on existing practices instead of trying to do away with the old order and introduce a completely new pattern of living. In order to achieve this, a sound knowledge of traditional patterns of living is necessary. This includes an understanding of the motivations behind the existing patterns. In efforts to improve women's position in rural areas, the starting point must naturally be an understanding of women's present situation. Understanding of the reasons behind the position and status of women in the society is also essential.[66]

Training through work experience
KEVIN TAYLER

Sudan is the largest country in Africa, and its Southern Region, with an area of approximately 650,000 square kilometres, includes about a quarter of the land area and has a population of about four million. The population is predominantly rural but Juba, Wau and Malakal, with approximate populations of 120,000, 80,000 and 60,000 respectively, are sizeable towns. Several other towns have populations in the range 10,000 to 20,000.

Juba, the seat of the regional government, is over 1,200 km from Khartoum and communications are difficult, both within the region and with the rest of the country.

Like other African countries, Sudan has been adversely affected by the recession in the world economy and it is currently faced with severe financial problems. At the same time, there is a shortage of trained people, particularly in the Southern Region where development was seriously set back by the civil war that ended in 1972. In view of these facts, it is inevitable that the Region relies heavily on the assistance of aid organizations and this is certainly true in the case of urban water supplies.

The water supply systems at Juba, Wau and Malakal are based on river abstraction with rapid gravity sand filtration, and were originally designed to serve populations of around 10,000. Although there have been additions to the original systems, facilities have failed to expand to match the growth of the towns so that large areas in each are without piped water. The systems are in a poor state of repair, due partly to the difficulties in obtaining parts and materials and partly to the lack of well-trained maintenance staff.

Some, but not all, of the smaller towns have piped water supplies. In areas without piped water supplies, a variety of water sources is used, ranging from boreholes to rivers and streams. Water carriers operate extensively in Juba and Malakal and their price for water is up to fifteen times the official rate for piped water.

Consultants have prepared reports on water supplies to Wau and Malakal which will lead to large reconstruction schemes if finance can be arranged. The reports recommend measures to be taken to improve water supplies to the towns in the interim period. A feasibility study is also planned for Juba where GTZ, the German technical aid agency, is carrying out a programme of interim measures. GTZ have also been involved with water supply schemes for Yambio and Maridi, two of the smaller towns.

Until recently, urban water supplies were the responsibility of the Public Electricity and Water Corporation (PEWC), a public corporation based in Khartoum. The southern area of PEWC was based in Juba and covered the whole of the Southern Region. Water and electricity services are in the process of being decentralized but the new arrangements have not yet been

finalized. The Regional Ministry of Housing and Public Utilities (RMH &
PU) has been involved with the schemes for water-supply improvements,
particularly those funded by GTZ.

The southern area has an operational deficit which has been met partly by
PEWC, Khartoum and partly by the regional government. A priority of any
development programme must be to take measures to reduce this deficit.

Southern Sudan programme

Assistance to Sudan in the fields of urban water supply and sanitation has
until now taken two forms. The first is the provision of finance for consultants to carry out feasibility studies, intended to lead to the detailed design
and then construction of new facilities. A consultant's report can provide a
useful statement of the overall strategy to be followed but the procedure has
drawbacks for a poorly developed area like Southern Sudan. It tends to
concentrate development into discrete periods of intense work at widely
spaced intervals, precluding the substantial involvement of local institutions
and ensuring heavy dependency on expatriate personnel.

Thus, the procedure does nothing to build up local expertise and increase
a country's self-reliance. The concentration of construction also tends to
push the need for correct operation and maintenance procedures and
training into the background. Two effects of this approach are that local
engineers and technicians are underworked, quickly becoming demoralized
and losing interest, and that the inflexibility of the procedure leads to delays
in execution while problems remain unsolved and water services deteriorate.

The second form of assistance, scholarships for academic study abroad,
has little relevance where consultants are used as described above. All
technical disciplines require a combination of practical experience and
theorectical knowledge and the knowledge gained through study is rapidly
lost if not put into use. Lasting development can only occur if steps are taken
to fully involve local personnel in schemes to improve water and sanitation
facilities.

Aid programmes must operate as far as is possible through local institutions which must be strengthened and supported where necessary to enable
them to function effectively.

A small team of engineers has been set up within the RMH & PU to work
on the planning, design and construction of water supply projects. Support
and guidance is provided by an experienced engineer recruited by VSO, a
British volunteer organization, and employed by the RMH & PU. Kevin
Tayler, the author, was the first such engineer. He started work in March
1981 and was replaced in early 1983. Both Kevin Tayler and his replacement
have been recruited from British water authorities.

Plans are in hand to extend the programme to include the training of
mechanical and electrical maintenance technicians. VSO or the organiza-

tion Water Aid, based in the British water industry and intended as a response to the Water Decade, will be used to recruit experienced technicians to assist in this part of the programme. The first priority will be to improve and repair existing facilities. This will enable correct operational procedures to be introduced so that the training programme can be extended to include operational staff.

As the reliability of water services is increased, their profitability will improve and it should be possible to reduce the operating deficit. Some attention will also have to be given to the training of accounting and administrative staff. Once the present position has been consolidated, it will be possible to start to expand services.

The aim of the team is to give engineers and technicians a grounding in the principles and practice of water supply and, at the same time, improve the state of water supplies in the Southern Region. Training is given as far as possible through the work of the team, but inevitably there are gaps in the knowledge gained in this way and directed reading and design examples are used to fill these gaps. A task which has been carried out by one member of the team may be repeated by another if it illustrates important principles. The intention is to cover a range of subjects including the planning of overall water strategy, hydraulic design of waterworks and distribution systems, a knowledge of the available plant and materials, preparation of working drawings, drawing office procedures and construction techniques.

The disadvantage of working alongside an already established programme is that work cannot be followed through from beginning to end. The decisions as to which work is required, how it should be executed and which materials are required have already been made. A more comprehensive approach is possible for Wau and Malakal. Programmes of essential work are being prepared by the team, based on the consultant's proposals for immediate measures but including other items, identified after examining the water supply system in each town.

Malakal is a good example of improving the functioning of a system without incurring large expenditure. The town is flat and extends about 5 km along and an average of 1 km back from the River Nile. At present, the distribution system is fed by gravity from a 15 m high tank at the waterworks. The main features of the original distribution system were 4 in. and 6 in. mains running parallel to the river. An 8 in. main laid in the early 1970s also runs the length of the town but the number of connections to it are not as many as its size would allow.

Water pressures throughout the town are extremely low. Approximate calculations indicate that they could be improved by dividing the distribution system into two zones. The zone nearer the waterworks can be served by gravity from the high-level tank and new pumps with a delivery head of around 40 m supply the further zone directly via the 8 in. main. Some new connections will be required, both at the waterworks and in the distribution system. This improvement provides a useful exercise, requiring estimates of demand, approximate hydraulic design, pump selection and some detailed design. If implemented successfully it will also provide greater income since improved pressures will bring an increased demand for house connections and public water points.

Operation and maintenance

Mechanical work requiring attention includes the repair of pumps, filter control mechanisms and bulk meters and the maintenance of tools and vehicles. Routines and maintenance schedules must be established. As with the electrical installation work, it is planned that this work will be carried out by Sudanese trainees working alongside experienced expatriate volunteers.

The most obvious problem in Southern Sudan is the difficulty of obtaining materials for even the most basic improvement schemes. Apart from the physical distance to hinder ordering and transporting materials, there is an acute lack of finance because many materials require foreign exchange for their purchase. Manufacturers' catalogues and other technical information are being gathered in the Juba design office to assist in ordering equipment and materials, but there remains the problem of financing and transporting purchases, particularly those which must be imported.

The problems caused by inadequate finance will undoubtedly continue to occur in many countries throughout the Water Decade and beyond. Repaying interest on large loans may be difficult for Sudan. It will therefore be reluctant to put large-scale projects into practice.

Consultants should be asked to produce proposals which can be implemented over a period as a series of small contracts combined, where appropriate, with the use of direct labour rather than in concentrated blocks. This will ensure development, albeit at a slow rate. If arrangements are made for the supply of imported materials such as pipes and fittings, much of the work can be carried out by local contractors, thus adding the knowledge and experience available in the country for continued development.

Unless there is this emphasis on starting in a small way and involving local institutions and manpower, the Water Decade will fall far short of its aims in urban areas in many countries in Africa.

(*Waterlines* Vol. 2 No. 1, July 1983)

Planning intensive training courses
FRED ROSENSWEIG

In this article a workshop is defined as an event, one to three weeks in duration, in which the participants acquire new skills and knowledge to help them carry out their everyday jobs more effectively and efficiently.

Once a general need for improving knowledge and skills has been determined, a specific needs' assessment should be carried out. This assessment should focus on determining the overall goals of the project and the specific knowledge and skills that personnel should have to reach those goals. It should emphasize the tasks that the workshop participants will be assigned in their jobs and which the workshop can address. Once these tasks have been determined and their importance to the project assessed, the overall goals and objectives of the workshop can be established.

The goals and objectives should address what the participants need to be able to do rather than just increase their knowledge of subject matter. A careful needs' assessment will greatly assist in establishing overall goals and objectives. These must be explained to the appropriate manager(s) to ensure that they are in keeping with project goals.

Selecting participants and trainees

Where possible WASH tries to make reconnaisance visits to the countries where the workshop will be held two to four months prior to the event, in order to assess needs and reach agreement with programme officials on the goals and objectives of the workshop. The rules and responsibilities of the host country groups sponsoring the workshop and the training consultants brought in to do the workshop are also discussed.

The selection of participants may appear on the surface to be obvious, but there are several key considerations.

○ Are the participants in the right job to make use of the skills and knowledge they will acquire at the workshop?
○ Will the participants have such varied educational backgrounds and experience that it will be impossible to satisfy everyone?
○ Will the various jobs of the participants (such as managers and line positions) be so disparate as to inhibit learning?

The maximum recommended workshop size is 20 to 25 participants. If there are more participants it is difficult to find a suitable training site and the amount of 'hands-on' experience for each is likely to be less.

After the trainers have been selected, the workshop designed, and the training site chosen, a three- to five-page description of the workshop should be sent to the participants two to four weeks beforehand. This information greatly influences the participants' expectations and alleviates much of the uncertainty that participants feel about such things. In a workshop run in the Dominican Republic, half of the participants did not receive this description because of administrative problems. Those participants came with an unrealistic set of expectations as to the content of the workshop which created initial problems for the trainers and other participants. Those who received the description had none of these problems.

When planning its workshops, WASH has set certain standards for the selection of trainers. A trainer-to-trainee ratio of one to 10 is recommended. Workshops with more than 10 participants should use two trainers. When using two trainers, a balance of technical expertise and training skills is suggested. Most training teams for WASH workshops have consisted of a technical specialist with a fair amount of exposure to training and a training specialist experienced in the design and delivery of workshops. In this way both the technical content and the training process are well represented.

Trainers with experience in doing short courses or workshops are preferred. Teachers who have worked only in formal academic settings often tend to be too lecture-oriented in their approach and are not used.

WASH has attempted to identify local trainers to work with its training consultants. For example, two Togolese trainers were identified and worked as co-trainers during a rain-water catchment workshop in Togo. Following the workshop, the WASH training specialist worked with these local trainers to develop a French version of the WASH Trainers Guide on Rain-water Harvesting. The result was two local trainers with skills to conduct the workshop and a trainers guide tailored to local conditions.

Designing the workshop

Before designing the workshop it is important to determine what time limitations it may suffer. For instance, the maximum amount of time available for the workshop in view of participants' work schedules and time available per day, and scheduling factors such as holidays that fall within the workshop period, weather (it might be too hot in the middle of the day), and protocol (opening and closing ceremonies).

Once the amount of time available has been determined, the trainers should begin to design the workshop. Table 10.1 is a checklist of the key considerations in designing a workshop.

A highly participatory, interactive approach is used in workshops. In a short period, the more participation there is in both classroom and in field activities, the more learning is likely to occur and the longer the knowledge will be retained. Lectures and other didactic learning methods are not emphasized. In a latrine construction workshop conducted in the Dominican Republic, the Dominican participants cited the participatory training approach as the most significant strength of the workshop. The same

Table 10.1

Design process based on the goals and objectives
Appropriate choice of exercises/activities
Appropriate choice of training materials/aids
Sequencing of activities
Integration of sessions
Varying the exercises
Pacing of activities
Allocating adequate time for sessions
Blend of theory and practice

comment was made by the participants in a latrine construction workshop in Senegal.

In the workshops WASH has conducted, a key element has been to hire a local mason and work crew to assist the participants to complete the construction. In Senegal, three labourers and a mason were hired to finish digging the pits, haul the sand and gravel, and complete the foundation for the shelter. The work crew supplements the labour of the workshop participants so that when opportunities for further learning are exhausted and only the labour remains, the participants may move to another session while the work crew completes the activity. This is not meant to deny the value of manual labour for the participants.

Training materials

Before developing any new materials, it is recommended that existing materials available to the trainers are examined. In many cases, materials may already exist which can either be adopted as they stand or easily adapted to the situation. Existing materials should be surveyed not only for accuracy and appropriateness of the technical content, but also for whether they fit in with the proposed training process.

After the materials have been surveyed they must be put together for use in the workshop. It may be concluded, after examining existing material, that new materials must be developed. Adequate time must be allowed since this is time-consuming.

The WASH Project is developing four trainer guides for workshops on latrine construction, handpump installation and maintenance, spring capping, and rain-water catchment. These guides contain all the information a trainer needs to plan and conduct a skill-building workshop including workshop designs, trainer guide-lines, hand-outs to participants, lists of supplies and material, and reference materials for trainers. Each training programme is about two weeks long and includes field construction projects as well as classroom time. These guides have been developed as part of an effort to provide sound training models adapted to important low-cost rural water supply and sanitation technologies. All of these guides will be field-tested and revised twice.

Importance of organization

If organization of a workshop, especially a practical one, is not good, the workshop and learning will suffer. Below is a list of the most common things which need to be taken into account. They vary depending on the nature of the particular workshop.

Transport. Will vehicles be needed during the workshop? How will participants get to and from the classroom and work sites?

Room and board. Is the accommodation adequate for the number of participants? Is the training site suitable for study after workshop hours? Are the arrangements for meals satisfactory?

Training site. Is the training site close enough to the area where hands-on work will take place? Is there a suitable classroom with movable chairs and tables? Does the room have good ventilation and lighting? Does the site have the necessary training equipment, such as flip-charts, blackboards, typewriter, and duplicating machine?

Purchase of materials. Have all tools and materials been purchased and transported to the site in advance? Is there a good place to store them before and during the workshop?

Supplementary labour-force. Have arrangements been made for a work crew, and has a local mason been identified to supervise the work force?

One of the most critical conditions for a successful workshop is the staff preparation before the beginning of the training programme. This preparation, which is in addition to the time spent designing and preparing materials for the workshop, should consist of the following:

O Discussing the trainers' roles, ways of working together, their expectations, and the division of responsibilities.
O Making a list of the tasks that need to be completed prior to and during the workshop.
O Reviewing the workshop design for any last-minute changes.
O Contacting local officials for protocol purposes.

In the Dominican Republic, for example, a three-day staff-training session was held. The result was that several questions were answered and it was a lot easier for the Dominican co-trainers and the WASH consultants to work together.

If all the planning steps described above are carried out then the workshop should proceed without major problems. During the workshop there should be:

Activity Month	4	3	2	1 Workshop start
Carry out preliminary needs assessment	■			
Select trainers		■		
Conduct a detailed needs assessment	■			
Establish goals and objectives		■		
Identify participants			■	
Design workshop			■	
Prepare training materials			■	
Locate training site			■	
Arrange participant and staff room and board			■	
Work with local community to obtain co-operation (if there will be field-work)				■
Carry out technical survey on site (if there will be field-work)				■
Arrange transportation				■
Identify and obtain needed tools and materials				■
Arrange for storage of supplies				■
Staff preparation				■

Figure 10.2   *Suggested timetable (to be completed before the workshop)*

○ Daily meetings for the trainers to review the day's events and to plan for the next day. This meeting should focus on the training process as well as the workshop content. What worked well? What didn't work? What should be done differently the next day?
○ A mid-course workshop evaluation with the participants. This should take no longer than 30 minutes and should attempt to obtain the participants' reactions up to that point.
○ A system of keeping daily notes. These notes will help in revising the workshop in the future.
○ Devoting an hour at the end of the workshop to an evaluation with the participants (oral and/or written) and focus on what the participants have to say about the workshop.
○ A review of the workshops' results with key programme managers as a means of debriefing and linking the workshop back to the realities or work.
○ A brief report should be written documenting the workshops' successes and areas where improvement is needed.

As a general idea for the timing of the steps described above, a timetable (Figure 10.2) is proposed. Although the timetable will vary according to the nature of the workshop, it should give the reader a good indication of time to allow for the planning stages. The timetable assumes that the programme managers will carry out a preliminary needs assessment and that the trainers will do a more detailed assessment.

Within a water supply and sanitation agency or institution, training workshops represent one of the best ways of increasing the skills and knowledge of personnel. Courses in academic institutions are usually not geared to the needs of people who are already working. The steps recommended in this article suggest the key elements of carrying out an effective workshop. In the experience of the WASH Project, these steps lead to water supply and sanitation workshops which have a significant impact on participants and programmes.

(*Waterlines* Vol. 3 No. 1, July 1984)

Malawi: Demonstration for self-help

J. GUS LIEBENOW

Even before the IDWSSD, Dr Banda, Malawi's president, committed the Malawian government to improving the supply of clean water to the rural countryside in both good years and lean years to enhance the quality of rural life and thereby keep people in those areas of the country where they could be most productive. The task is an enormous one, considering that most Malawians live in dispersed rural settlements far from the major lakes.

The programme has been imaginative. In addition to using gravity-fed systems (the principal subject of this article), the government has invested in pumping water from Malawi's lakes and rivers, and has built dams (most significantly to provide water to the new capital city of Lilongwe). Further, the number of boreholes drilled and maintained by the government for rural communities has increased significantly.

This article focuses on the development in Mulanje District, where the first major efforts took place. Today, over ¼ million people in the district now have clean water no farther than one quarter of a mile away from any homestead. Some one million people will be served in all regions by 1985.

The genius of the Mulanje and other gravity fed water schemes is that they work with, rather than against, nature. The primary source of energy is gravity, and thus there is no need for pumping equipment, which has a high initial cost, high costs of petroleum fuel to operate it, and high costs of labour and parts to maintain and repair it.

Maintaining the purity of the water is also relatively cost free. Since the main pipes are placed in mountain streams at an altitude above most human habitation, there is little pollution at the source and hence no need for chlorine or other chemicals. All that is required is a sedimentation tank to remove natural debris and sediment before the water enters the main conduit.

Constant surveillance of the water in the storage tanks and immediate repair of any break in a pipeline or a tap are further guarantees against pollution. The tanks, which hold about 50,000 gallons of water, are routinely emptied and cleaned twice a year as a further precaution against the build up of algae and other organisms.

The other major factor in the low cost of the Mulanje and other gravity fed schemes in Malawi is the central importance of creative community self-help both in the initial construction and in the maintenance of the system.

Political will

The labour of literally hundreds of thousands of villagers enormously reduced the cost of construction, but self-help, to be successful, must be supported by external agencies. In this instance, it was not only the psychological and material support provided to the people by President Banda and the Malawi Congress Party leadership in the area, but also the skill of the political leadership in convincing external donor agencies of the worth and feasibility of the project. Indeed, the result was an impressive collaboration on the part of the Malawian and foreign government aid agencies, the UN and both religious and secular private donor groups.

Many of the donor agencies look upon the Malawi gravity-fed water system as ideal from the standpoint of their overall development philosophies: the project is aimed primarily to help the rural poor; it focuses on improvement of health as the key to the developmental process; and it has elicited a continuing spirit of community cooperation which can be transferred to other development projects. Its results, moreover, become visible in a relatively short period of time and the low costs per person show maximum use of the funds available.

Technical problems

Unskilled and semi-skilled voluntary labour—no matter how well motivated and energetic—can accomplish little unless skills are introduced which can guarantee the success of enterprise.

Many technical problems had to be resolved in order to close the gap between inspiration and its fruition. First, statistical data and oral tradition had to confirm that the mountain streams which it was planned to use could be guaranteed to flow all year round. Second, extensive aerial photography had to be done to insure that there was a feasible route for a pipeline from the source high on the mountain to the plains below. In selecting the appropriate sites from the aerial survey maps, the engineers had to take into account the configuration of the terrain, the clusterings of population, the food-producing capacity of the area to be served and existing local political boundaries.

Next, decisions had to be made on the appropriate piping for the system and to place advance orders so that the piping would arrive at the same time as the work was carried out. It was decided that asbestos piping would be the best for the segment from the mountain source to the storage tanks. Asbestos was thought to be the most resistant material to corrosion and would be strong enough to withstand the weight of stone and sand piled into the trenches to protect the pipes from breaking.

More flexible plastic tubing was adequate for those stretches of the system that carried the water from the tanks to the village taps. Finally, before the volunteer community labour could be involved, a limited number of technicians had to be trained in rudimentary hydrology, geology, and other subjects so they could provide informed supervision of the volunteer labourers. Since the piping would be buried under three feet of stone and dirt, it was absolutely essential for the laying and joining of the pipes to be done carefully and skilfully. The technicians would also have to be trained in the art of maintaining the commitment and enthusiasm of the volunteers until the scheme was actually in operation.

Self-help

The involvement of community labour in the project took place in two stages. First, an area for a small pilot project was selected, partly on the basis of the terrain but, more important, on the strength of commitment of the community to self-help projects previously demonstrated. In the pilot scheme at Chingale on Zomba Mountain—as was true of work on the subsequent major schemes—no community labour was actually involved until it had been demonstrated that strong community commitment existed.

This meant that there had to be numerous village meetings in which local leaders, Members of Parliament and traditional chiefs attempted to explain the benefits for the villagers in terms of health, access to water during the dry season, and other factors.

It was also explained what would be required of the people should they decide to participate in the self-help scheme. Throughout the discussions, ran the message: 'This is not the government's water scheme, it is yours. It will only work if you are willing to work. And it is you, rather than government, that will make the decision on whether to proceed, to organize yourselves into committees, and to decide the order in which various villages will participate.'

The project would not work if the people felt that this was just another imposition on them by the government. This attitude was also in keeping with Dr Banda's philosophy of 'helping those who help themselves'.

Demonstration effect

With the success of the pilot scheme (which had also provided invaluable field experience for the paid staff), it became relatively easier to persuade the people of the Mulanje area that the gravity flow water system did work and that it had brought water to within a quarter of a mile of every homestead in the pilot area. The 'demonstration effect' upon political and other leaders who saw the pilot scheme was dramatic, and it was a significant factor in getting the local committees in the Mulanje area organized quickly and in maintaining enthusiasm until the water actually reached the villages. In the larger projects at Mulanje and other areas, the anticipated benefits were to be up to two years in arriving.

In addition to the demonstration effect, other techniques were employed to sustain the villagers' enthusiasm. The work, for example, proceeded from the mountain downward. This meant that at the end of each day's laying of pipe, the water was turned on. This had the dual effect of flushing out the pipes as work progressed (which was technically sound) and of graphically demonstrating that the mountain water was now that much closer to the villages.

Second, it was necessary to maintain a certain rhythm in the work schedule so that the various phases could be co-ordinated, the quality of the work maintained, and the best use could be made of the paid technical and supervisory labour while maintaining some flexibility.

Without flexibility, it would be hard to instil the notion that this was the villagers' project, not just government's. Account had to be taken, for example, of the demands which the various phases of the agricultural cycle placed upon the volunteer labour.

For each day's work, the paid supervisor would indicate by two parallel pieces of string the digging that was to be accomplished. Each village, in rotation, was expected to give a week's work to excavating the trenches from the mountain source to the storage tanks, as well as doing the shallower digging on the branch lines that led to the village taps. Much of the digging was done by women, who in many cases worked with babies wrapped to their backs. Men did, however, participate in both digging, and laying and joining the pipes. During Youth Week—an annual March event in Malawi—many school-age youngsters committed themselves to digging trenches as part of their service contribution. Even pre-school children carried the lighter plastic pipes.

Blending technologies

The construction of the system was a remarkable blending of modern and traditional technologies. Hydrologists and an aerial survey analysis were used with other aspects of modern technology, while the digging was done largely with the *jembe*, or short-handled hoe, supplemented by a pickaxe where the ground was very hard. In an area where large granite boulders obstructed the path of the pipeline, some very ancient African technology came into play to split the boulder into manageable pieces for removal. This consisted of building a huge bonfire atop the rock and letting the wood burn for about six hours. Then cold water would be thrown on the heated boulder, causing it to crack along its fault lines. Workers with hammers, crowbars and pickaxes then reduce it to small pieces.

The construction phase was also used to further reinforce the message that this was the people's project and not the government's alone. For example, each village committee was told that it would be responsible for reimbursing the scheme for any pipe that was broken during its work period.

As in the construction phase, maintenance required a blending of paid, technically trained personnel with a spirit of community self help. Without it, the ultimate objective of providing clean water to the rural population of Malawi cannot be realized.

Typical, perhaps, of the trained supervisory personnel for the Mulanje and other gravity-fed systems was Mr Nkhoma. Since he had been a participant in the project, he had first-hand knowledge of the general problems and knew the route of the pipeline so he could quickly find major breaks in the system should they occur. He was a resident of the area who elected not to migrate in search of more lucrative employment. His primary school education reinforced the respect and confidence the people of the area had in him. This was important, for in addition to the routine tasks of supervising the cleaning of the storage tanks twice a year or checking on the condition of the taps, he had the responsibility of teaching the villagers about the importance of sanitation and clean water in maintaining good health.

Tap committees

Responsibility for continuing the spirit of self-help fell largely on the women. Since it was they who had had the major burden of finding, digging for, and carrying the water during the dry season, they appeared to embrace their responsibilities with enthusiasm. Several I interviewed in the villages said they now had more time for their families, and had gardens to supplement the family food supply.

Each tap has its committee of women, who see that the tap is not left running, that people do not leave standing water that might become a breeding ground for mosquitoes or snails, and that the cement slab around the tap (a gift of the government) is kept clean.

No-one is permitted to wash clothes, bathe, or do anything other than draw water in the tap area. Each committee has responsibility for disciplining offenders, but it appears that the women's pride in their contribution to the water scheme, as well as social pressure, constitutes the major deterrent. The pride of each tap committee was shown, moreover, by the friendly competition in landscaping the edges of the cement slabs with flowers. As with the local supervisor, the knowledge that the women had acquired of the position of the trenches ensured that the pipe would be quickly located in the event of a break.

Maintenance costs are being kept low. The only thing a village may have to pay for is the replacement of a tap. It is reasoned that the breakage (as well as wastage of water) can normally be avoided by replacing used washers with new ones provided free of charge by government.

Voting with their feet

One further common sense index of the success of the programme is the fact that people are literally 'voting with their feet' in its support. There is a considerable migration of Malawians into the areas already served. Although this may strain existing facilities, there is probably enough flexibility to accommodate them. And they will hopefully not only be healthier for the move, but will remain in rural areas, improving agricultural productivity rather than migrating to the towns.

Other systems

The supporters of the concept of a gravity-fed scheme would be the first to acknowledge that it cannot be replicated throughout the rest of Africa or even all Malawi, although there are perennial mountain streams above fertile plains in many parts of the continent. In accomplishing the goal of clean water for every Malawian, resort will have to be made to more costly pumping systems, deep well drilling, and catchment dams.

In the long run, however, the greatest benefit derived from the way in which the Mulanje and other Malawian schemes were carried out is the spirit of self help so apparent. People realize not only that their lives can be changed for the better, but that they themselves can be a significant factor in making that change.

(*Waterlines* Vol. 3 No. 1, July 1984)

CHAPTER 11
Planning and Management

In the first article, the ITDG Water Panel stress that future management is the key to the planning of rural water supplies in developing countries and should therefore have an overriding influence in the selection of projects. The article sets out some basic principles. Bill Wood expresses the problem succinctly in the title to his article 'Who will look after the village water supply?'. He was Chief of the Community Water Supply Unit for the WHO in Geneva and his constructive suggestions warrant full consideration.

Louise Fortmann outlines the lessons from Botswana in managing seasonal man-made water sources and comes to the conclusion that management by the community and the use of familiar methods are likely to be successful strategies. John Williamson compares the three approaches of community involvement in the drinking water programmes of the Nawal Parasi Hill Project in Nepal. He concludes that development agencies should be more willing to give control and responsibility to the community. Latrine building has been encouraged by adopting the villagers' advice that only households with latrines should be supplied with water, thus leading to a combined programme. Reference is made in the article to the evaluation of the project on completion to ascertain whether it is achieving its aims. WHO have developed a minimum evaluation procedure for water supply and sanitation projects.[67]

The final article relates to a multi-disciplinary study financed by Petroleum Development (Oman) Ltd. Sally Sutton carried out the field work on which her article is based while she was working with Durham University's Oman Research Project. A *falaj* consists of a tunnel, perhaps many kilometres long, which taps aquifers and leads the water to the surface. The gradient must be less than that of either the water-table below ground, or the water surface. The design of the tunnels, therefore, has to be very precise and they require regular maintenance, but operate without any mechanical device. Construction, maintenance and administration are hereditary jobs in the community. Major changes have occurred which have placed the *falaj* at risk; drought has speeded up the process. There are important lessons to be learned from this traditional system.

Guide-lines on planning and management of rural water supplies in developing countries

THE ITDG WATER PANEL

The term 'rural water supplies' covers a wide category of schemes ranging from a well with bucket supplying a few isolated huts to river pumping schemes with piped supplies to several villages. The latter range from such simple treatments as communal standpipes to taps in individual homes, and even provision for livestock and vegetable gardens. The problems of preparing guide-lines for these different cases is further complicated by the diversity of climatic and socio-economic factors prevailing in the developing countries. In this article, the guide-lines will be limited to rural community water-supply schemes, based on experience gained from existing projects, and the practical application of appropriate technology principles. The article will only highlight some of the basic principles: a selection of the more important publications which provide useful guidance in planning and management. These can be found in the list of References on p. 276.[75,76,77,78,79,80]

Future management—the key

Operation and maintenance are usually the most neglected aspects of any form of development. Poor or non-existent administrative and technical support and lack of funds for proper operation are cited as the most frequent causes for the failure of rural water-supply systems.

During the planning, design and construction phases of a rural water scheme, future management considerations must have an overriding influence in the selection of the optimum solution, although this is often overlooked. Suitable local personnel must be fully trained in the skills required to operate and maintain the plant, and the technology should be kept simple so that they will be able to manage the system over long periods of time in the absence of a qualified engineer. The method and materials of construction, together with the future organization and financial considerations, are also critical factors.

Appropriateness of technology

Rural water-supply projects are crucial to raising the standards and well-being of the vast majority of people in developing countries. Appropriate technology is that which makes the best use of available resources, such as labour (skilled and unskilled), capital, and natural assets, taking into account operation and maintenance as well. Appropriate technology is not just a method of production, but a way of life; therefore a detailed knowledge of the country involved is also required. The proper identification of the appropriate technology for a particular rural water supply necessitates the evaluation and comparison of alternative methods, including all costs and benefits.

The optimum selected will largely be determined by the social framework and the valuation allocated to the various inputs and outputs. A rural water-supply project designed, built and maintained using appropriate technology should be more labour-intensive than high technologies, more efficient than traditional methods, and should have the following characteristics:

○ Simple, robust and reliable.
○ Relatively labour-intensive with low capital cost and little import of foreign material and skills.
○ Acceptance and support of the local community with minimum change to the social fabric.
○ Capable of organization at local level with relatively simple training.

The implementation of appropriate technology projects is not necessarily a question of new inventions or methods, but requires the sensible use of an existing technology with basic developments and changes. It involves not only supervision of construction but also the establishment of the requisite organizational structure including the training of staff and management. Evaluation in planning is directed towards the optimum use of resources, and to this end it is absolutely vital that the views of the local people should be sought and their advice heeded so that there is no doubt that the scheme is acceptable to them. Their assistance and co-operation in planning and in construction, preferably through self-help, should ensure that the scheme does not become yet another failure.

Survey of local conditions

Appropriate technology, although simple in concept, may sometimes be difficult to implement efficiently because of complex procedures and relationships involved in a particular country, where, for instance, methods involving a more intensive use of labour may ultimately require political direction. In some situations, the structural change of the society may be a necessary precondition, and the engineering problems will probably not be the key issue. In these cases, a comprehensive survey of local conditions is a fundamental requirement. Important points to investigate in surveys are:

○ Available and potential water sources.
○ Examination of patterns of water use (for example, where do people do their laundry, how much water is carried and how far?).

○ Health problems which may focus on particular requirements for the water supply (precautions regarding schistosomiasis).
○ Skills of local people.
○ Availability of local materials.
○ Study of institution infrastructure for management.

The very important part played by women should always be remembered, as it is almost invariably women who have the responsibility for obtaining water, and for its use in the home for general hygiene. Planners in the past have mostly been men, and, in many communities, religious and cultural attitudes make it virtually impossible for the views of women to be ascertained by male planners. Future planning must therefore make full use of women for social research and investigation. Education in improved hygiene and optimum water use should also start in the home.

During the survey of local conditions, the planning team should endeavour to employ a woman speaking the local language to interview local women about the way they use water and the requirements they think a new supply should serve. She should also have a role in the educational process necessary to ensure that the water supply is fully and properly used; she may be a local person with some training in hygiene or health education.

The type of supply to be provided depends on water availability, costs, and climatic/social factors. Data on water use for design should be derived from existing village supplies with similar culture, economic and climatic conditions. It is preferable, also, to provide adequate supplies for cleaning and washing, rather than just for potable purposes, as this will greatly improve hygiene with consequent reduction in disease.

Demand forecasting is a necessary but uncertain exercise. Population and future growth are the basis of forecasting, but water availability itself will influence future settlement. Water use greatly depends on the method of supply. For instance, demand from communal standpipes, involving the carrying of water, will be much less than that from individual house connections. Wasteful use can lead to severe shortages in even the best planned schemes unless adequate controls can be implemented. Also, in many rural and even urban situations, if more water is made available to people with inadequate sanitation the health situation deteriorates. The development of water supplies can go only as far as local sanitation justifies.

Source selection

When selecting a supply, preference should be given to naturally pure sources which can be protected from pollution, as purification of unsafe water under rural conditions can be both expensive and difficult to organize. The algorithm in Figure 11.1 can be recommended as a rational method for the assessment of possible sources.

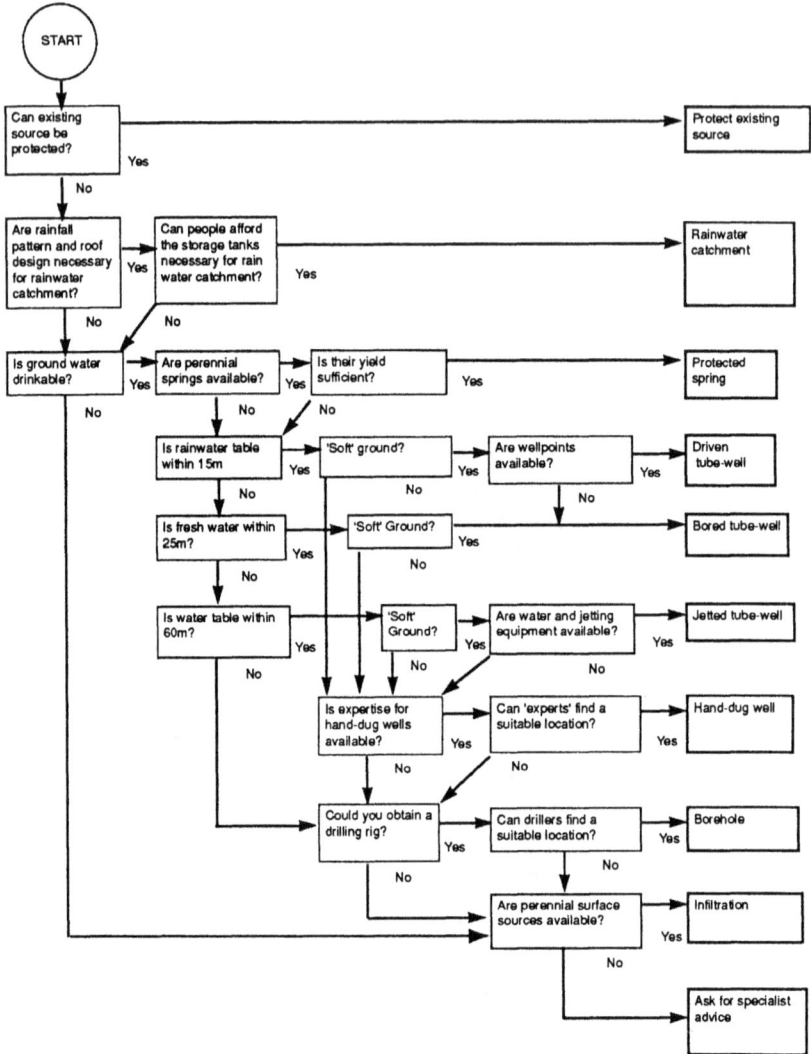

Figure 11.1   *Choosing a source of water. Follow the arrow corresponding to your answer to the question in each box (Chart: S. Cairncross and R. Feachem, see Reference 71)*

Ground water is usually the first practicable choice, either from perennial springs, or from wells or boreholes. To avoid pollution, measures such as the exclusion of surface runoff by constructing a diversion channel above the spring, or, in the case of boreholes, lining the top of the well to prevent contamination by seepage from the surface, are essential.

Abstraction from river sources introduces problems of pollution by disease-causing micro-organisms, turbidity and extreme variation between flood and drought levels. To minimize these problems, consideration should be given to abstraction from boreholes or infiltration galleries in the immediate vicinity of surface sources.

In all cases, it is desirable to obtain bacterial and chemical analyses of water sources over a period to determine whether any noxious or undesirable chemicals may render the source unsuitable. Special treatment, however, should only be considered if it can be afforded and reliably operated.

Ideally, the source selected should have a reliable yield sufficient to satisfy future growth over several years. This will avoid difficult choices in the future between either superseding an existing small scheme by a larger scheme with a consequent waste of resources, of having to operate and maintain two or more separate schemes simultaneously.

Staged development is recommended as the basis for any new rural water-supply project so as to introduce new ideas gradually with robust and simple equipment. If villages start off with a large, sophisticated supply there is a strong probability that breakdowns will occur. In the least developed areas, staged development must mean emphasis first on public water stations with house connections to priority consumers only, such as schools and dispensaries. More extensive connections can only be made if the adequacy of the supply and disposal systems are able to handle the increased volume that will be involved.

Reliability of supplies

Storage is the simplest method of treatment as the quality of water can be improved by allowing it to stand in an open tank or basin. If the water can be stored in a closed tank for more than 48 hours then it will be free of schistosome larvae and will contain considerably fewer viruses, bacteria, protozoal cysts and helminth eggs. Storage near to the point of demand is also strongly advocated to balance the fluctuating demand against fixed pumping and treatment rates, thereby enabling schemes to be designed for average, *not* peak demands. Additional storage is useful at times of breakdown or flash floods when excessive turbidity may make surface sources untreatable for short periods. It may be argued that the cost of standby storage would be better spent in improving supplies elsewhere, but the health benefits of a water supply can be adversely affected if a temporary failure forces the villagers to revert to inferior polluted supplies.

The same standby considerations apply to pumping and treatment plants. Standby capacity should be sufficient to enable single units to be taken out of operation for maintenance without unduly affecting supply. There should be sufficient pump spare units to facilitate rapid replacement and despatch to headquarters in sequence for repair or comprehensive overhaul. Obviously, a balance must be struck between standby on a particular scheme and extension of supplies elsewhere. Standardization of equipment can greatly reduce the number of spares and standby sets to be carried.

Furthermore, the careful selection of simple robust equipment and materials, together with close supervision of construction and installation reduces the risk of breakdowns. For example, pipe materials should be carefully selected for local conditions and self-help should be limited to trenching and the carrying of pipes. Pipe-laying must be left to trained personnel to minimize pipe failures and excessive leakage.

Treatment and storage are linked to the source and method of abstraction. If preliminary storage and simple sedimentation are insufficient then consideration can be given to slow sand filtration. Equipment for this process requires careful design and operation but the method is unsuitable for water of a high turbidity or varying rates of flow. The reliable production of a pure wholesome water from a polluted source is normally achieved by chlorinating water of low turbidity, often necessitating chemical coagulation, sedimentation and filtration.

To be effective, these processes must be continuous and failsafe, thus requiring careful monitoring of sophisticated equipment and regular supplies of chemicals. For the vast majority of rural water-supply schemes, these standards are just not attainable. Hence, where sources are less than pure, the best that can be done is to attempt to achieve the highest unvarying standard possible. Intermittent treatment is useless and it is far better to concentrate on pollution control measures and simple effective treatment to minimize disease-causing micro-organisms.

Operation and maintenance

For most schemes these can be only infrequent supervision from central headquarters, and control must be decentralized to village headmen or a locally-elected authority. They, in turn, will usually delegate responsibility to a volunteer caretaker, who will have little or no assistance, but should always be encouraged and given moral support. This person should be provided with the tools and materials necessary for the job, and furthermore must be fully trained, preferably through in-service training during construction and commissioning stages, supplemented by formal training at headquarters or on an existing scheme.

For any water supply, unremitting care is mandatory. The first requirement is to have as many lines of defence as possible to avoid the dangers of pollution. With simple methods of abstraction and treatment the lines of defence are strictly limited and greater emphasis should be placed on control routines with rigid checks and counter-checks. The caretaker should have a comprehensive check-list of controls and procedures, such as inspection and maintenance of channels to divert surface water from spring sources, and the

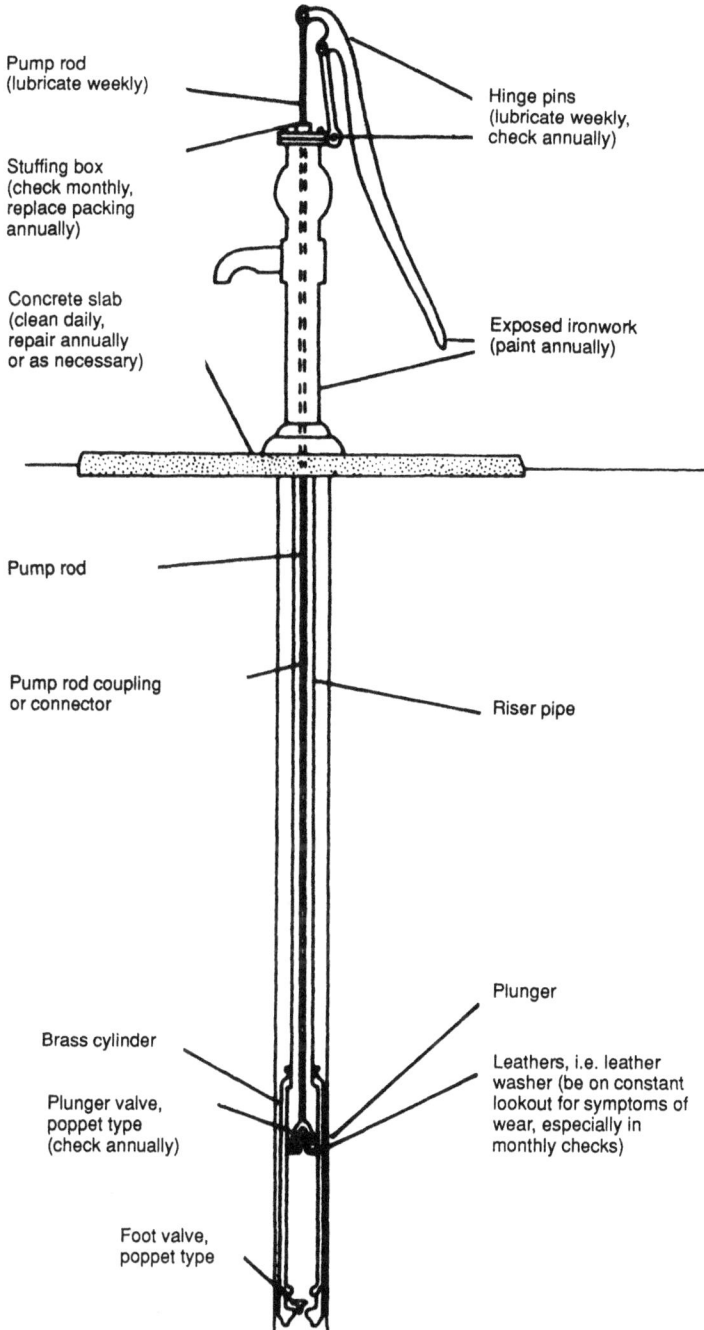

Pump rod
(lubricate weekly)

Hinge pins
(lubricate weekly,
check annually)

Stuffing box
(check monthly,
replace packing
annually)

Concrete slab
(clean daily,
repair annually
or as necessary)

Exposed ironwork
(paint annually)

Pump rod

Pump rod coupling
or connector

Riser pipe

Plunger

Leathers, i.e. leather
washer (be on constant
lookout for symptoms of
wear, especially in
monthly checks)

Brass cylinder

Plunger valve,
poppet type
(check annually)

Foot valve,
poppet type

Figure 11.2   *Maintenance points on a simple hand pump (photo: Arnold Pacey from* Hand Pump Maintenance, *Reference 47)*

villagers should be kept informed of the health risks of pollution to their supply.

Rules and regulations must be clearly defined and be enforceable for both pollution control and water use. However, petty rules should be vigorously excluded, as they will lead to disrespect for all regulations.

As regards maintenance, the caretaker should be competent to undertake day to day routines but arrangements should be made for regular preventive maintenance to be undertaken by visiting skilled personnel. Operation and maintenance procedures should be clearly defined in manuals which should be simple and concise. The equipment suppliers should provide the technical information on which the manuals are based. If they are accompanied by suitable diagrams or even photographs they are more likely to be consulted and understood.

Every aspect of the water supply and every item of equipment should be analysed in terms of noting places where wear, blockage, or malfunctioning is likely to occur. Every point that needs cleaning, removal of debris, etc. should also be noted. A comprehensive list of maintenance points should then be drawn up, and, as shown on the hand pump diagram (Figure 11.2), a desirable frequency of maintenance should be noted.

It should then be decided which of these maintenance tasks should be left to the caretaker and which tasks should be carried out by visiting technicians employed by the central water-supply agency. Some such procedure is the only way of ensuring that responsibilities are allocated clearly, and that nothing is left to chance; it will make sure that the training and manuals provided cover all the essential points.

It should, however, be emphasized that everything does break down soon or later. Facilities for repair are therefore vital and should be a major consideration in the choice of equipment.[35,47,68,69,70,71]

(*Appropriate Technology* Vol. 7 No. 3, December 1980)

Who will look after the village water supply?

W. E. WOOD

There are few ways in which the health and general well-being of small communities can be so improved, at such a relatively low cost, as by providing them with a safe and reliable water supply. Unfortunately there is sometimes a difference between constructing an installation capable of supplying the needs of a village and the actual provision of water to individual consumers.

That this distinction is not an imaginary one can be seen in many parts of the world. Water-works can be found, apparently well designed and properly constructed, which have degenerated through neglect or misuse and are now either partially or wholly inoperative. A frequent cause for such deterioration is that insufficient thought was given at the planning stage as to the way in which the completed works would be operated, maintained and financed—in a word, how they would be managed.

Any water supply, however large or small, consists of three essential parts:

○ A source of water.
○ The physical works which bring the water from the source to the consumer, treating and storing it en route as necessary.
○ The organization that manages and operates the service.

These three parts are interdependent and indispensible; failure of any one of them means failure of the whole system.

This is more obviously true in the case of larger works that incorporate pumping and other mechanical plant, chemical dosing reservoirs and complex distribution systems. Neglect or unskilled handling can quickly lead to breakdowns, and insufficient financing may mean understaffing or complete shutdown if fuel and chemicals cannot be purchased.

In the case of smaller works the results of inadequate management may not be so immediately apparent, but can be just as disastrous in the long run. Just as no planner of any water undertaking would allow construction to start until the adequacy and reliability of the proposed source has been thoroughly tested and proved, so should the system of management be laid down and approved by all concerned at an initial stage of planning. Only too often the principle that 'details can be worked out later' has led to the corollary 'it's too late to change now' when difficulties in working have become manifest.

Ownership

One of the most obvious questions about any water supply is 'who owns it?' This might seem of minor consequence until the question is rephrased as 'who is responsible for it?' The answer is not always as straightforward as it should be.

Water supplies may be financed and constructed in a number of different ways. Government grants are often available for rural works, sometimes with assistance from international or bilateral agencies (such as UNICEF or one of the regional development banks). Charitable funds may be used, and the actual construction may be carried out by a missionary (or similar) society.

It frequently happens that the body providing the capital cost has neither the inclination nor the facilities to continue to operate the works for an indefinite period and prefers to hand over the responsibiility to the local community. Often, too, a government will prefer to construct and then transfer a completed supply to the village council or some other local authority in order to strengthen the sense of responsibility at village level (and, dare one say it, to acquire some political advantage by so doing). There are inevitably occasions when the local community representatives are inadequately prepared and equipped to accept the responsibility of the gift thus temptingly offered.

A water supply, on being completed and put into operation, is a considerable local asset. There should be no need here to detail the health, social and economic advantages that may be attributable to a reliable, ample and convenient supply of safe water to members of a community. On the other hand the ownership of this asset can be (paradoxically) a liability in itself, implying the continuing commitment for operating, maintaining, extending and eventually renewing the asset. Once having experienced the benefits conferred by the improved service the members of the community will be most reluctant to go back to the earlier situation.

Hence it is important that the ownership of the waterworks should not be 'foisted' on to a reluctant and unwary body. The full implications, both as regards finance and individual involvement, should be worked out in advance. The benefits and the liabilities should be set out in detail and incorporated into the 'handing over' documents. This exercise has another advantage in that it throws the onus of planning the subsequent operation on to the original designers of the plant.

Possible problems

Obviously the relevance of these remarks will vary according to the degree of complexity of the new works. We are considering small projects alone, but even these may differ widely. At one end of the scale may be a village well, or a weir and apron across a nearby stream. In other areas (where water-borne or water-related diseases are endemic) pumping, storage, treatment or chlorination may be necessary. Between these extremes there may be tube-wells and handpumps, animal- or windmill-operated pumps, steam impoundments, spring improvements, rain-water catchments, stream-operated hydraulic rams, and other installations with low running costs.

Because of their simplicity there is a danger that those systems that do not require staff, fuel, added chemicals or other obvious recurrent expenditure may be installed and forgotten, and that they will be expected to continue to work indefinitely without attention of any kind.

But every item of construction has a finite life. This may be extended by careful maintenance or shortened by misuse or neglect. It is plain that moving machinery, whether power-driven or hand-operated, needs regular lubrication and servicing, but it cannot be assumed that in the absence of machinery no action is required. For example, an impoundment will gradually silt up and requires periodically cleaning out or it will eventually fill and become useless. A concrete apron (such as that around a well or stand-pipe, or below a weir) may become undermined by erosion of the surrounding ground, and the edges will crack and crumble if not attended to in good time. Metal tanks or exposed pipes need painting at intervals; building and roofing materials exposed to the elements cannot be expected to last for ever. Concrete well-tops must be inspected occasionally to deal with rollers that need replacement, and with incipient cracking or deterioration of the concrete surfaces.

In addition to deterioration due to age or weathering there is one hazard that is unfortunately becoming more widespread—that of vandalism or deliberate sabotage. This danger is greater when the authority with reponsibility for the supply is remote from those using it, but it can be minimized when the consumers have a strong sense of communal ownership. One of the best safeguards against wanton damage is an appreciation by the women of a village that it is to their own interest to protect their installations from outside interference. In the same way mischievous damage by children can be controlled by public opinion much more effectively (and cheaply) than by watchmen or police action. Time, effort and expense spent in putting over this message to all consumers are rarely wasted.

Considering the community

For these various reasons the planning of a village supply should start with the most important consideration—that of the people who will benefit from it. There are three stages at which the villagers themselves should be involved—at the initiation and planning stage, during construction, and during use.

First of all it is important to recognize the need for improving the supply and deciding upon the best method of satisfying it. This need may not always be as obvious as it sounds.

It must be remembered that what is intended is almost always the improvement of an existing supply rather than the introduction of something entirely new. Wherever a community exists there is already a supply of some sort, otherwise there would not be people living there. It may be inadequate in quantity, dangerous to health, unreliable, inconvenient (or all of these), but basically water is there and is being used. While certain deficiencies will be obvious to the villagers, for instance the seasonal drying up of a stream or well, or the distance that water has to be carried from the source to the home, other factors may not be so generally appreciated.

The connection between water quality and the prevalence of endemic bacterial or parasitic diseases is not always understood by the consumers, whose outlook may be summed up as 'it was good enough for my father and grandfather, why should it be changed now?' Thus though the desire for an improved supply may be shared by the health authorities and the consumers themselves their reasons for wanting the improvement may be quite different.

For a community supply to operate successfully the improvement must be acceptable to the users, and this acceptability usually depends on the degree to which it was genuinely wanted before it was installed.

The attitude of country people all over the world is surprisingly similar in a number of ways. Anything imposed from outside (and to the villager any body or authority beyond his own small community is usually 'foreign') is regarded with suspicion and accepted with reluctance, even when it is obviously to the villagers' benefit. If, however, the villagers have made an effort to obtain it, and if they feel that they have achieved a 'victory' in forcing or persuading the outside body to install it for them, acceptance is much more whole-hearted. If, in addition, people have been consulted on the details of the proposals that most affect them, such as the precise siting of the wells or stand-pipes, their sense of ownership is enhanced.

The wise planner will therefore start with local consultation with the village council or other representatives of the people. Persuasion rather than dictation should be the key to ensuring that what the villagers want coincides with what the constructing body is prepared to provide.

In some countries in the Caribbean it is customary for a public gathering with a definite 'fiesta' atmosphere to be held; concessions are made on both sides and the meeting is counted a success if the villagers disperse with the impression that they have 'got away' with advantages that they would not otherwise have obtained. Before this meeting rural health workers (a doctor, nurse or sanitarian) will have done some groundwork by informing schoolchildren and parents about the health implications of the proposals. Arising out of the meeting (and follow-ups must be speedy if the euphoria is not to be lost) agreement is reached on the contributions to be made by the villagers in the form of finance, materials and labour. Some degree of local participation is essential to foster the sense of ownership.

Before embarking on consultations (whether privately with village heads, or at a public meeting) the planner must have worked out the full implications of his proposals, together with any possible alternatives that may be considered, if time-consuming arguments are to be avoided in the future.

Costings

If wells, tube-wells or similar units are planned the cost of each must be estimated (both as a lump sum and as contributions per individual) so that the effects of increasing or decreasing the number of facilities can be considered. If the scheme is to comprise pumping, mains, storage, treatment, stand-pipes and the like, figures should be available to demonstrate the effect on the individual contributor of increasing or reducing the facilities to be provided, not only as regards the initial outlay but also in the cost of running the supply in the future. For example, if villagers are expected to provide gravel and sand for concrete aggregate an idea of the quantities required should be available. If they are to supply labour for construction or mains-laying they are entitled to an estimate of the numbers of people and length of time they are agreeing to. An important point may be the time of year during which work will be carried out—labour readily available in the 'off' season may be unobtainable during the cultivation or harvest periods.

It is at this initial stage that planners should ensure that management commitments are understood and prepared for by the village authority. Whatever the proposals there is bound to be some cost and effort required in the future. In the case of simple structures, such as wells or spring collection chambers, it may be sufficient for regular (though not necessarily frequent) inspections to be made to forestall concrete deterioration and erosion around the apron. There must also be an arrangement for periodically cleaning the structures and their surrounds. Handpumps require more frequent inspection and lubrication of bearings. Spare leathers, washers and pivot pins should be held in stock and somebody given the responsibility of making minor repairs.

Pumps and treatment plant need more in the way of management. Labour (pump attendant, filter cleaners) must be recruited, trained, paid and supervised. Fuel must be purchased, properly stored, allocated and periodically checked—the same applies to chemicals, lubricants and other materials. Arrangements must be made for machinery to be regularly inspected and serviced by a competent mechanic. Spare piping, gland packing, tap washers and similar items should be held in store, and, again, there must be someone capable of using these to make minor repairs.

In short there will be a regular expenditure, even though this may be relatively small, and this expenditure must be balanced by an equally regular income. Such income may be by direct payment from village or other public funds, but it is more usual that it will be collected from the consumers themselves by tax, rates or payment for water received according to local customs and circumstances. It is most important that the method of collection is agreed before construction commences and that individual liabilities are known, at least approximately. Unexpected demands are always unwelcome, and will prejudice consumers against the supply.

Income and expenditure call for an accounting system, which may be of the simplest kinds but none the less essential. They also call for an individual to be responsible for the supervision of the accounts, collection of the income, payment of the operator(s) and other expenses, ensuring that fuel and material stocks are adequate and kept so by ordering in advance of need, and that the installation is maintained in good and clean condition.

The 'manager', or responsible officer, may well combine his water supply duties with some other post if the supply is a small one, but it is essential that he should have some knowledge and experience (gained, perhaps, by secondment to some operating supply elsewhere) and the status to exercise his responsibility on behalf of the village authority. It is often an advantage if he has been actively engaged at the construction stage of the works. It also makes for smoother working in the future if his responsibilities and duties are agreed and set down in writing in consultation with the planners before work commences.

Management

With regard to the construction phase of the work some management as well as purely technical supervision is called for, and this is often overlooked. It is only too easy to agree that villagers should contribute materials and labour, but not always so straightforward to ensure that the contributions are forthcoming as, when and where they are required. It is not unknown for a large number of volunteer workers to present themselves at an early stage before they can be properly used, with the consequences that many of them quickly lose enthusiasm and are unavailable as the tempo of work increases.

Another difficulty is that, being volunteers, the labourers are not always amenable to the discipline necessary if the work is to proceed smoothly. The 'supervisor', or whoever is in charge of the technical aspects of concrete construction, pump installation or plumbing, needs to concentrate on his/her own responsibilities and should not be diverted to settling the minor disputes that inevitably arise among the work-force or to 'chasing up' absentees who are holding up part of the work.

Another point is that the supervisor is usually someone from outside the village, who may find it difficult to impose discipline or even to communicate adequately with local people, especially when they speak a different dialect.

For these reasons it will often be found advantageous for a nominee of the local village council to take over as 'manager', working closely with the 'supervisor' and acting as a direct link between him and the village authority and with the volunteer labour force. Thus the supervisor pegs out the line of a trench or the foundations of a filter bed, checks levels during excavation and gives technical guidance to the workers shaping the finished bottom surface, while the manager allocates the duties of the labourers carrying out the work and ensures that they are fulfilling the tasks allotted to them. Similarly the supervisor indicates where and when and how much concrete, gravel or filter sand will be needed while the manager will be responsible for the arrangements for gathering and stacking the material.

Perhaps 'management' is an excessively grand title for these duties; the point being made is that someone should take the responsibility for them. There are other management duties that cannot so easily be undertaken by a local person. These come under the heading of site planning: for instance the allocation of the supervisor to the project and his payment; loan of picks, shovels and other tools for the labourers; provision of cement or other materials that are not available locally; transport of labour, materials and equipment. It may be thought that listing these details is unnecessarily complicating a simple project, but all should be considered in advance as the omission of any of them may hold up the whole of the work.

When construction is completed, the work is tested and handed over to the village authority (possibly with some ceremony—it all adds to the pride of local possession). Provided that the design and construction are soundly based technically, and that arrangements have been made along the lines suggested for future operation and maintenance, the improvement to the village water supply can be one of the soundest investments possible, producing dividends both in health and in economic well-being that will continue indefinitely.

(*Waterlines* Vol. 2 No. 2, October 1983)

Managing seasonal man-made water sources: lessons from Botswana

LOUISE FORTMANN

Botswana is a semi-arid country the size of France with a population of just under a million. Most of the population lives in a 100 km wide strip running north to south along the eastern border. After minerals, cattle are the most important export commodity and the basis of the rural economy. Under the traditional settlement pattern, people maintained two or three homes. The non-agricultural season was spent in a village. A second home was maintained at the 'lands' where farming was done. Wealthier households which kept large herds of cattle generally had a third hut at a cattle post where boys and young men looked after the cattle. Today only a small minority have cattle posts, most herds are being kept at the lands where they are used for draught power and milk.

Traditionally all natural water sources—seasonal streams and rivers, pans, puddles and springs—were communal; that is, their use was open to all. A water source developed by a private individual such as a *hafir*, a pit where runoff water is trapped, a dam, or a well (and later, a borehole) was the property of that individual. However, the custom was to allow travellers to drink or water their cattle even at private sources as long as they asked permission. Similarly, neighbours who were experiencing trouble with their own water sources were generally allowed to use those of others.

The practice of sharing with others was a form of insurance in a country characterized by periodic and localized droughts. Survival necessitated the ability to move one's household and livestock to an area with better grazing and/or water.

Thus, although water was a scarce commodity, it was rarely one which was sold. Rather its free exchange, through a system of mutual obligation and benefit, provided the whole population with the flexibility of movement necessary for survival. This norm has survived to the present day. Today, owners of boreholes which represent considerable capital investment still feel under pressure to allow neighbours access to drinking water and to let travellers water their cattle.

Government's managerial plans

In 1974 the Government of Botswana adopted a policy of constructing dams in the lands areas. Each dam was intended to water 400 head of cattle and to be managed by a small group of farmers. It was assumed that a group of farmers who considered a dam to be theirs would be willing to manage it according to what government considered good management principles. In this way the government hoped to solve the problem of the shortage of drinking water for cattle. It was also assumed that by imposing management requirements on the groups, the management of the range would follow. The government saw management in terms of a series of technical steps which were focused on a single water source. Groups were supposed to manage the dam in three ways.

○ Maintenance and repair. This meant planting grass on the dam wall to prevent rill erosion, keeping the fence and gate in good repair, and keeping animals off the dam wall and out of the reservoir. Where there was a pump and water trough, the pump was to be kept in working order.
○ Revenue collection. They were to collect 72 thebe (10 thebe = 1 pula) per year from each member for each adult animal watered at the dam.
○ Regulation. They were to limit the number of stock watering at the dam to the equivalent of 400 adult cattle.

Agricultural extension workers were responsible for forming the dam groups. Generally, the extension worker would talk with farmers in the area until a group of 15 or so had signed up. There was nothing particularly deserving about these farmers, they were simply willing to form a group. Generally, they were male and did not come from the poorer section of the community which lacked access to land and owned few cattle.

By 1979, the government was convinced that management of dams by groups was causing environmental damage. A multidisciplinary team undertook a nine-month investigation of the rural water sector including 24 dams, 21 of which were managed by groups. In fact group-managed dams did not

Construction of a platform for a handpump in Bahr-el-Ghazal province, Sudan (UNICEF/Martin Beyer)

A well-tended and maintained village pump in Senekedougou, Sierra Leone (UNICEF/Murray-Lee)

Education and sanitation are essential if the new water supply is to benefit the community fully (UNICEF/Bernard Wolff)

appear to cause any more environmental damage than other livestock-watering points.

Groups did manage their dams effectively but not in the way government thought they ought to.

○ Maintenance. Ten groups (48 per cent) undertook some sort of maintenance. Generally this took the form of protecting the fence and dam wall by hiring a caretaker or by reinforcing the fence with thorn bushes. Only one group planted grass and only one handpump was in use. Almost all maintenance activity took place at the end of the dry season when other sources dried up and dams became an important part of the water system.
○ Revenue collection. No group collected the government-mandated fee. Nine groups (43 per cent) said they charged fees particularly for use by non-members. In practice these fees were rarely, if ever, collected.
○ Regulation. No group limited livestock to the government-recommended 400 head. In a sense this did not matter since, contrary to expectation, the water in most reservoirs dried up midway through the dry season. This had essentially the same effect on preserving the grazing as the Government regulations would have had.

This is not to say that groups did not undertake any regulation. In fact, every group did. There were four types of regulation. The first was limiting the number of users. This was done by preventing certain categories of people from using the dam—either non-members of the group or people from other communities, more often the latter.

The second regulation was restricting type of use. Although these dams were intended for livestock, six dams were limited to domestic use either permanently or seasonally. Sometimes calves and smallstock were allowed to use these water points. Since people use less water than cattle, this lengthens the time there is water in the dam.

Controlling the manner of use was the next rule. Where water is used for both livestock and domestic purposes, cattle were typically kept out of the water, being watered from troughs either inside or outside the fence. Although this was done to keep water clean for human consumption, it had the added benefit of reducing the amount of silt carried into the reservoir.

The final point was regulating the time of use. Some dams are closed (generally by padlocking the gate) entirely during certain seasons—generally the rainy season. Other dams are used in sequence. The dam most likely to go dry is used first, followed by other more reliable sources.

Thus, through different types of regulation the quality and quantity of water is preserved as the more plentiful and convenient rainy season water supplies diminish.

Some lessons

The experience with dam groups in Botswana poses a set of questions which should be answered before setting up a group management strategy for seasonal water sources.

What factors vary seasonally?

In the Botswana case, four critical and interrelated factors varied by season: the location of the people and their herds, the demand for water, the availability of labour, and the availability of water in that particular water source.

For part of the year there were no management activities at the dams for the simple reason that people were not there. They had returned to the village after the harvest. This factor would be especially operative with nomadic people and others who must move in search of grazing.

Demand for dam water varied seasonally not only because of the location of the people, but also because at some times of the year other water points provided cheaper, more convenient water. This was particularly true during the rainy season when water is readily available in puddles, pans and rivers. When demand for dam water is low, there is unlikely to be much management activity. Rather efforts will be directed to those sources which are in use.

During parts of the year all available labour may be involved in other activities. The agricultural season with its need for large amounts of labour for ploughing, weeding, bird scaring and harvesting is the most striking case. During such times only emergency maintenance of absolutely crucial water supplies is likely to be undertaken.

Seasonal water sources by definition hold water only at certain times of the year. When they are dry, management activities are likely to be directed only at sources which are providing water.

The answers to these questions about seasonality should indicate *when* it is reasonable to expect management to take place.

What other water resources do people use?

All too often, planners think only about the particular water source they are concerned with. But in many of the rural areas of Africa, people use a series of water sources depending on where they are, what the season is, and whether the water is being used for domestic or livestock purposes. Even people who have access to a mechanized system with stand-pipes will have a back-up water source to use when the system inevitably fails.

By establishing the relative importance of a water-point in the overall system, it will be possible to estimate the relative importance attached to its management. This should reduce any unrealistic expectations about the probable levels of management.

What quality and quantity of labour is available?

The rural areas of Botswana are characterized by a high out-migration of young and middle-aged males searching for wage employment. Thus for the better part of the year, the available labour force consists largely of very young boys, old men, women and girls. The physical strength of most available males is limited. Women are quite capable of undertaking heavy physical work but certain tasks are defined as socially inappropriate for them. The technical skills available in the community will also vary. In smaller communities obviously there is simply less labour available.

By finding out what labour is available, it is possible to determine what kinds of management activities are physically and technically possible.

What is the users' perception of the water point?

The government's rules for dam management would have been quite reasonable if taking care of the dam was all people had to worry about. A few questions would have shown that one of the reasons people like dams is that they do not take much labour to use or to manage. An appealing feature of dams is that cattle can water themselves without human assistance except in the form of opening gates. When labour is short, the 'self-watering cow' (as Charles Bailey, our economist, put it) is very appealing indeed. The immediate return to an activity such as planting grass on the dam wall is unlikely to be perceived as worth the labour invested in it.

People's attitudes to dams also affects the likelihood that fees can be collected. Dams in the semi-arid conditions of Botswana have a relatively long life. Walls only rarely break and silting-up is a reasonably slow process. Thus collecting money for repairs in the far distant future has little urgency about it.

The answers to questions about user perceptions will indicate what kinds of management activities users think it is necessary to undertake.

What are the local rules about water use?

Because water in Botswana was traditionally considered a free good, it is often difficult to charge for it. According to traditional notions about water, government-built dams were perceived as communal water sources because they were dug on communally-held land, by the government (which should serve everyone) and were filled with rain-water.

This perception made both fee collection and the exclusion of non-members almost impossible. Important questions to ask are: Who has what rights to use water for what purposes when? Under what conditions may water be sold? What responsibilities do users have for the maintenance of a communal water point or a private water point?

Answers to questions such as these will indicate which types of management are culturally acceptable.

Are all members of the community around the water point allowed to use it? If not, what is the relationship between the group of users and the community as a whole?

In many rural areas, residents are highly dependent on acts of neighbourliness to get through the many and unpredictable emergencies of life. These ties of mutual obligations are unlikely to be broken lightly. In such a situation, an attempt to restrict users to only part of the community is bound to fail. The authorized users will be loathe to turn away neighbours whose help they may need in the future.

Related to this is the problem of enforcement. Who has the authority to punish those who do not abide by the rules of use and management? The type of people with authority will differ from community to community. They may be elected officials or traditional leaders or leaders of a subdivision of a community such as a ward or they may be heads of family groups. A group which cannot by right call on the authority of such leaders may have a very difficult time enforcing its regulations.

In the case of Botswana, communities which managed dams were fairly successful in enforcing their rules. When a small group of individuals had control of the dam, the resulting sense of inequity on the part of the other community members led to cut fences and other violations of the regulations which the group was powerless to prevent.

By ensuring that the group of users is an accepted subdivision of the community or consists of the community as a whole, it is more likely that there will be authority to enforce regulations.

How are the use and management of the water point related?

There is a tendency to think of management as a separate activity from use. In fact except for special cases, use and management are often part of the same activity. (An example of 'pure management' would be by paid employees running a large municipal water system. An example of 'pure use' is using water from puddles caused by a rain shower.)

Often, the manner of use is a form of management. For example, by watering livestock from a trough instead of allowing them into the reservoir, the life of the dam is lengthened and the water can also be used for domestic purposes. No-one fetching water from a well or *hafir* surrounded by a thorn fence would think of leaving without replacing the thorn bush which serves as a gate. These and other actions which are simply considered part of responsible water use, are forms of management as well. Depending on what the water is used for (domestic or livestock or irrigation), the manner of use is likely to differ. The customary ways of using water should be observed.

From this management can be incorporated into existing patterns of responsible use.

Management of water sources by the local community or a local group is an appealing strategy in water development projects. It has the potential for better management at lower cost than could be provided by paid employees. In general, a good rule of thumb in setting up such a management strategy is to try to fit it as closely as possible into existing community structures and customary patterns of water use. Management groups may need to develop new skills and roles which will require changes in some traditional forms. However, the use of forms which are familiar and functional is likely to increase the success of group strategies.

(*Waterlines* Vol. 1 No. 4, April 1983)

Towards community-managed drinking-water schemes in Nepal

JOHN R. WILLIAMSON

A community that manages its drinking-water system from the beginning has a greater likelihood of successfully operating and maintaining it. In Third World countries, drinking-water projects are very expensive and poor communities cannot afford them. These communities usually depend on government or development agencies to provide all or a large proportion of the cost of the project.

Because so much is supplied from outside the community, the water users may not feel the responsibility to maintain the system, depending instead on outside help. However, when a community takes responsibility for planning and building the system, it will also take charge of maintaining it. The development/government agency needs to relinquish control and encourage communities to manage their drinking-water systems from the earliest stages.

The United Mission to Nepal (UMN), in co-operation with His Majesty's Government of Nepal, is operating the Nawal Parasi Hills Development

Table 11.1 Summary of the Nawal Parasi drinking-water programme

	Number of projects completed	Number of villages served	Population served	Budget expended[1]	Cost per capita[1]	Number of latrines built
1975–8	12	14	2,500	_[2]	_[2]	0
1981	6	14	2,072	$39,300	$18.90	50
1982	4	6	2,513	$23,500	$9.40	350
1983[3]	20	34	5,957	$62,166	$10.40	900

Notes: [1] in terms of US dollars   [2] not available   [3] first six months of 1983 only

Project, an integrated rural development project which evolved from medical work begun in 1969. The first drinking-water system was installed for its medical dispensary in Bojha in 1970. Since then the project has installed about 42 drinking water systems supplying water for 68 villages of the Nawal Parasi hills, serving a population of 11,000 (see Table 11.1).

The people of the hills of Nawal Parasi find the scarcity of drinking water a major problem. These hills, along with the rest of Nepal, depend on the monsoon rain during the summer months to replenish their water sources. Because of an increasing population and 'slash and burn' agriculture which causes deforestation on the steep hills, nearby village water sources have dried up. As a result, women sometimes need to walk an hour or more to the nearest water source below their village. The water source is also used for bathing and feeding water buffaloes and other livestock, and may have a run-off from the village draining into it. The jungle around the village is used as a toilet. In most villages, pigs are allowed to roam freely within the village. After eating human faeces, the pigs spread disease throughout the village. The incidence of roundworm, diarrhoea, infected sores and abscesses and dysentery is high.

Drinking-water systems in Nawal Parasi are gravity-flow and consist of high-density polythene pipe laid from the source down to a storage tank located above the village. The source is often a spring or spring-fed stream. A distribution system delivers water to taps throughout the village. Each tap provides water for about ten houses. Depending on the distance of the village from the source, a system can vary in size and cost. A couple of systems have been built which include over 10 km of pipe, while some systems may use much less than 1 km.

Three approaches

The first water system built for a number of villages was seen by the people who used the water as being owned by the government. No wonder! The government provided the design, materials and overseers, and the labour was paid for by 'food for work'. The villagers made no investment. When maintenance problems arose the water users did not feel responsible for fixing the system. Due to lack of maintenance, water is now very scarce and does not flow at all from this system during the dry months.

For some time the mission attempted to use the participatory approach and encouraged community involvement without giving it control and responsibility. Communities participated by providing advice and free volunteer labour. Decisions on the design and the management of construction were made by project staff. When the drinking-water project was completed the village was expected to operate the system and carry out maintenance. All the systems constructed in this way continue to operate, some better than others. How well a village maintains the system depends upon its management ability.

The project has now evolved into a third phase: it is relinquishing control of drinking-water systems to communities. The project has not reached the point of handing over everything to the community, and still provides the necessary building materials to villages. However, the community itself manages the construction of the system by organizing and supervising its volunteer labour. Design decisions are made by the village.

The experience of taking responsibility for the overall drinking-water project has helped the villagers to work together and to develop their organizational ability. It has created community pride and developed self-reliance. However, much time is needed for communities to carry out their own management. Project personnel have to meet villagers more often to make sure they understand their responsibilities. Most of the these visits take place before beginning construction of the system.

Building a drinking-water system consists of many stages—request, survey, design, latrine building, construction, maintenance and evaluation. The UMN Project has had to change its way of doing each stage as it tries to move towards community management of drinking-water systems. Each of these stages will be described separately.

Request and survey

In some areas of Nepal, villagers feel that development projects such as drinking-water schemes can only come about through exercising status, position in the social hierarchy and personal connections. Many of the first drinking-water schemes came through the influence of the district *panchayat* representative of the region. He had good contact with project staff and the government. He personally requested drinking-water surveys for villages which supported him. Villagers often did not know that a request for drinking-water had been made for them and were surprised when surveyors appeared.

Now the project only works in one small area at a time. Village leaders from within that area are called to a meeting and informed that they are eligible to make a request for their drinking-water system by sending a letter to the project.

Surveys for small gravity-flow drinking-water systems are quite simple to carry out. The only technical data necessary is the size of the dry season water flow at the source and a profile showing the distance and height elevation from the source to the village.

The surveyor's work can be made easier by involving the villagers. Even illiterate people who could not count past 20 came up with a simple method of measuring long distances. They counted the number of rope lengths by putting a pebble in their pocket for each rope length. Other villagers cleared a path through the jungle. Water flow was measured using local units: litres per minute meant nothing to farmers, but measuring the water flow by the number of *pathi* (local unit used for measuring the volume of grain) was far more real. Villagers also suggested the location of the water tank and tap stands.

Design

The task of the designer is to produce a workable system represented by a drawing from the information compiled by the survey. In the early years, the foreign short-term engineer returned to his office and, using guide-lines from WHO studies for water demand, made his designs. Drawings in the English language were prepared and sent off to government offices and donor agencies for approval. When it was time to begin building these systems, the drawing was given to the mason-technician who knew no English, so the drawing made little sense to him and none at all to the community.

Designs should be done by the villagers with the assistance of the engineer. Perhaps sizing the pipe may be puzzling to illiterate people, but they should be able to determine how much water in terms of *pathis* per day they want to flow from the source to the tank, or from the tank to each tap.

Instead of relying on the WHO regulations for water demand, villagers should be asked how many *pathis* of water an average household needs daily for cooking, feeding animals, bathing, and washing clothes. The total daily village water demand can be estimated by multiplying the number of houses by the average household need. This can be checked against the amount of water the source will provide. If it is not large enough, the villagers can then decide to develop another water source if there is one nearby. The community can calculate the water storage volume needed in the same way and select the most appropriate tank size.

Latrine building

The greatest change has taken place in the latrine building programme. When, only a couple of years ago, the project decided that latrines should be built, staff were very sceptical that villagers would be interested. But then a village leader suggested that everyone in his village should build a latrine as a precondition to receiving water. In the first year of latrine building, 52 latrines were built in six villages for demonstration as a condition to receiving materials for drinking-water.

But standards were low. The latrines were used for a short period and then abandoned. In evaluating the latrine-building programme, villagers said that all households should be required to build their own latrine before they were supplied with water. This advice was followed the next year. Again the quality of construction was poor, but project staff were still amazed at the willingness of the villagers to build the latrines.

During the third year of latrine-building, dramatic changes were made. High construction standards were set within the constraints of locally available materials and construction skills. Latrine pits had to be dug to a minimum depth of 2m. The wooden planks for the floor had to be well-joined, avoiding any cracks. Covers for the hole had to fit snugly. The superstructure had to be built with stone and mud masonry and/or with wooden planks. A door had to be put in.

A competition was held among the different villages and drinking-water projects were started only in those villages which completed their latrines. Rather than project staff having to decide which village should have first opportunity to get pipe, materials and technicians, the villagers themselves decided the order on the basis of who finished building latrines first.

Several observations were made on the latrine-building programme. First, this was good experience and a test of organization for the village. Village leaders had to show each household how to build a latrine. Villagers were better able to manage the construction of their drinking-water system later.

A few villages did not build their latrines, even after two years. These villages share similar characteristics—leadership is weak, and factional conflict is present. If water systems were built in such villages they would be likely to fall into disrepair. The requirement for latrines has helped to prevent this sort of thing happening.

Another observation is that the higher the standard of latrine construction the better chance it will have of being used. Many latrines were built only in order to meet the conditions for obtaining a water system. These barely passed the minimum requirements and were often abandoned soon after.

Construction

Building a water system is hard work. Pipe, cement and fittings need to be carried in from the nearest road. This can take up to three days for one trip. Building materials such as sand, gravel and stone need to be collected. The trench for the pipe has to be dug. Joining the pipe with cement masonry may call for a skilled technician.

For most of the earlier systems, each village was responsible for providing unskilled labour while the project provided a technician to do the skilled work. The project technician also supervised the work and the villagers followed his command. The villagers learned no new skills except indirectly by observing the technician. Working in this manner was both quick and efficient.

Nowadays the community is responsible for managing the construction.

The technician's role is to instruct others on how to join pipes and do masonry work. The technician may advise the village on scheduling the work, but village leaders organize and supervise the work.

A year after one system was built, a devastating rainstorm occurred which caused the nearby river to flood. Bridges and a 200 m section of pipe which stretched across the river were carried away. Within the next few days the villagers mobilized themselves. They temporarily replaced the lost high-pressure pipe with a low-pressure plastic pipe which had been left over from the construction.

When the water started to flow through the pipe many of the joints began to leak because of the high pressure. Out of thicker plastic pipe the villagers then made their own sockets to reinforce each joint. The system started to supply water again. However, the people were still afraid that another flood might wash away their pipe, and they had no more pipe left for repairs. They knew of a spring located on their side of the river in the jungle, several kilometres above the villages, so they removed 4 km of pipe from the original source to the new source on their side of the river. All this work was done without any assistance or outside funding. The people were able to do this themselves because they had learned new skills and had had experience of organizing themselves.

Maintenance

The importance of maintaining projects in developing countries is being stressed much more these days because many projects failed in the past as a consequence of lack of thought on maintenance procedures. This has also been the experience with the UMN Project's drinking-water systems.

Villagers have always selected their own maintenance people to be responsible for overseeing the maintenance of their drinking-water system. In the past, these people lacked both the skills and tools necessary to fix leaking pipes and broken taps. Sometimes communities lacked the organizational ability to oversee the maintenance.

Now the village selects two or three maintenance people to work alongside the project technician before construction begins. A set of pipe-joining tools (heating plate, hacksaw, file, pipe wrenches, pincers) and masonry tools are also provided. The technicians shows the village maintenance workers how to join the pipe and put together fittings. The village decides on payment for the maintenance person: this usually follows the tradition of paying a quantity of grain annually to village workers.

Evaluation

When a drinking-water project is completed it should be evaluated to see if it is achieving its aims. By involving the villagers in the evaluation they can

CWD—S

Table 11.2 Three approaches to implementing drinking-water systems

	Agency—managed (centralized)	Limited community—involvement (people's participation)	Community—managed (decentralized)
Flow of ideas	AGENCY → COMMUNITY	AGENCY ↑↓← COMMUNITY	AGENCY →↓ COMMUNITY
Basic assumption	Local people know nothing and can't learn new things	Local people have knowledge which can be used in design. They can also provide labour for construction	Local people have management skills and quickly learn needed technical skills
How need is realized	Agency decides community needs water	Local political official decided community needs water	Community realizes own need
Who makes decisions	Agency	Agency and local leaders	Community
Strategy	Survey, design are done by agency staff. Little time is spent in community. Design is done in office	Survey is done by agency staff with advice given by local leaders on location of water sources, tank and tap stands. After design is completed in office it may be sent to community for information.	Community asks agency for survey. Local people assist and understand survey. Community makes decisions about design. Design is prepared in the community; everyone is able to understand it.
Construction	Construction is done by contractor hired by agency	Agency provides technician who organizes all work and does skilled work himself. Community provides volunteer unskilled labour	Agency provides technician who teaches necessary skills. Community organizes all work
Maintenance	Agency provides for maintenance by placing own staff to look after own system	Maintenance is left for community to work out	Maintenance is organized by community who have skilled persons able to make repairs
Approval of designs	Agency	Agency	Community and agency
Primary beneficiaries	Agency—its 'good name' Contractor—profit	Agency—its 'good name' Local political leaders	Community
End result	Dependence on agency	Continued lack of initiative	Self-reliance

Note: 'Agency' refers to government or development agency which is implementing the drinking-water project then continue to monitor the system. Villagers can measure water coming into the storage tank to see if the pipe is delivering the amount of water it was designed to. In this way, the flow can be monitored over the years. Evaluation is another area where the project is beginning to encourage more community participation.

The three approaches of community involvement in drinking-water schemes are compared in Table 11.2. This is drawn from the author's own experience in Nawal Parasi hills and from observing other systems which have been built in Nepal. Planners and implementers of drinking-water systems can use this table to evaluate their programme's level of community involvement.

Community-managed drinking-water schemes are different from schemes with community participation. When the community manages the scheme it has control and owns the system from the beginning. However, in community participation projects, the development agency invites villagers to participate in whatever way they want to—mainly supplying labour. Throughout the project, ownership, control and responsibility of operation and maintenance is unclear for both the community and the developing agency. This may result in conflict between the community and the development agency.

Development agencies, hoping for more successful water systems should be more willing to give control and responsibility to the community. Also, development workers must have greater patience and flexibility and adapt to the pace of the community.

UMN staff have learned that most communities in the Nawal Parasi hills have the ability to manage their own drinking-water systems. When the community has responsibility for planning and building the system, the water users feel that they own the system. They, the owners, realize that they are responsible for maintaining it themselves and are not dependent on an outside agency.

Project staff expect that the systems built and managed by the communities will continue to supply water. Who knows what other development initiatives may start, within the community as a result of the experience of managing construction and maintenance of latrines and water systems together? Only time will tell.

(*Waterlines* Vol. 2 No. 2, October 1983)

The falaj—a traditional co-operative system of water management

SALLY SUTTON

The *qanat* or *falaj* systems of Oman have provided communities with water for irrigation and domestic purposes for 1,500 to 2,000 years. Many of the systems are over a thousand years old and owe their continued existence to the well-established social and financial structures which have evolved over the years and which take care of administration and maintenance.

The longevity of these systems is in direct contrast to many of the village-level water supplies established world-wide in the 1970s and early 1980s, both for agricultural and domestic purposes. In both cases it is apparent that, despite adequate (and sometimes even appropriate) technology, breakdown and abandonment of systems is common, and organization of finance and maintenance is seldom successfully accomplished.

In common with many modern schemes, *falaj* systems were an imposed technology, and one whose methods of construction the present users can neither understand nor copy. Nevertheless, the communities that depend upon them have kept many of these precarious water supplies running for over a thousand years, and it may therefore be that the organizational aspects of these long-lived co-operative water based systems may have some features which modern schemes might consider. They do, however, also have some features which can be seen to be putting whole systems at risk in the rapidly changing economic climate of the present day.

Physical structure

A *falaj* consists of a tunnel to tap ground water and bring it to the surface for distribution to crops and housing (Figure 11.3). It is designed to raise ground water to the surface without any mechanical device or costly expenditure on fuels. This is achieved by excavating a tunnel (usually several kilometres long) which taps concentrated lines of ground-water flow and leads water to the surface along a channel at a lesser gradient than either the ground surface or the water-table. The design of these tunnels has to be very precise, and their excavation is a mammoth task, particularly without modern technology.

For ventilation during excavation and for removal of debris, access shafts were generally sunk every 20 metres or so. These shafts, while essential during construction, lead to instability of the tunnel and divert flood flows into the system, causing roofs to collapse and major blockages in the underground section. Constant maintenance of this fabric is required, as is the removal of tree roots which proliferate in the channel, fracturing the walls and roof and blocking the water flow. Additionally, in years of water

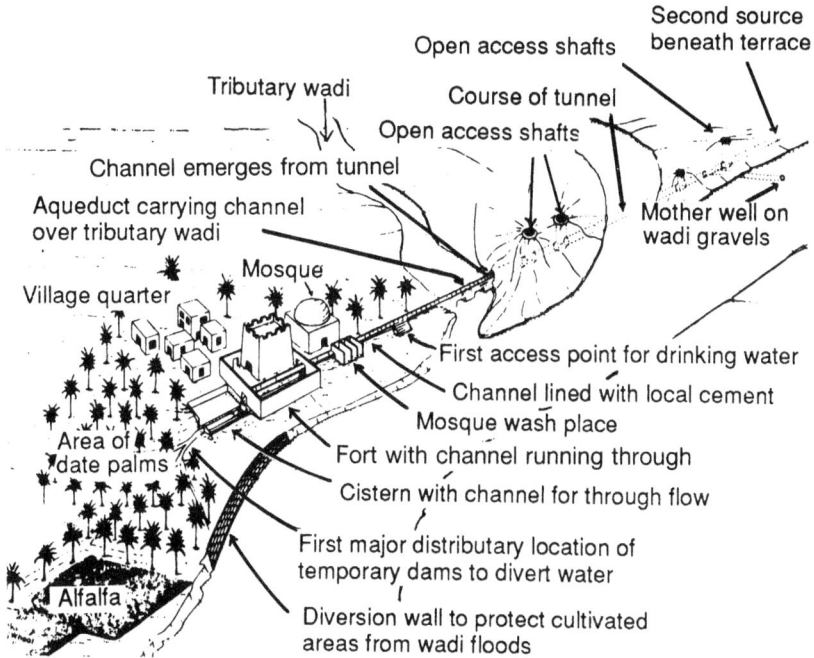

Fig. 11.3 *Sketch of a typical small* falaj

shortage intake tunnels require extension, and in periods of flood, whole sections of tunnel may be swept away. To keep this underground part of the system operating requires administration and finance which can respond not only to the regular demands of basic maintenance but also to the major disasters to which each system is subject at times.

On reaching ground-level, the main channel splits into many smaller channels, which in turn divide to supply individual gardens. In almost all systems the water is led to only one garden at a time. The distribution channels, and especially the diversion dams to gardens, need constant attention to control leakage, and the distribution of water to each plot of land. Points for the collection of drinking water and those set aside for washing also require maintenance.

Each system, while simple in concept, is complicated to operate and maintain. To keep it working, to ensure the availability of unpolluted drinking water and to distribute the water equitably to all landholders requires the co-operation of the whole community. A social structure has therefore grown up in each settlement to organize the water-supply system, and to fund both regular maintenance and the sporadic, unpredictable emergencies requiring immediate and major works.

Administration

As mentioned above, the original design and construction of *falaj* systems was a major task requiring a high level of technology and work-force control. A powerful central government to establish the administrative structure[72] was a prerequisite provided by the Achaemanid and Sassanid invasions of Oman from Persia. The present settlement pattern and social structures in Oman date back at least to the second of these invasions and the development of a stable central government in the fifth century AD, while some may own their origin to the first invasion perhaps around the fifth century BC.[73]

Since then, the care and operation of each system has been the responsibility of the tribal community which depended upon it, and it is only in the past decade that central government has again become significantly involved in providing technology and funds. During the period in which the community had sole control of the system administrative and financial structures evolved in it and a traditional workforce, whose organization dated back to the Persian period, became established for routine maintenance of the system, and for the distribution of water.

Falajes (the Arabic plural is *aflaj*) vary in size from those supplying just one or two families and their crops, to those providing water for several thousand people and several hundred gardens. For the smaller systems one man may undertake all the management and operation, but for the largest a committee may be required. In both cases the aspects of management are similar. At its largest the management committee consists of a *wakil*, a *qab'th*, two *arif* and a work-force of *biyadir*. The structure of the *falaj* organization changes little from region to region, although the names for the different posts vary.

The *wakil* is the overall administrator, who is responsible for the organization of *falaj* affairs, the ownership and rental of water rights, the arrangements for distribution of water according to such rights, the maintenance and sale of *falaj* property, and policy decisions on *falaj* repairs. He is of high standing in the community, but is not usually the head (or *shaykh*) of the village. The *qab'th* is the treasurer dealing with receiving money for *falaj* funds and spending them. In smaller systems there is no *qab'th* and the *wakil* fulfills both roles.

The *arif* is equivalent to the 'foreman'. He is in charge of the physical structure and knows its weaknesses, assessing the method and timing of repairs and maintenance. On the largest systems two people fulfil this role, one being responsible for the underground section and one for the above ground part, but both will work with the maintenance teams, rather than simply managing them. On smaller systems one man is responsible for the whole fabric, and on the smallest, the *wakil* himself has considerable knowledge of both the underground and surface sections, and may be found working on repairs.

Below this administrative superstructure are the *byadir*. Again on the larger sytems there may be a division between those who work at the surface and those who work underground, but on most systems there is no such division and the team of labourers is responsible for the state of repairs of the whole *falaj* and for water distribution to each garden. Most *biyadir* are descendants of members of the early Persian feudal system adopted at the time the *falajes* were established.

Their persistence as a comparatively separate group in the community stems partly from the fact that the job requires a self-discipline which many find difficult to adopt. This includes shift work and routines which cannot be broken. Few who are not born to it become *biyadir*, and their numbers are on the decline.

The whole social structure for running the water supply is usually heredit-ary. In this way the experience of one *wakil* or *arif* is easily passed on to the next. Payment for the managerial posts is usually in water rights that are inherited with the job, and are a valuable asset which can otherwise only be rented at considerable cost. They can very rarely be bought. In contrast, payment for *biyadir* tends to be on a share-cropping basis for the distribution of water: the man who irrigates alfalfa receives one-fifth of the crop. This method of payment in kind seldom provides more than subsistence, but has the advantage that a constant rate of payment can be maintained regardless of rates of inflation and the *biyadir* will still be able to maintain approxi-mately the same standard of living (as long as the market prices for agricul-tural produce are roughly linked to inflation). The same is true for payment of water rights. Work on the underground section is generally less regular and may be paid for in kind from *falaj*-owned date groves, or with money raised from them.

Other influences

While payment for services is mostly independent from the state of the economy, so the management hierarchy of the *falaj* is often independent of, but complementary to, the traditional tribal hierarchy of the community.

At certain times, however, the *falaj* systems calls upon, or may be influenced by, the other social organizations within the village. For instance, in some cases the *shaykh* may regard the whole system as his own rather than being the property of the tribe or community. So the income of the *falaj* may be appropriated and only a proportion be available to finance running the system. Even where the *falaj* is owned by the *shaykh*, however, the management structure outlined above will still operate.

If a dispute over water rights arises which the *wakil* cannot resolve, the *qadi* (expert on koranic and/civil law) or another government official such as the *wali* (governor), who are completely separate from the tribal hierarchies and from the water-supply management, will give judgement.

With this structure a team of twenty people can operate and maintain a complete system producing 10,000 cu m/day for the domestic and irrigation requirements of some 3,000 people. This same team will also prune, fertilize and pick the fruit of most of the 20,000 or so date palms in the groves they irrigate, and distribute water to them night and day.

While the general operation and maintenance of the system is financed by payment in kind, the *falaj* requires a regular income of capital to pay for materials, so that it can take on extra labour in emergencies, and for major repairs which are too big for the regular work team to undertake. By tradition the *falaj* institution owns property from which the income necessary for its continued survival comes. This property may include houses, palm trees or water. In all cases the property is rented out, generally on an annual or half-yearly basis.

Cycles of irrigation are mainly based on eight- or 16-day retention, particularly suitable for date palm, alfalfa and wheat irrigation. Of the eight days, the *falaj* institution will usually own one or two days water, the rest being hereditary water rights for which there is no payment. Thus the *falaj* gains some of its income from auctioning water (usually in half-hour units). This is rented by people who have insufficient water rights to irrigate the crops they wish to grow. It is used mainly for seasonal crops, such as wheat.

Water rights are not measured by volume, but by time. During seasons when water flow is low everyone receives proportionally less water but at the same time intervals. Thus at periods of low flow the water available for rent is much in demand to augment individual supplies, and the auction price rises.

The income of the *falaj* is therefore highest in periods of water shortage and so provides funds for extending the system, improving its efficiency and maintaining flows. This is the opposite of the situation with many modern systems of water supply which sell water at a fixed rate for a given volume, and whose income therefore declines when the flow is reduced. Where renting date palms provides the *falaj*'s main income, the position is reversed and systems are less capable of surviving drought. The best date harvests are in years of plentiful water, and the income is highest at this time (date prices varying relatively little in relation to available water). The pattern of income from date palms is, however, complementary to that from the lease of water, so systems which combine the two tend to be the healthiest financially. Renting houses provides an additional uniform but generally low income and is not as common.

The income from each system is such that the average cost of a cubic metre of water—approximately 0.04p (0.06 US cents) compared with 2.8p (4.2 US cents) for well water. This is to some degree an artificial comparison, because the cost of construction has long ago been covered for the *falaj*. The chief outlay is now on maintenance, where the amount of work undertaken is generally governed by the short-term availability of funds rather than by the long-term requirements of the system. Consequently, the demands of emergency repairs are becoming more frequent as the shortfall on regular maintenance increases.

Socio-economic factors

The *falaj* system is an integral part of village life. It provides water for crops and domestic use and because the community depends upon it, codes of social behaviour have become established. One user does not pollute the system for another. For instance, the uppermost access point in the settlement is set aside for the collection of drinking water, and no-one should wash in or otherwise dirty the water above this point. Then there is the mosque and the main washing point for men, followed by points for the women to wash and to take clothes and pans for cleaning. The last point on the channel before it divides to take water to the crops is generally the washing place for the dead.

The walk for water may be long (especially in summer when families live among the date groves) but the point for the collection of drinking water is a meeting place for the women, and anyone seen to collect water from downstream would be regarded as lazy and with dirty habits. Social ostracism is a strong persuader in a close-knit community, and the value put on clean water is high. Indeed even if there is a good well nearer home, most women prefer to walk the extra distance to 'running water' which they see as a healthier source.

The role of women within the system is essentially passive. In no case did we find that they were involved in the distribution of water. Women only use water for domestic purposes in *falaj* areas, carrying clothes and pots to the water for washing and carrying drinking water to the house. They are not involved in the agricultural use of water or the maintenance of the system.

The community acknowledges its dependence upon the *falaj* and it is not uncommon for a landowner to bequeath date palms and water-rights back to the *falaj* institution to augment its income and ensure its continued survival. The mosques of the villages also frequently own palms and water rights and may contribute a proportion of the annual income raised on these to the *falaj*. Thus the *falaj* system impinges on all aspects of life within the village.

The management and financial structure outlined above have enabled the *falaj* system to survive during a variety of socio-economic changes. In the past thirty years, however, and particularly in the past decade, very major changes have occurred as a result of employment opportunities offered by the development of the oil industry, within Oman and in neighbouring countries. These have led to both a serious shortage of local labour and a major increase in cash flow within the rural communities. As a result:

○ Landholders often now have enough capital to establish private water well supplies, so removing their dependence on the *falaj* water and undermining the stability of the system by reducing its income.

○ The labour available consists only of the oldest and youngest members of the community. Those who are physically fit and of normal working age tend to be working away from the home. When they return they are often only prepared to work for the very high wages.

Because of this, the traditional institutional structure of the *falaj* is at risk, and the fabric prone to neglect. This underlines the fact that the financial structure which has supported the *falaj* system over so many centuries is geared to a pressing need for water. When the pressure of demand is suddenly removed, the system has to readjust if it is not to fail. This illustrates that a prime necessity for the successful introduction of a rural water-supply scheme is education, to create the feeling of need for the supply. Once the feeling of need for the supply is established within the community, the motivation to absorb the technology is there, and the operation of the system can become a target of community effort.

The other point perhaps is that it is not necessarily the young, better-educated sons of the village who contribute the most to such systems. They are the one most likely to go and seek jobs elsewhere (if only temporarily) and so to leave a vacuum which cannot easily be filled if the system relies upon them. Older members of the community, although perhaps less formally educated, are less likely to want to move away, are more aware of the pride of the people and are perhaps more likely to wish to improve their standard of living within the village, rather than moving out to towns and cities where such facilities are already established. In addition, the jobs which can be done by the old and the blind are not numerous in rural societies, and therefore they may be better suited to regular, repetitive and fairly simple tasks of operation and maintenance than those people who have other interests and are likely to give priority to other higher paid jobs if they are offered them.

Levying water rights

As a result of the present economic situation the chief readjustment necessary to the system is that its income should not depend only on water rental, which is a minor proportion of the total supply, but that those owning hereditary water rights should also contribute to the upkeep. This has already been instituted for some systems. The levy instituted on water rights may be in money, but may alternatively be in labour, with inputs proportional to the water rights held. While the latter system causes problems through the large number of absentee landowners in most villages, it is a system which is independent of outside labour costs and is, therefore, less at risk from inflation. It has been found to work well.

Communities still tend to avoid changing the character of a *falaj* system, so that it becomes even more vulnerable to inflation. The communities concerned are trying to keep responsibility for the system. Although central government may need to inject capital to counteract the neglect of the past thirty years in some cases, it would be unfortunate if this led to greater centralization of management and operation. The factor which has best helped the *falaj* system to survive is probably its close ties to the community, and its management by those most familiar with it and most affected by its state of health. It is one of the oldest co-operative systems in the world and its demise would have far-reaching social effects for those depending upon it.

(Waterlines Vol. 2 No. 3, January 1984)

References and further reading

1. E.F. Schumacher, *Small is Beautiful: a study of economics as if people mattered* (Blond & Briggs, London, 1973).
2. Marilyn Carr, Ed., *The AT Reader: theory and practice in appropriate technology* (IT Publications, London, 1985).
3. S.B. Watt and W.E. Wood, *Hand Dug Wells and their Construction* (IT Publications, London, 1977).
4. *Shallow wells* (DHV Consulting Engineers, The Netherlands, 1978).
5. H. de Iongh, *Small is difficult* (TOOL, The Netherlands, 1979).
6. A.T. Kruft, *Appropriate Technology: a ten-year case study* (TOOL, The Netherlands, 1985).
7. *Low-cost Water Supply, part 1: survey and construction of wells*, (DHV Consulting Engineers, The Netherlands, 1985).
8. H.A. Cochrane, 'The Technique of Well Sinking in Nigeria', *Geological Survey of Nigeria*, (1937).
9. *Wells Manual: programme and training journal* (Action P.C., Washington DC, 1974).
10. Bob Mann, 'The Gambia Western Division: the falling water-table and the need for well-deepening (unpublished report, Gambia Christian Council, 1982).
11. Bob Blankwaardt, *Hand Drilled Wells: a manual on siting, design, construction and maintenance* (Rwegarulila Water Resources Institute, Dar es Salaam, 1984).
12. R.G. Koegel, *Self-help Wells* (FAO, Rome, 1977).
13. R.E. Brush, *Wells Construction: hand-dug and hand-drilled* (Peace Corps, Washington DC, 1979).
14. Y.M. Stemberg, R. Knight and R. Middleton, 'PVC Well Screens for Local Manufacture in Developing Countries', *Appropriate Technology* Vol. 7 No. 1 (IT Publications, London, 1980).
15. John Collett, 'Oil-soaked Wood Bearings', *Appropriate Technology* Vol. 2 No. 4 (IT Publications, London, 1976).
16. Andrew Metianu, 'A Simple Method of Jetting Tube-wells', *Waterlines* Vol. 1 No. 1 (IT Publications, London, 1982).
17. E.J.P. de Nooy, *Handbook for simple water engineering in Kitui district, Kenya* (Diocese of Kitui, Kenya, 1977).
18. R. Wiseman, 'Kano's Jet Set', *World Water* (Liverpool, 1983).
19. *BSADP Northern Zone Fadama Seminars* (July 1983, March 1984).

Reports of these meetings are available from BASRA, 28 Old Church Street, Chelsea, London SW3 5BY, UK.

20. *Installation of Wash Boreholes for Small-scale Irrigation in the Riverine Areas of Kano State* (KNARDA, Nigeria, 1983).

21. D.B. Tinker, *Sri Lanka Trials of Simple Water Jetting Equipment for Domestic Wells* (NIAE, Silsoe College, 1982).

22. 'Well-sinking made easy in Bangladeshi's ideal terrain', *World Water* (Liverpool, 1979).

23. H. Bell, 'Design and development of a low-cost jetting technique for shallow borehole construction' (unpublished, Silsoe College, 1984).

24. Arnold Pacey with Adrian Cullis, *Rain-water Harvesting: the collection of rainfall and runoff in rural areas* (IT Publications, London, 1986).

25. 'Man's Influence on the Hydrological Cycle', *Irrigation and Drainage Paper No. 17* (FAO, Rome, 1973).

26. G.P. Kalinin and V.D. Bukov, 'The World's Water Resources, Present and Future', *Impact of Science on Society Vol. 19 No. 2* (UNESCO, Paris, 1969).

27. Economic Commission for Asia and the Far East, *Water Resources Journal*, ST/ECAFE/SER.C/83 (United Nations, New York, 1969).

28. A.S. Kenyon, 'The Iron Clad or Artificial Catchment', *Journal of the Department of Agriculture* (Victoria, Australia).

29. C.W. Lauritzen, 'Collecting Desert Rainfall', *Crops and Soils* (American Society of Agronomy, USA, 1961).

30. C.W. Lauritzen, 'Plastics in the Development and Management of Water Supplies', *Proceedings of the Second International Congress on Plastics and Agriculture* (Pisa, 1966).

31. Doxiadis Associates, 'Village water tanks, land and water use survey in Kordofan Province of the Republic of Sudan', *Document DOX-SUD-A42* (UNSF/FAO, 1965).

32. ITDG, 'The Introduction of Rain-water Catchment Tanks and Micro-irrigation to Botswana' (unpublished report, ITDG, London, 1969).

33. *Village Water Supply* (World Bank, Washington, 1976).

34. D. Ray, *The Socio-economics of Rain-water Harvesting, Volume II: India* (ITDG and Wye College, Reading, 1984).

35. R. Feachem et al, *Water, Health and Development* (Trimed Books, London, 1978).

36. L. Fortmann and E. Roe, *Water Use in Eastern Botswana: policy guide and summary of the water points survey* (Ministry of Agriculture, Botswana, 1981).

37. G.K. Maikano and L. Nyberg, 'Rain-water Catchment in Botswana', *Rural Water Supply in Developing Countries* (IDRC, Ottawa, 1980).

38. Arnold Pacey, *Report on the State of the Botswana Catchment Tank Project after Three Years of Operation* (ITDG, London, 1971).

39. Peter Stern, 'Rain-water Harvesting', *Waterlines Vol. 1 No. 1* (IT Publications, London, 1982).
40. E. Nissen-Petersen, *Rain Catchment and Water Supply in Rural Africa: a manual* (Hodder and Stoughton, London, 1982).
41. N.W. Hudson, *Field Engineering for Agricultural Development* (Oxford University Press, Oxford, 1983).
42. Evenari, Tadmor and Shanan, *The Negev—A Challenge of a Desert* (Harvard University Press, USA).
43. *Dam Construction Handbook* (Agritex, Zimbabwe).
44. Bill Kennedy and Traudi Rogers, *Human-powered Water-lifting Devices: a state of the art survey* (IT Publications, London, 1985).
45. Peter Stern, *Small-scale Irrigation* (IT Publications, London, 1979).
46. 'Crop Water Requirements', *Irrigation and Drainage Paper No. 24* (FAO, Rome, 1977).
47. Arnold Pacey, *Handpump Maintenance in the Context of Community Well Projects* (IT Publications, London, 1977).
48. *Hand/Foot-operated Water Pumps for use in Developing Countries* (Consumers' Association, UK, 1981).
49. Gary Cockett, *Report of Secondment to OXFAM in Somalia* (Anglian Water Authority, 1982).
50. Robert Fraser, *Interim Report of the Utilization of Solar Pumping Equipment in the Oxfam Water Supply Programme for Refugee Camps in North-west Somalia* (Oxfam, Oxford, 1981).
51. *Community Water Supply: the handpump option* (World Bank, UNDP, Washington DC, 1987).
52. *Handpump Testing and Evaluation Bulletin No. 15* (International Reference Centre, The Netherlands, 1979).
53. *Rural Water Supply Handpumps Project: laboratory testing, field trials and technological development*, Report No. 1 (World Bank, Washington DC, 1982).
54. *UNDP/World Bank Rural Water Supply Project for the Testing and Technological Development of Handpumps:* Interim Report (World Bank, Washington).
55. Donald Sharp, *Village Handpump Technology: research and evaluation in Asia* (IDRC, Ottawa, 1983).
56. Simon Watt, 'The Mechanical Failure of Village Water Well Pumps in Rural Areas', *Appropriate Technology Vol. 4 No. 3* (IT Publications, London, 1977).
57. Val Curtis, *Women and the Transport of Water* (IT Publications, London, 1986).
58. S.B. Watt, *Ferrocement Water Tanks and their Construction* (IT Publications, London, 1980).
59. Thomas D. Jordan Jnr, *A Handbook of Gravity Flow Water Systems* (IT Publications, London, 1984).

60. Christine van Wijk-Sibesma, *Participation of Women in Water Supply and Sanitation, Roles and Realities* (UNDP, 1985).
61. G.F. White, P.J. Bradley and A.U. White, *Drawers of Water* (Chicago University Press, 1972).
62. A. Sinclair, 'Domestic water in North Kitui, Kenya' (unpublished, ITDG, 1983).
63. T. Abdullah and Zeidenstein, *Village Women of Bangladesh—Prospects to Change* (Pergamon, Oxford, 1982).
64. Hans-Erik Gram, Hakan Persson, Ake Skarendhal, *Natural Fibre Concrete* (SIDA, Sweden, 1984).
65. Colin Glennie, *A Model for the Development of a Self-help Water Supply Programme* (World Bank, Washington, 1982).
66. Carolyn Hannan-Anderson, *Development of Water Supplies in Singida Region, Tanzania, Part 2: the realities for village women* (Institute of Resource Development at the University of Dar es Salaam, 1984).
67. *Minimum Evaluation Procedure for Water Supply and Sanitation Projects* (WHO, Geneva, 1983).
68. Arnold Pacey, Ed., *Water for the Thousand Millions* (Pergamon, Oxford, 1977).
69. Sandy Cairncross (et al), *Evaluation for Village Water Supply Planning* (John Wiley and Sons, UK, 1980).
70. Robert Sanders and Jeremy Warford, *Village Water Supply Economics and Policy in the Developing World* (Hopkins, Baltimore and London, 1976).
71. Sandy Cairncross and Richard Feachem, *Small Water Supplies* (The Ross Institute, London, 1978).
72. K.A. Wittfogel, 'The Hydraulic Civilizations', in W.L. Thomas, Ed., *Man's Role in Changing the Face of the Earth* (University of Chicago, 1966).
73. J.C. Wilkinson, 'Water and Tribal Settlement in Southeast Arabia', *Oxford Research Studies in Geography* (Clarendon Press, UK, 1977).

www.ingramcontent.com/pod-product-compliance
Lightning Source LLC
Chambersburg PA
CBHW072054020426
42334CB00017B/1508